P9-DFU-599

Holm, Don.
     Fishing the Pacific; an angler's guide
to Pacific marine fishes. [New York] Winchester Press [1972]
     241 p.   illus.   21 cm.
     Bibliography: p. 239-240.

     1. Fishing - Pacific Coast (North Ameri-
ca) 2. Fishes - Pacific Ocean.   3. Saltwater fishing.   I. Title.

                              72-79361

Fishing the Pacific

Fishing the Pacific

an angler's guide to Pacific marine fishes

DON HOLM

WINCHESTER PRESS

Library of Congress Catalog Card Number: 72:79361

ISBN: 087691-044-4

Published by Winchester Press
460 Park Avenue, New York 10022

Printed in the United States of America

FOR REBECCA LEE AND DOUGLAS KIMBALL
AND THEIR OWN, WITH THE HOPE THAT
THEY WILL BE ABLE TO ENJOY IT ALL, TOO.

Introduction

The American poet Archibald MacLeish once wrote, "No man can come to the Pacific coast of this continent . . . and feel that he has come to the end of anything."

Certainly, with 32.4 per cent of the earth's surface, the Pacific Ocean can't be ignored. It has always been the *Ultima Thule* of America's westward expansion, has always connoted a promise or a mystery or a romance. Perhaps because of the name given it by Balboa, *Pacific*—a misnomer if there ever was one—perhaps because of those romantic tales of gold from the North Pacific or of avid, willing maidens on South Pacific islands—the name has been magic. Even today, Alaska and Hawaii, the 49th and 50th states, are known as "frontiers," offering promise and opportunity.

One thing is certain: The Pacific *is* a frontier, as far as the sportfisherman and seeker of elbow room is concerned.

One of the paradoxes of the Pacific is that, although it has been one of the most explored, probed, and written about regions on earth, much of it is still little known and, yes, mysterious and romantic — especially that part beneath its long blue swells.

Putting it in perspective, for nearly two centuries before there was a United States, the Pacific was virtually a Spanish "lake," from which other nations were excluded. There was even regular galleon service between the west coast of Mexico and the Philippines. A generation before the Jamestown colony was established, Sir Francis Drake had sailed up the west coast of South and North America as far as Cape Blanco, Oregon. Before the Declaration of Independence was signed, the Danish navigator Vitus Bering discovered Alaska, and naturalists attached to his Russian-backed expedition classified numerous fish and wildlife then unknown to science. Spanish and Russian settlements were established in Alaska, California, and British Columbia before Washington crossed the Delaware. Two decades before Lewis and Clark trekked across the continent, Yankee trader-adventurers were making regular trips to the Northwest coast, and Nantucket whaling ships were prowling among the islands and atolls of Micronesia, Polynesia, and Melanesia.

And, of course, these island natives, who were among the world's greatest navigators, were crossing long expanses of the open Pacific hundreds of years before Columbus, Cook, or Magellan were born.

Today, the Pacific still seems as remote and undiscovered as ever. For the sports angler, yachtsman, seeker of relief from the pressure cooker of modern society, perhaps it is. While big-game fishing probably dates back to the days when the great Zane Grey opened up such areas as the California islands, Central America, New Zealand, and Australia, it has only been within the past decade that the average saltwater aficionado has discovered the superb angling of Baja, Panama, the Humboldt current, Hawaii, New Zealand, Fiji, and the Great Barrier Reef. This was, of course, made possible by modern jet transportation, which makes such trips within the means of the medium-income bloke.

Since World War II, scientific research in marine biology, oceanography, and other disciplines has boomed in earnest around the Pacific rim and offshore. General knowledge of the Pacific and its resources is rapidly being accumulated. Until recent years, the saltwater angler had concerned himself with only half a dozen marine game fishes, although it is apparent now that the true sportfishing potential includes around 200 species, plus another 100 of at least some interest.

Secretary of State John Jay once wrote: "The Mediterranean is the ocean of the past; the Atlantic the ocean of the present; and the Pacific the ocean of the future."

His foresight has proved accurate. This is the Age of the Pacific—politically, economically, scientifically. The fleets of half a dozen nations have already begun the race to exploit its resources with Space Age efficiency. Some species have already been depleted or nearly so by the commercial fishing fleets of Japan and the U.S.S.R. Other nations such as South Korea and Red China are moving in on the kill. There is much talk among politicians, editorial writers, conservationists, commercial and sportfishing leaders about international controls and treaties.

Today, because of this scramble to exploit the Pacific's fisheries, not only by commercial fishing cartels but by the sportfishing industry and the recreation-oriented sectors of society, the need for an up-to-date field guide is apparent. Now that the marine ecology of the Pacific has attracted the attention of the lay public, as well as the ubiquitous saltwater angler, a basic source of information is needed.

This is what this "fishing book" attempts to be. Although designed primarily for sportsmen, it should serve as a convenient introduction to the region and its marine resources for the visitor or tourist, as well as students, conservationists, editors, legislators, and amateur explorers.

This field guide represents the first attempt to bring together in one book a complete source of information on saltwater sportfishing and recreation covering the entire American Pacific region. It includes, for the first time, a cataloging of more than 300 marine fishes common to the Pacific, corrected up through the most recent scientific reports, described and illustrated to make for easy identification by the layman.

It should be noted that much confusion still exists in even the scholarly and scientific journals over the identification and naming of Pacific marine species. Biologists and zoologists do not always agree with each other or even with themselves from year to year—as Dr. David Starr Jordan coyly admitted years ago. The right to change one's mind has long been extended by scientists to include the right to change one's nomenclature, even if it comes to challenging Linnaeus himself.

Standardization by the International Commission on Zoological Nomenclature, the American Fisheries Society, and similar groups attempts to bring order out of chaos in the face of almost hopeless opposition. Over the centuries common names have been applied to species by local custom, by commercial and sportfishermen, often out of whim or humor. Fish marketing practices have added to the confusion.

For this field guide, we are indebted to the latest and best authorities on the subject: *Manuscript List of Fishes of California* by Dr. Carl L. Hubbs and W. I. Follett; *Fishes of the Pacific Coast of Canada* by W. A. and G. V. Clemens; *Some Common Marine Fishes of British Columbia* by G. C. Carl; *Atlas of Eastern Pacific Marine Game Fishing*, Circular 174, Bureau of Sport Fisheries and Wildlife; *Field Guide to Common Marine and Bay Fishes of Oregon* by Alan J. Beardsley and Carl E. Bond; *A Field Guide to Some Common Ocean Sport Fishes of California* by Daniel J. Miller, Dan Gotshall, and Richard Nitsos; *A List of Common and Scientific Names of Fishes*, American Fisheries Society Special Publication No. 6; and *The Fishes of North and Middle America* by David Starr Jordan and Barton Warren Evermann.

In addition, innumerable technical reports and bulletins of the many state and federal agencies concerned with Pacific fisheries were studied in detail, particularly those of J. E. Fitch and J. L. Baxter of California. In case of conflicting information, the latest and most commonly accepted was selected. In some cases the decision was made arbitrarily by the author.

Other sources included the Scripps Institution of Oceanography, the Oregon State University Marine Science Center, the University of Oregon Marine Science Division, the California Academy of Sciences, the American Fisheries Society, the Fisheries Research Board of Canada, the U.S. Fish and Wildlife Service, the University of Washington marine research department, the Smithsonian Institution Press, and the fish and game departments of Alaska, British Columbia, Washington, Oregon, California, Hawaii, New Zealand, and Australia.

Outdoor writers and fishing experts in many local areas were most helpful and too numerous to mention individually here, but sources for further periodical reading are listed elsewhere in this volume.

It was the aim of the author to provide the newcomer with as complete a guide and reference work possible to our "last frontier," the ocean which Vasco Nunez de Balboa first looked upon on September 29, 1513 and called *Pacific*.

*It is the age of the Pacific Ocean
—mysterious and unfathomable in
its meaning to our future.*
—Frederick Jackson Turner

Contents

CHAPTER ONE

The Frontier Ocean

A FISHERIES biologist friend, who migrated to the Marine Science Center at Newport, Oregon, from his native New England where he spent his youth on a North Atlantic trawler, confided to me, "I just can't get used to the idea of sailing west to go fishing!"

Had he wished to pursue the idea further, he could have pointed out numerous other characteristics of the earth's largest ocean. North of the Equator, its prevailing winds are westerly, blowing onshore, often bringing in great seas with an unbroken fetch of thousands of miles. The coastline from the tip of the Baja Peninsula to the Bering Sea traces an incredible 60,000 miles of ocean border, but with few exceptions is relatively unbroken by natural harbors, inlets, and coastal waterways.

Some exceptions of note, of course, are Puget Sound, San Francisco Bay, the fjords and islands of British Columbia, Alaska's Inland Passage, Cook Inlet and the Alaska Peninsula, and Prince William Sound.

The North Pacific, for all its mysterious and majestic elements, is truly one of the last great frontiers for the fisherman and recreational escapist. Its climate varies from the subtropical to the arctic, from exotic islands to frozen tundra, from dark green forested coastal mountain ranges and

1

winding fjords to endless stretches of empty white beaches and sparkling blue water.

The climate varies from the browns and tans of the Baja California mountains and desert beaches to the rain forests of the Olympic Peninsula, British Columbia, and southeast Alaska, to the violent extremes of the western Alaska and Bering areas, to the ice pack of the Arctic—not overlooking those enchanted subtropical islands of the fiftieth state, Hawaii.

The oceanography of the vast North Pacific shows clearly defined ocean currents forming a clockwise "river" around the almost circular continental rim, with semipermanent back eddies here and there, and weaker counter currents, all of which are the result of tidal phenomena and the Coriolis effect of the earth's rotation.

The prevailing currents include the Kuroshio (meaning "black") or Japan Current, the North Pacific Drift, the California Current, the North Equatorial Current, all in a clockwise rotation around the rim. Along the North American continent there is usually a weak counter current alongshore, such as the Alaska Current of the Gulf, and the southward flowing Bering Current along the Siberian coastline.

The result is a permanent high pressure cell between the Hawaiian Islands and the mainland U. S., and a permanent low just off the Alaska Peninsula, which shift with the seasons and perform as the North Pacific's "weather factory," affecting not only the prevailing climate, but the seasonal weather patterns of Washington, Oregon, California, Baja, British Columbia, Alaska, and Hawaii.

This, in turn, has a direct effect on the fishing. The seasonal winds, swinging around these weather cells, often determine where bars and inlets are safe for running and which anchorages can be used. They also determine whether or not there will be precipitation, and even have an effect on the upwelling of cold nutrient-filled waters alongshore which determines when the fish go on the bite.

Tides also greatly affect navigation and fishing. In some regions such as the Hawaiian Islands and west coast Baja

they may rise and fall only a few feet, but in Cook Inlet and Prince William Sound the changes are as great as thirty or forty feet. These tidal changes are unnoticed on the high seas, but on inshore waters such as the Inland Passage of British Columbia and Alaska they cause terrific currents that sometimes funnel through passes at speeds of eight to ten knots. At the upper end of the Sea of Cortez, where the Colorado River empties into salt water, hazardous tidal bores are a common phenomenon.

These North Pacific phenomena affect the feeding and spawning habits of the alongshore marine fishes, and also have a definite effect upon the pelagic species of game fish such as marlin, sailfish, swordfish, tuna, and albacore and the bait species upon which they forage.

These game fish generally swim a counterclockwise pattern around the North Pacific, well offshore in the blue water of the open sea, appearing in Mexican waters early in the year, moving northwesterly against the prevailing current.

Hooking into a "hot" marlin off Mexico is one of life's unforgettable experiences.

Tuna and albacore move closer to shore along the sixty degree isotherm as far north as the Columbia River "plume" of warm brackish water, then swing westward to Japanese waters and southward toward the Equator. Billfish swing westerly off Southern California toward Hawaiian waters, and albacore are frequently found as far north as Vancouver Island.

A marlin once tagged off Baja in an experiment was caught off Hawaii sixty days later. Similarly, a thirty-five-pound albacore tagged off California was caught six months later off Japan at which time it weighed nearly sixty pounds.

Recent studies have shown that the North Pacific's famed anadromous species such as salmon and steelhead are also affected by these currents and ocean conditions. The five species of North American salmon migrate for thousands of miles along the colder waters of the continental shelf from the Columbia River to the tip of the Aleutian chain, and return. A steelhead caught and tagged by a Japanese research vessel at about 177° East was caught recently in a Washington river at a longitude of about 125° West—an astounding revelation that upset many previously held concepts.

If nothing else, this demonstrates dramatically how little is known about the fisheries of the North Pacific at this moment when a great surge of interest in its game fishing and recreational potential has begun, and at a time when the commercial fishing fleets of several nations are engaged in international competition to exploit the marine resources, with little regard for wise conservation.

For the sports fisherman, instead of being limited to the various species of salmon, the tuna and big-game species, and a few popular surf and bottom fishes, the North Pacific provides between 200 and 300 marine species of fish of interest and potential sport and recreational value. Its attractions, including these hundreds of marine species of game fish and dozens of undeveloped and unspoiled sport fishing provinces, are a challenge even to catalog and describe.

It is, without doubt, the ocean of the future—especially for the saltwater sportsman.

CHAPTER TWO

New Fishing Frontiers

Alaska

THAT THE Pacific rim is a region of vast distances suddenly impresses the first-time visitor to Alaska, the forty-ninth state. Its 230,000 people rattle around in 586,400 square miles of mountains, tundra, and glacial river valleys, stretching from 55° North to 72° North and from 130° West to the westernmost point of Cape Wrangell at 172° 26′ East on the other side of the International Dateline.

Lumber, furs, minerals, fisheries, oil production and exploration support the economy, with tourism emerging in this decade as a major source of "outside" income. Most transportation today is by air or water, and this is likely to be the case for the rest of this century.

For the yachtsman and saltwater angler, Alaska offers a general coastline of 5,770 nautical miles with 29,482 miles of shoreline. The Panhandle section alone, from Dixon Entrance to Cape Spencer, although only 250 nautical miles long and eighty miles wide, has a tidal shoreline of 11,085 miles! About one-third of the geographic size of the "lower forty-

6

eight" if superimposed on a map of the mainland U. S., Alaska would stretch almost from the Atlantic to the Pacific. Instead of being isolated, it is obviously a strategic part of the globe. Separated from the U.S.S.R. in the Diomedes by a mile or so of water, Alaska is closer to Asia and Europe than to the United States. The city of Fairbanks, for example, is only 900 air miles from Moscow.

"North to Alaska" is a common phrase, but the traveler will find himself traveling more west than north when leaving the lower forty-eight. In fact, he will touch three time zones on his way westward.

The decade of the seventies marks the emergence of Alaska as a major nonresident sportfishing, hunting, and boating area. New facilities are being developed to meet the demand. Most of the population is concentrated in towns and cities, which means that the "good" areas are mostly primitive and that air travel and private boating are expensive for the visitor. At this writing, most nonresident hunting and fishing is done from fly-in dude camps, scattered American-plan resorts, and on packaged tours offered by airlines and travel agencies.

Future facilities will include these, plus more access roads, expanded auto ferry service, and the promising field of charter cruiser and houseboat service from major coastal ports, and even from Seattle. Even now, there is heavy private boat traffic up the Inland Passage from Puget Sound through British Columbia to southeast Alaska.

Visitors at any time of the year should expect frequent and often unexpected changes in weather. The best weather in most areas is from May to October, with the peak of sunshine and mild days coming in July and August. The general climate ranges from mild and wet on the southeast coast to wild and wet on the Aleutian chain (the tip of which is almost due west of Seattle and only 1,800 miles from the Hawaiian chain), to arctic conditions in the Bering and North Slope.

As far as the angler and tourist are concerned, Alaska can be conveniently divided into three parts: southeast or Pan-

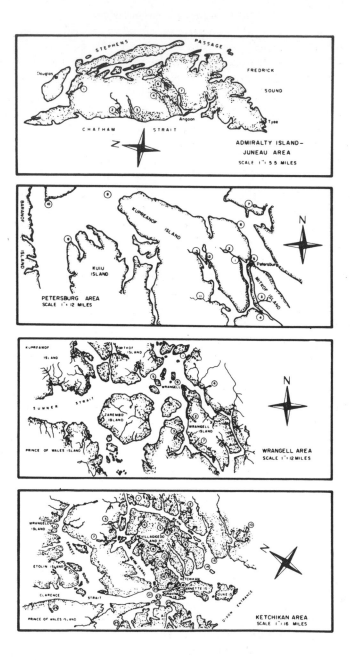

A crewman from the famed Jacques Cousteau expedition examines a sockeye salmon in spawning condition, on the Russian River, Alaska.

handle, southwest or "westward," and the Bering coast.

Panhandle. A strip of rugged, forested mainland, bordered by a chain of hundreds of islands, most of the southeast coast is contained in the Tongass National Forest. The district's 50,000 citizens live in sixteen towns and villages, surrounded by mountainous terrain covered with dense stands of spruce, hemlock, and cedar that make possible large pulp and lumber operations.

The mainland mountains are higher than those on the islands, have less dense forests, and are usually snowcapped and glacier-strewn. The snowline is at the 3,000-foot level in midsummer, and glaciers are frequently seen along the fog-shrouded mainland shore, some dropping right down to the salt chuck.

The waterways are deep—without shoals, except off rivers —and the straits are often narrow, with violent tidal currents and overfalls. The islands form a complex maze of

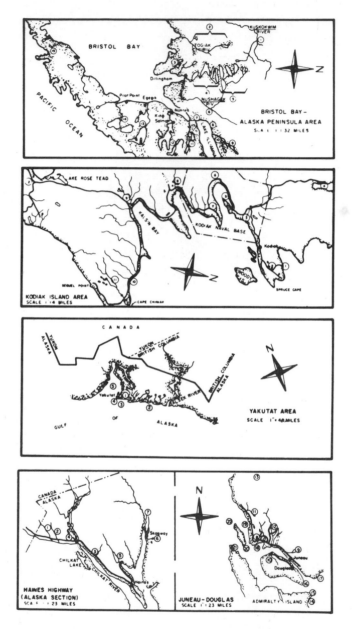

BRISTOL BAY

PACIFIC OCEAN

KUSKOKWIM RIVER

KOGIAK

Dillingham

Pilot Point Egegek

King Salmon Naknek

NUSHAGAK RIV

AKE ILIAMNA

BRISTOL BAY –
ALASKA PENINSULA AREA
SCALE 1 : 1 : 32 MILES

AKE ROSE TEAD

FALS'N BAY

KODIAK NAVAL BASE

Kodiak

SEQUEL POINT

WOOD

SPRUCE CAPE

CAPE CHINIAK

KODIAK ISLAND AREA
SCALE 1 : 4 MILES

CANADA

YUKON
ALASKA

YUKON
BRITISH COLUMBIA

BRITISH COLUMBIA
ALASKA

Yakutat

EK RIVER

GULF   OF   ALASKA

YAKUTAT AREA
SCALE 1" : 48 MILES

CANADA
ALASKA

Skagway

CHILKAT LAKE

CHILKAT RIVER

Haines

HAINES HIGHWAY
(ALASKA SECTION)
SCALE 1 : 23 MILES

N

Juneau
Douglas

ADMIRALTY ISLAND

JUNEAU – DOUGLAS
SCALE 1 : 23 MILES

passages, with thousands of coves, inlets, and natural harbors. Transportation is by float plane, ferry, and boat. There is much marine transportation, especially during the summer, with thousands of commercial fishing boats, logging vessels, gillnets, and private boats. Almost every island has its logging and fish camps. Constant hazards to boaters are the log rafts, floating debris, and deadheads.

The principal ports are Ketchikan, Sitka, Petersburg, Wrangell, Juneau, Skagway, Metlakatla, and Ward Cove for the large vessels, with perhaps another dozen major small settlements. The sportfishing centers include Ketchikan, Petersburg, Sitka, and Juneau, where charter boat, float plane, and guide services are available. In the outlying areas, the Forest Service operates wilderness cabins, which are available by reservation with that agency in the major cities.

The Panhandle has a marine climate, with high humidity, fog, heavy cloud cover, small range of temperature, and lots of rain. The waterways are subject to sudden and often violent winds, including the downslope *williwaw.* A local wind around Juneau is the *taku*, which tears down off Taku Glacier.

Summer weather and temperatures, however, are generally mild, and the period of most cloudiness is from September through December. All ports are ice-free all year, although slush and glacier ice are frequently found in Frederick Sound, Stephens Passage, Cross Sound, and Icy Straits.

During the summer, the channels are busy with boat traffic and alive with marine life—whales cavorting, porpoises, sea lions, seals, fish jumping, birds swooping and wheeling. Deer are often seen swimming between islands, even through strong tidal currents.

Saltwater angling is for chinook (locally called king) salmon, coho salmon, humpbacked or pink salmon, steelhead, sea-run cutthroat and dolly varden, bottom species such as halibut, lingcod, rockfish, flounder, cod, greenlings, hake, tomcod, turbot, sole, dogfish, shark, and sculpin. The salmons and sea-run trouts are the most sought-after species, with halibut also much prized. Alaskan waters also have fine

This handsome chinook, or king, salmon, was caught in southeastern Alaska.

crabbing for king and Dungeness varieties, plentiful shrimp in several varieties, and many kinds of clams and mussels.

During the spring and summer months, usually starting in May, most towns conduct salmon "derbies" offering astonishing prizes for the biggest fish, running to thousands of dollars.

Anglers will find the chinook abundant from April to August, coho from July to September, dolly varden from May to September, halibut from May to August, steelhead in the spring and fall. A large number of steelhead are known to be caught as "salmon" in Alaskan waters. A young angler from Seattle recently caught a forty-two-pounder that was thought to be a salmon until identified by a taxidermist a week later. Otherwise the lad would have qualified for an official world record. (Refer to the field guide section for an easy way to tell the difference.)

Up-to-date information on local areas can usually be obtained from the airlines serving Alaska, from chambers of commerce at Sitka, Skagway, Wrangell, Petersburg, Juneau, and Ketchikan. The Forest Service regional office in Juneau can supply maps and information on recreational opportunities. The local newspapers in the above-mentioned cities carry fishing news and sports advertising most of the year. The national outdoor magazines carry the ads and notices of guides and outfitters. The Alaska Visitors Association, Juneau, and the Alaska Department of Fish and Game, Juneau and Ketchikan, can provide angling information and maps.

I'm often asked the best way to fish the Panhandle, and my answer has to be by private boat. You can come and go as you please, you have your "camp" with you, and it's the best way to see the country. The next best way is to fly to a major center such as Juneau or Ketchikan and link up with a fly-in outfit. Either way it's expensive for the pilgrim from the outside.

Westward. Cape Spencer, located across Cross Sound from Lisianski Inlet, is the jumping-off point for boats crossing the Gulf of Alaska, but few private yachts pass this way. The town of Pelican is located up in Lisianski Inlet, and is an important center for commercial fishing boats with air and mail service to Juneau and other points.

From Cape Spencer the coastline is deserted and forbidding, with few shelters. Lituya Bay, a narrow inlet with an active glacier, is the main fishing boat haven, especially for the salmon trollers working the offshore Fairweather Banks —one of the most productive grounds in the entire North Pacific, about fifty miles off Lituya.

From Cape Fairweather to Ocean Cape at the entrance to Yakutat Bay, the only other major break is Dry Bay at the mouth of the Alsek River. The village of Yakutat is located just behind the cape. Icy Bay is the next point on the rim, followed by Cape St. Elias, Cordova, and Valdez in huge Prince William Sound; Whittier and then Seward at the head of Resurrection Bay on Kenai Peninsula.

The shoreline of the Kenai is one of Alaska's most popular sportfishing areas, from Seward, on the south side, to Seldovia, near the southwest tip of Cook Inlet. Other good areas are at Homer, a little farther up the inlet, and in the Anchorage vicinity at the head of the inlet on Turnagin Arm. On the mainland, Illiamna Bay and Kukaka Bay at Cape Ugyak, Portage Bay, and Port Wrangell are outlying fishing campsites.

Kodiak Island, off the tip of the Kenai Peninsula, is also a sportfishing and hunting area. Air service is available from here to the outer Aleutian settlements, and to points across the Alaska Peninsula on Bristol Bay in the Bering.

Kuskokwim Bay at the mouth of the Kuskokwim River; the Yukon Delta in the vicinity of St. Michael; Nome, Teller, and Norton Sound on the Seward Peninsula; Kotzebue on Kotzebue Sound at the mouth of the Kobuk River; Point Hope, Wainwright, and Point Barrow—all are popular "adventure" points for the tourist and sportsman, but offer nothing especially spectacular to the saltwater angler. With the development of the North Slope oil reserves, the Arctic coast from Barrow to Beaufort Sea will also attract the adventurous angler looking for new waters, as it already has attracted the hunter and the new husband-and-wife teams of ecologists.

The most spectacular scenery will be found crossing the Gulf of Alaska and on the Kenai and Alaska peninsulas. Westerly winds are common in summer, easterlies in winter, with squalls or *williwaws* all year. In the fall and winter, the winds are often tempestuous—after all, the Gulf of Alaska and the Aleutians make up the North Pacific's principal "weather factory." Precipitation is heavy in the coastal areas. The mean average temperature is forty degrees with a summer maximum of seventy-five degrees. Sea-water temperature is usually four degrees higher than that of air in winter, and one degree lower in summer.

None of the harbors of the Gulf freeze over in winter, although river mouths may be ice-bound for a few weeks in winter. Fog is worse from June through September, with

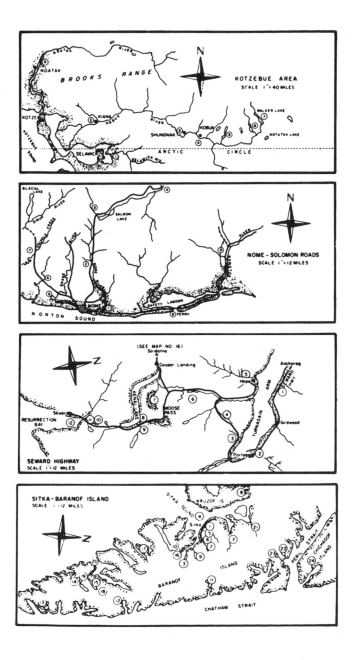

some periods of fog lasting ten days. Floating ice is common in Prince William Sound in the spring. Cook Inlet is noted for heavy winds and considerable cloudiness most of the year. Kodiak is one of a group of islands, and is about fifty-five by 155 miles in size, with many bays and inlets. Fishing is the major industry, followed by sheep- and cattle-raising. The city of Kodiak is the main center. The annual precipitation is about sixty-seven inches, and the temperature often reaches eighty-five degrees in summer. Fog and cloudiness are common.

The south coast of the Alaska Peninsula is rugged and spectacular with many bays, islets, inlets, and a number of fish camps, canneries, and settlements. The weather is extremely variable and unpredictable, and the coastline is hazardous for boats. In fact, the weather in all this coastal region can be summed up as "miserable," most of the year, and the navigation as "hazardous" for strangers.

The principal saltwater sportfishing centers are Cordova, Valdez, Kodiak, Anchorage, Seward, and Homer. Chinook are found from April to August, coho from July to September along with pinks or humpbacks. Rockfish, starry flounder, atka mackerel, lingcod, greenlings, soles, Alaska pollack, and halibut can be caught all year. Dolly varden and sea-run cutthroat are found in the tidal rivers, except on Kodiak where there are no cutthroat trout.

The Kenai Peninsula, one of the most popular areas, is accessible by a network of roads from Anchorage. These waters contain chinook, steelhead, coho, and halibut. Here the sockeye will readily take lures and flies during the spawning runs—uncommon in most salmon waters. Steelhead run in winter; coho, dolly varden, and humpbacked salmon in the fall. Some of the chinook salmon caught in these waters run to enormous size.

There are many charter boat services, launching ramps, and rental skiffs at Cordova, Valdez, Seward, Homer, Anchorage, and Kodiak.

On the Alaska Peninsula, the fishing is mainly for coho salmon, dolly varden, and halibut. The Adak Navy Base area is noted for its coho and humpbacked salmon and halibut.

There are several fishing camps and lodges on the Peninsula can be reached from Anchorage or King Salmon by air. They all operate on the American plan, or are part of package tours offered by airlines and outfitting firms. Usually, big-game hunting, freshwater fishing, and photographic opportunities are available, and there is a surprising amount of traffic in the summer season.

Bering Area. The Aleutian Islands, one of the most remote regions under the U. S. flag, are at this time of little interest to the saltwater sportsman, although there is a smattering of yacht traffic here. The best-known settlements or anchorages are Akutan, Dutch Harbor, Nazan Bay, Kuluk Bay on Adak, Constantine Harbor on Amchitka, Kiska, and Massacre Bay on Attu. The chain is marked by hazardous coastline, heavy swells and surf, extreme tidal currents, thick fog, and violent winds.

Hunting, fishing, trapping, and stock raising are the main sources of livelihood. There are a number of military and Atomic Energy Commission reservations, but the region is definitely only for the more adventurous visitor.

The Bering Sea is only partially surveyed and charted, and is generally shallow—that is, under 100 fathoms—which means short choppy seas in contrast to the long swells of the open Pacific. Weather and currents are extreme and unpredictable. There are few navigation aids, and most of the villages on the mainland shore and off islands are served only by air. Oddly enough, winter is the best time for access to these outlying villages, as then they can be reached via snowmobile, dog team, and tractor.

There are a number of fishing camps maintained along the Bering Coast by airlines and outfitters from King Salmon or Anchorage, usually as part of package tours. One of the more popular spots is Bristol Bay, the scene of the famed commercial sockeye salmon operations. Saltwater fishing is for chinook and coho salmon, steelhead, dolly varden, sockeye, and whitefish. Trips into this area are usually of a week or ten days' duration, and current prices average around $200 a day per person.

Northward on the mainland, the Kuskokwim is also a

popular mecca for the adventurous and fairly well-heeled sportsman. It is accessible only by air. Guide service is available at the villages of Sleetmute, Bethel, Stony River, and McGrath. The Kuskokwim delta has some fine fly fishing for Arctic grayling, and the rare sheefish, or *inconnu*, often called the Arctic tarpon because of its fishing qualities. It is caught through the ice in the early spring and in the summer on lures of all kinds. The lower tidal sloughs and channels also contain northern pike.

In the Yukon watershed, an enormous drainage on a scale of the Columbia, the fishing is for salmon, chinook, coho, sockeye, grayling, sheefish, and pike. The area is accessible only by air and by riverboat with experienced guides. The offshore fishing in the Nome area is mainly for tomcod and halibut. Crabbing is good here for king crabs.

The Kobuk, Selawik, and Noatak in the Kotzebue area are noted for sheefish, pike, and dolly varden, with access only by air. The delta area of the Kobuk and Noatak also have some pike fishing. There are many fishing camps in this area, served from Nome and Fairbanks. A party of four, for example, would pay about $500 a day, in the season from June through August. There are some settlements, including Allakaket, Beetles, and Alatna, but the main reason a sportfisherman would go in here would be for a big sheefish, with some recorded up to sixty pounds.

Around Point Hope and Point Barrow, one gets into the Arctic, and from here to the Beaufort Sea on the Canadian border you are on the remote North Slope with all streams flowing into the Arctic. The best-known streams are the Meade, Colville, Canning, Ikpikpuk, and Sagavanirktok. Under increasing pressure in the traditional search for "new" places, these may become important in future years.

British Columbia

Similar to Panhandle Alaska in most respects, including climate, scenery, and gamefish species, British Columbia contains some of the finest fishing and boating in the world.

It is also much more accessible than Alaska at this time. The saltwater fishing is found around huge Vancouver Island, which extends down into Puget Sound—mainly on the inside or eastern side—in the island-dotted inland passageways between Vancouver Island and the mainland, in the spectacular fjords along the mainland, and around outlying islands such as the Queen Charlottes.

Most fishing spots are reached only by boat or by air to outlying camps. The exceptions are the east shore of Vancouver Island, the "Sunshine Coast" on the mainland from Vancouver northward, and the immediate vicinity of Prince Rupert, the busy ship and railroad terminus in the North.

Coastal British Columbia is a region of countless wooded islands, thousands of miles of rugged coastline, secluded coves, logging and fishing camps and Indian villages, and a large commercial fishing fleet in operation during the summer months. The climate is mild, but usually wet except in midsummer. Vancouver Island has regular car ferry service from Washington and mainland B.C. points, and a road network from Victoria to as far north as Campbell River, with access at one or two points across the island to the west side. There is a road up the mainland for some distance, but for the most part travel by car is restricted. A new ferry service operates from the northern end of Vancouver Island to Prince Rupert, which connects with the new Alaska ferry service, as well as to the terminus of the transcontinental highway. There is also regular ferry service to the Queen Charlotte Islands.

There is little red tape for the U. S. citizen visiting British Columbia, and fishing licenses are relatively inexpensive for nonresident aliens. Canadians are generally friendly and hospitable, in spite of heavy American investment in real estate and local industries, which occasionally generates

---

*As a result of a new regulation aimed at American private boat owners, alien sport anglers are now subject to exorbitant fees if they bring their own boats into British Columbia.

some heat. Many British Columbia resorts and fly-in hunting and fishing camps are owned by U. S. citizens or immigrants from the West Coast United States. Almost all are operated or managed by experienced Canadians.

Saltwater angling is mainly for salmon and steelhead, with

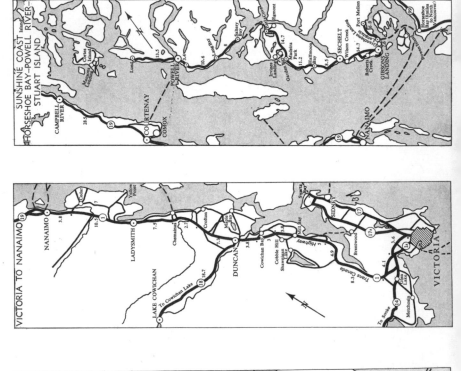

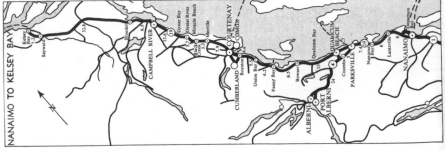

sea-run cutthroat and dolly varden also abundant. About
fifty species of bottom fish are common to these waters, but
at this time only halibut, flounder, lingcod, some perch, and
rockfish are regularly sought by sports anglers. Albacore
tuna are found off the coast in late summer and early fall,
but no sport fishery has yet been developed for these. Crabs,
clams, shrimp, and oysters are abundant.

Vancouver Island. This 280-mile long island hangs like an
appendix alongshore. Reached by ferry from many mainland
ports, it is popular with tourists and anglers alike. The best-
known spot is Campbell River, which can now be reached
by auto, and the original lodge has been supplemented by
forty or fifty new motels. Located at the mouth of the Campbell River, this is the home of the famed Tyee Club. Almost
all salmon fishing is done in rowboats with local guides, but
all services are available.

The town overlooks Discovery Passage, a narrow channel
through which the main salmon runs travel both from the
North and the South all summer long. The coho fishing here
is superb in summer, especially with flyrods and saltwater
streamers. In the spring there is a heavy run of grilse (locally
called bluebacks). These are actually immature fish, however,
and should not be taken. Coho fishing is from June to October; the big chinooks come in June and July; spring salmon
are present from December to March. The "tyee" fishing
starts in August, when this big race of chinooks moves into
Frenchman's Pool at the mouth of the river. This is the big
action, when the river is covered with boats, and when hundreds of fish are caught, some as large as sixty pounds.

The Tyee Club, founded in 1927, supervises the competition trophy fishing and makes awards.

Some common lures used locally are the Buzz Bomb,
Lucky Louie plugs, Canadian Wonders, whole and cut herring, spoons with dodgers or flashers, coho streamers, and
similar designs. At times casting can be done right from the
downtown docks and log booms. Surf casting is possible
here, too. Fishing the Narrows and Brown's Bay can be hazardous for amateurs without guides, due to tidal currents
and bores.

This 32-pound chinook salmon won the $25,000 grand prize
in a Vancouver, B. C., salmon derby.

The remote west coast of the island can now be reached
via a road across the middle to Port Alberni at the head of
a long fingerlike inlet. This spot is famous for its big chinooks
and there are complete sportfishing facilities here, including
boat rentals. This is also an outfitting point for Barkley
Sound, Ucluelet, Tofino, Clayoquot, and other points, and a
mail and passenger boat makes regular trips to many points
on the outside.

Gold River, a small settlement on the west coast, can be
reached by a road from Campbell River, and from this point
the historic settlements of Nootka Sound, Tahsis, and Zeballos can be reached by boat.

There is some superb fishing in the area of Port Alice, a
logging settlement at the head of Neroutsos Inlet. It can be
reached by a restricted road from Port Hardy, but the best
way is by airplane or boat.

Kelsey Bay, just north of Campbell River, is the end of the paved highway and the terminus for the new ship ferry to Prince Rupert. It is a fast growing sportfishing center with motels, resorts, boat rentals, and guides. Fishing is for coho and humpbacked salmon in June, July, and August; chinook most of the year; bottom fishing for cod, rockfish, and red snappers all year; and sea-run cutthroat and dolly varden fly fishing in the spring, summer, and fall.

Nanaimo is the ferry terminus for the city of Vancouver on the mainland and is also a sportfishing center for George Strait. It is also a popular stop with yachtsmen coming north and has all facilities and marinas for this purpose. The mouth of the Nanaimo River is best for big chinooks, as is Nanaimo Flats.

Courtenay, just north of Nanaimo, is a sportfishing center with chinooks found all year around, the best months being May, June, July, and August. Coho fishing starts in June, lasts to September.

Victoria, the capital city at the southern end of the island, has rapidly modernized since World War II but still retains its old Victorian charm. It is the cosmopolitan center of island life, a tourist mecca, favorite entry point for yachtsmen, and ferry terminus. There is excellent coho fishing alongshore from June through September. Sea-run cutts and dolly varden are found all summer long, and there is bottom fishing all year around.

Mainland British Columbia. The south coast is locally called the "Sunshine Coast," and is the scene of extensive resort and recreational development, centered around Vancouver city. The mainland stretches along Georgia Strait from the U. S. border to Bute Inlet, with hundreds of islands, islets, coves, and fjords. The peak of the salmon fishing is in the summer. A highway leads north as far as Lund, opposite Campbell River—assisted by several auto ferries—but the best way is by private boat or float plane. There is a steamer or mailboat service to many remote villages, lumber camps, and canneries, and some Vancouver outfitters now offer modern houseboat cruises to many good fishing areas.

British Columbia offers some of the world's most spectacular scenery. The inlets, bays, fjords and channels, pushed up against tall glacier-draped mountain ranges, the countless rivers and creeks stocked with a variety of salmon, bottom species, and shellfish, all add up to a fisherman's paradise. The local saying is, "When the tide is out the table is set."

From the jumping-off point of Vancouver, some of the more popular spots are Texada Island, Howe Sound, Jervis Inlet, Powell River, and Stuart Island.

North Coast. The inland passage north to Alaska is a maze of channels, narrow passages, and sometimes frightening tidal races between densely wooded islands, with long fingerlike fjords penetrating deeply into the coastal mountains. These are lonely waters, with few people and limited facilities. From Powell River to Prince Rupert, some 400 airline miles, there are only two towns of any size: Bella Coola at the head of North Bentinck Arm, which can also be reached via adventure road from the interior; and Ocean Falls, on the north side of King Island.

Prince Rupert, terminus of the new highway from the interior and the Canadian National Railroad, is a busy world port. It is connected by road to Kitimat, the huge aluminum complex, at the end of Kitimat Arm. Several outfitters operate from Prince Rupert, with both float plane and surface transportation. The usual method is to take clients by houseboat or cruiser to a floating camp at outlying points where the fishing is done from skiffs.

Rivers Inlet, just north of the tip of Vancouver Island, is one of the most famous salmon sportfishing spots in the world, and from here came the ninety-two-pound record chinook. There are many villages, canneries, and gas floats in the area, with ferry and mail service from Port Hardy on Vancouver Island.

Namu, at the mouth of Burke Channel, has an air strip and a mailboat with limited supplies and services. This is a popular yacht stop on the northward run.

Ocean Falls can be reached by air and mailboat. The facilities here are mostly company-owned, but it is a good jumping-off point for superb salmon fishing.

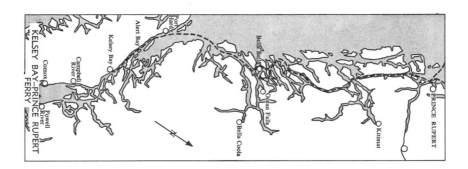

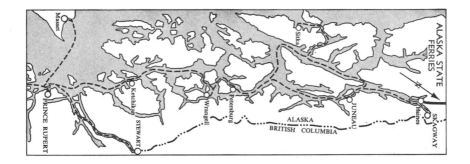

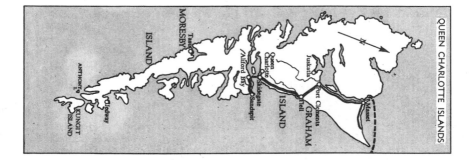

Kitimat, site of an old mission, now a booming industrial town with the Alcan aluminum smelter, is rated a fair to good fishing center. It is accessible by ferry and air, and by road from Prince Rupert.

Queen Charlotte Islands. Little known to the tourist and sportfisherman, these remote offshore islands can be reached only by boat and air. The two main islands of Graham and Moresby are divided by a narrow passage at Skidegate. The main settlements are connected by road, and there is an airport at Sandspit. The islands are mountainous, rugged, and densely forested. The several short streams, the Copper, Tiell, and Yakoun, have superb steelhead angling, but the islands are most famous for the coho fly fishing. The ocean or west side of the islands is deeply indented with inlets and bays, with heavy surf at times, and is one of the most remote and primitive sections on the North Pacific.

Stuart Island, one of the least-known of all B.C. fishing areas, has a really fabulous run of big chinook, some up to seventy and eighty pounds, beginning in June and lasting through August, with the best fishing up Phillips Arm. Local knowledge is needed and few services or accommodations are available, except at Stuart Island proper.

Washington

The state of Washington, in the image of most outsiders, is synonymous with the Pacific Northwest, with the queen city of Seattle the center of it all. This, of course, would be disputed by local residents of Oregon, Idaho, British Columbia, Alaska, and north California.

The coastal area of Washington is dominated by huge Puget Sound, an inland sea reaching 200 miles in from the Pacific. On the shores of the Sound live almost two-thirds of the state's population. Because of this, the area is sometimes referred to as "Pugetopolis." The climate features cool summers and mild, wet winters. The Olympic Mountains shield much of the area from the ocean and collect most of the rainfall before it gets to the interior. The "rain forest" of the

Olympics has some of the heaviest precipitation on the entire West Coast.

The Sound is connected to the open sea by the Strait of Juan de Fuca. The "outside" or ocean side of the Olympic Peninsula has few natural harbors or ports and is a surf-lashed coast broken by infrequent river mouths. Much of this coastline borders either National Park or Indian reservation.

Beginning at the Columbia River, the mariner will find the coastline broken by two large shallow estuaries—Willapa Bay and Grays Harbor—with long low sandy beaches in between. From Grays Harbor to Cape Flattery the coastline is more rugged, with brown and tan bluffs backed by heavy green timber, and many offshore sea stacks and reefs.

Washington's saltwater areas are subjected to heavy angling pressure, especially from May to October when the salmon runs are peaking. One can fish all year, however, for bottom species and for salmon, steelhead, or sea-run trout in one place or another.

West Coast Washington. Ilwaco, at the mouth of the Columbia, is a major world salmon port for sports fishermen, with a busy charter fleet that goes out daily from behind Cape Disappointment across the bar for coho and chinook, from May through September. The peak months are July and August, and a trip during the last two weeks in August is almost certain to bring limit catches. Every possible service and facility is available at Ilwaco and at several smaller centers close by. At this writing, no license is required for saltwater fishing in Washington. Ilwaco can be reached via the Astoria Bridge and U. S. 101, and from the north by other highway connections.

North of Cape Disappointment there is excellent chinook fishing around the north entrance to Willapa Bay, but the shoals are dangerous. Many charter boats from Westport fish off here.

Grays Harbor is a major lumber and shipping port, with the busy sportfishing and commercial fishing center of Westport just inside the bar. Westport is probably the world's

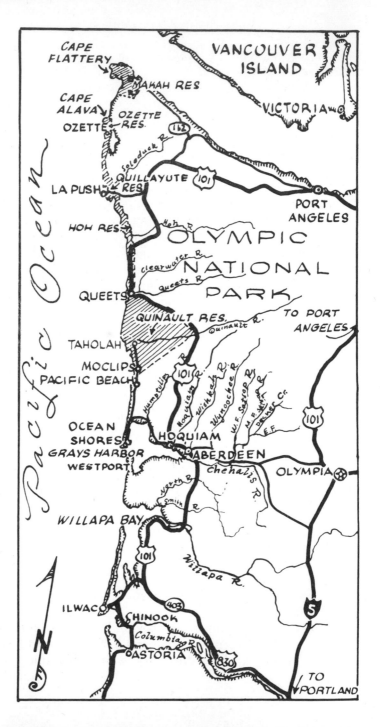

largest salmon charter fishing port, and from April to October it is a waterfront carnival with salmon anglers from all over the world here to get in on the bonanza. Ocean Shores, on the north side of the bay, is another new charter center.

Copalis Beach, at the mouth of the Copalis River, reached by State 209 highway, has minor access to the ocean fishing. Taholah, an Indian settlement at the mouth of the Quinault River, is a popular fishing point where Indian guides can be hired with dugout canoes. Queets, the next point north, at the mouth of the Queets River, can be reached from U. S. 101. The sportfishing is mostly winter steelhead. The Hoh River, just north, is another superb winter steelhead stream.

Forks, at the junction of U. S. 101 and a road leading to the Indian town and port of La Push, is a well-known sportsman's headquarters, especially during the winter steelhead runs. La Push, site of a Coast Guard station, is one of the most colorful and picturesque harbors on the Pacific, and an important sportfishing center. The best offshore salmon fishing is from July through September. The nearby Bogachiel and Soleduck rivers are two world famous steelhead streams.

The north coast of La Push is largely inaccessible to anglers. Around Cape Flattery and just inside the Strait of Juan de Fuca is Neah Bay, which can be reached from Port Angeles by road. This is a major sportfishing center, on the Indian reservation, and all services are available.

Farther down inside the Strait is Sekiu, another major salmon center at the mouth of the Hoko River. It is famous for the winter "blackmouth"—immature salmon—fishing that begins traditionally with the first frost, and lasts until May. Then come the big early spring chinooks, followed by various runs through the summer until October, when the coho salmon start in. From July until October in odd-numbered years, there is an excellent run of pink or humpbacked salmon. Humpies are two-year fish, coming back to spawn every other year.

Fishing in the Strait is done from boats operating close to shore where the ledges drop off sharply, and with lures deep down near the bottom.

One of the new type of offshore charter boats leaving from
harbors in Washington and other states in the Pacific Northwest.

Port Angeles is an important city with a protected harbor,
a ferry terminus to Vancouver Island and other islands in
the Sound, and every possible kind of accommodation and
facility for the sportsman. Agate and Crescent Beach close
by are top salmon and halibut fishing spots.

Sequim, pronounced "Squim," is known locally as the
"banana belt" of Puget Sound, due to a weather phenomenon
that somehow creates a pocket of mild, sunny weather regardless of prevailing conditions around it. This is a top
salmon and bottom fishing port, with all facilities.

Port Townsend, a historic waterfront town, is a ferry terminus, a major sportfishing center, adjacent to Discovery
Bay. Hood Canal, a long narrow arm, forms the east shore
of the Olympic Peninsula. Most of the canal is accessible
only by water, due to private ownership of the waterfront.
Hoodsport, at the southern end, is an important salmon
center.

Seattle, a major U. S. city and seaport, boasts salmon fishing right inside its harbor on Elliott Bay, as well as in Lake
Washington, which can be reached by a lock system. Winter
fishing is for blackmouth and bottom species such as cod
and rockfish. Coho and chinook salmon are present most of
the year, with humpies in the odd years. A rehabilitated

sockeye salmon run in Lake Washington holds promise as a sport, as well as a commercial, fishery. There is, of course, a high concentration of marinas, ramps, boat and fishing facilities in the Seattle area.

Tacoma Narrows, a section of the south sound area, has extensive sportfishing for salmon and bottom species, with several good winter steelhead streams nearby. Point Defiance, Dash Point, Browns Point, Commencement Bay, Fox Island, Day Island, Gig Harbor, and Wollochet Bay are all major sportfishing centers.

Bremerton, home of the big naval base, is a popular all-year fishing area. Blackmouth are caught from November through May, and sea-run cutthroat are found in the tidal currents under the sheer bluffs. Point No Point, located near Kingston, is best known for coho and blackmouth. Anderson Island, a large island off the Nisqually River between Olympia and Tacoma, is known mainly for blackmouth. Steilacoom, Shelton, and Olympia are major access points for salmon fishing from early spring to summer.

Whidbey Island, the largest in Puget Sound, is the home of the naval air station, and is surrounded by good salmon and bottom fishing. The island is reached by ferry at several points. Possession Point is popular for coho and hump-backed salmon, and chinooks; Mutiny Bay, Double Bluff, and Bush Point on the west side also rate tops. March through October is the normal season, although there are large concentrations of blackmouth in Holmes Harbor in early spring.

Edmonds and Mulilteo are major access points on the mainland. From July to September some really big chinooks pass the northwest tip of Whidbey Island bound for the Skagit and Fraser rivers.

Everett is a major city, headquarters for much saltwater fishing from July through November. During the winter, several adjacent streams have excellent steelhead fishing. Chinook and odd-year humpies are found close to the mainland shore. The mouth of the Snohomish River at Mission Bar is a hot spot for big chinook in August.

San Juan Islands. This delightful and picturesque group of islands and islets in Puget Sound between Whidbey and Vancouver Island is a paradise for the boater and sport fisherman. Like Sequim, the islands lie in a pocket of good weather, usually surrounded by other extremes. Blackmouth fishing is from December to March. July to September is best for odd-year humpies; September and October for coho. Many large fish are caught in these waters. There are numerous resorts, marinas, and other facilities, with ferry and air service to the mainland. Anacortes is a convenient access point.

North Puget Sound, Hope Island, just off the mouth of the Skagit River, was once famous for its big forty- to sixty-pound chinooks. There is good winter steelhead fishing in

A nice catch of assorted rockfish, including China rockfish in the foreground and (left to right) striped perch, pike perch, and quillback.

the Skagit. There are spring, summer, and fall runs of chinook, and odd-year humpies. Heavy tackle is needed in these waters, which have strong tidal currents. Resort facilities are limited.

Camano Island is a commuter's paradise, with most fishing done along the west side for small chinook and coho. In July and August some large chinook are taken. From March to September the coho, humpies, and chinook are present, with some winter blackmouth.

The city of Bellingham is a lumber, fishing, oil refining, and manufacturing center and the jump-off point for Lummi Island, Georgia Strait, and the northern San Juans. The west side of Lummi, the Bellingham Bay areas, and the Strait all have excellent salmon fishing. The salmon runs past here are headed mainly for the Fraser River and pass close inshore, from early spring until late fall.

Facilities and accommodations are plentiful at Bellingham, Blaine on the Canadian border, and Birch Bay. A remote and little-known piece of U. S. territory, Point Roberts, can be reached by boat or by road that detours into Canada and around Boundary Bay. The Strait of Georgia here separates the mainland from Vancouver Island.

Oregon

One of the most beautiful and spectacular coastlines in the world, Oregon's 430 miles of Pacific frontage alternates long, almost deserted stretches of sand beach backed by dunes and dense thickets of manzanita, salal, myrtlewood, and madrone, with bold bluff capes, and broken only by the outlets of twenty-two coastal streams. All but twenty-nine miles of this shoreline is in public ownership with unrestricted access. U. S. 101 runs the entire length of the coast, usually within sight of the ocean. With only nine bays, Oregon's estuarine resources are fragile and limited, and its natural harbors and safe havens are limited.

Oregon's top offshore saltwater fishing at this time is for salmon, chinook, and coho. Steelhead are taken during the

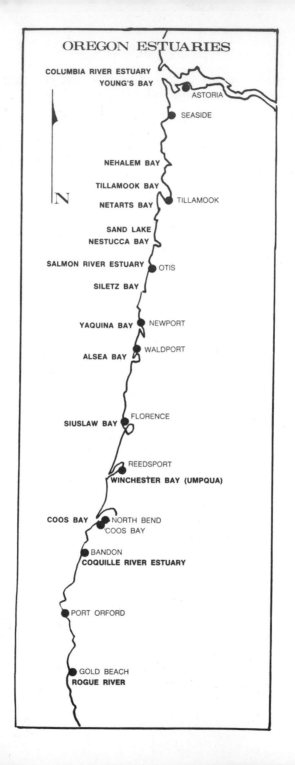

OREGON ESTUARIES

COLUMBIA RIVER ESTUARY

YOUNG'S BAY

ASTORIA

SEASIDE

NEHALEM BAY

TILLAMOOK BAY

NETARTS BAY

TILLAMOOK

SAND LAKE

NESTUCCA BAY

SALMON RIVER ESTUARY

OTIS

SILETZ BAY

YAQUINA BAY

NEWPORT

ALSEA BAY

WALDPORT

SIUSLAW BAY

FLORENCE

REEDSPORT

WINCHESTER BAY (UMPQUA)

COOS BAY

NORTH BEND

COOS BAY

BANDON

COQUILLE RIVER ESTUARY

PORT ORFORD

GOLD BEACH

ROGUE RIVER

N

runs in the tidal rivers. The third most popular fish is the sea-run cutthroat, which is found in all the estuaries and rivers and to some extent alongshore. Next in importance would be the bottom species, with halibut, lingcod, greenlings, and red snapper (rockfish) most commonly sought. The American shad and the striped bass complete the coastal gamefish bag. These two species are not native, but were introduced in the Pacific from the eastern seaboard about a century ago.

A "new" fishery rapidly developing off Oregon is the "bluewater run" for albacore tuna, which are present in vast schools off Oregon from July until October, although sport-fishing peaks in August. The commercial landings in Oregon alone amount to more than $30 million, and most of the tuna pack from U. S. waters nowadays is taken off the Pacific Northwest coast. As a sport fishery, however, it has become important only as recently as the late 1960s, although the first boats went out after tuna as early as 1936. Most regular charter fishing operators in Washington and Oregon offer tuna trips during July and August, in between salmon trips. At this time the albacore are found as close in as ten miles, with an average of twenty miles, depending upon winds and currents, and the upwelling of cold nutrient-filled waters. The albacore prefer a water temperature of from 58° to 65°, with 60° probably optimum, and they seem to follow the temperature gradients between the warm and cold water where the feed is most abundant. The commercial jig and bait boats commonly work the tuna from twenty to 200 miles offshore, staying out several weeks at a time.

One of the most adventurous sportfishing trips available anywhere in the world is the run out the blue water for albacore in one of the twenty-two-foot Cape Kiwanda dories that are launched through the surf near Pacific City.

The common bay and bottom fishes include twenty species of flatfish such as Dover sole, English sole, Pacific halibut, and starry flounder. There are also about twenty species of sculpin, including the red and brown Irish lords, and cabezon. The delectable lingcod is present in large numbers, as

Fishing off the rocks, on the coast of Oregon.

are the kelp greenling, sablefish, or black cod. There are at least fifty species of rockfish, the most common of which are the black, blue, and China rockfish, the bocaccio, and Pacific ocean perch (at this writing almost depleted by the Russian trawl fleets).

There are about ten species of surf perches, including pile perch, redtail, shiner, striped, walleye, and white surfperch.

Other marine species include Pacific tomcod, hake, pilchards, anchovies, skates, rays, and several kinds of sharks including blue, thresher, basking, and dogfish. There are green and white sturgeon in the bays, several kinds of smelts, sticklebacks, pipefish, gunnels and blennies, and *mola* or ocean sunfish.

The striped bass and shad, first introduced into the Sacramento system, are now found in Oregon rivers such as the Rogue, Coquille, Umpqua, Smith, Yaquina, Siuslaw, and Chetco. Over the years these two superb species have suffered from local public apathy, from commercial gillnetting, bay pollution, and destruction of watersheds by intense logging operations. The spawning period for both species in Oregon waters is from March through June, and frequently both species are found spawning at the same time in the same place.

The shad is the hardier and more prolific of the two species, and supports a substantial commercial fishery, especially in the Columbia River. About a half million are counted through the ladders at the lowest dam, Bonneville, each year. Since the creation of a series of impoundments on the Columbia and Snake, the shad have reached inland almost as far as Lewiston, Idaho.

The anadromous species common to Oregon are five species of Pacific salmon (chinook, coho, chum, sockeye, and humpbacked or pink), the smelts or eulachon, striped bass, shad, sea-run cutthroat, steelhead, and lamprey. Present, but rarely caught or identified, is the sea-run brown trout.

Salmon fishing starts in March and April and continues through November. There are two steelhead runs, summer and winter, with the action starting in early spring and continuing on and off throughout the year. Sea-run cutthroat fishing peaks in July and August, but the fish are generally caught from May through October.

The saltwater fishing in Oregon waters is good all year

Fishing fleet heading out for the Columbia Bar, early in the morning.

around, with some months better than others. There is no closed season for marine game species, no bag limit, and no license required (this does not include salmon, steelhead, and trout).

From south to north, the principal ports and river mouths are Chetco Harbor at Brookings with the Chetco and nearby Winchuck rivers; Pistol River and Hunter Creek; Gold Beach at the mouth of the Rogue, famous for its "spring hogs" (chinooks) and "half-pounders" (summer steelhead averaging four or five pounds), plus cohos, fall chinooks, and winter steelhead; Port Orford, a summertime port only; Elk and Sixes rivers; Coquille River, which enters the ocean at Brandon-By-The-Sea; Coos Bay, Oregon's largest estuary; Winchester Bay at Reedsport; Florence at the mouth of the Siuslaw; the Alsea River at Waldport; Yaquina Bay at Newport; Depoe Bay; Salmon River; Siletz Bay and Siletz River at Lincoln City; Nestucca Bay at Pacific City with nearby Cape Kiwanda; Tillamook Bay, which receives the Trask, Tillamook, Wilson, Kilchis, Miami rivers and has an offshore charter fleet at Garibaldi; Nehalem Bay; and then the mighty Columbia.

There are numerous smaller creeks and rivers that flow into the ocean, as well as a chain of about sixty freshwater lakes just behind the sand dunes. Clamming and crabbing are excellent most of the year in the bays and estuaries. While surf casting is still almost unknown on Oregon's coast, there are a number of excellent locations for rock and jetty fishing.

The Columbia River, which separates Oregon and Washington, has a five-mile wide estuary, and a tidal action that goes all the way inland to Bonneville Dam, about 150 miles upstream, and into the main tributaries such as the Willamette as far as the city of Portland. The river empties into the ocean across a bar considered at times one of the most dangerous in the world—fifty- to sixty-foot breaking waves are not uncommon during winter storms. The river "plume" fans out into the ocean, often extending in a warmer and fresher fan as far as 400 miles offshore.

Fishing for salmon, and ignoring everything but the tug of that line.

The Columbia spawns about eighty percent of all salmon caught in the Pacific Northwest, some of its runs traveling as far away as the Sacramento to the South and the Aleutian Islands to the North and West, before returning to complete the cycle. It is also one of the world's major sportfishing centers, with as many as 5,000 boats and 25,000 anglers found on or near the bar during the peak of the salmon runs. The river, which drains an enormous region extending to the Rocky Mountains, is an all-year around fishing river, with almost continuous salmon and steelhead runs. It is the home of sea-run cutthroat and jack salmon (immature fish return before they are able to spawn), plus shad, sturgeon, smelt, native trout, and the panfish including smallmouth and largemouth bass, crappies, bluegills, sunfish, and catfish. Marine species such as flounder and perch are found in the estuary, which is now spanned by a new toll bridge about four miles long.

The principal charter ports on the Oregon side are Astoria, Warrenton, and Hammond; on the Washington side, Chinook and Ilwaco. There are numerous "fish camps" where you can camp or park a trailer and launch a boat for fishing in the estuary or for crossing the bar to fish outside. The river is navigable as far as Portland, and this city, as well as Vancouver, Longview in Washington, and St. Helens, Rainier, and Astoria in Oregon, are major shipping ports.

The peak of the sportfishing season offshore is from June through August for salmon. During this period, the Coast Guard maintains a close watch on the fishing fleet with a fleet of rescue boats and aircraft, and a surf boat stationed right on the bar during hazardous periods. In spite of the danger, it is not uncommon to see sixteen-foot rowboats and rubber rafts offshore as far as the lightship.

There is a charter fleet of about 150 boats on the Washington side and about sixty on the Oregon side at this writing. They charge from $16 to $25 a day per person depending upon the boat and the services offered. Most of them furnish at least bait and a rod. Since limits of salmon are the rule during the peak season, an angler might bring home as much as fifty to 100 pounds of prime salmon, worth up to $2 a pound in the retail markets, so it's invariably a profitable "sport" fishing trip. During July and August, some of the boats also rig for tuna and make the run out to blue water often on the spur of the moment.

Tourists, sportfishermen, and private boat owners will all find complete facilities and services available at the Columbia estuary ports and communities. U. S. 101, the coast highway, crosses the river on the toll bridge. U. S. 26 and U. S. 30 connect with the interior points. It is about an hour and a half drive from Portland to the Oregon charter ports, and two hours to the Washington ports. The bridge toll is $1.50 at this time.

California

California's 1,000-mile coastline features one of the world's most varied and intense saltwater angling regions, ranging from the subtropical south coast to the central or midriff section to the redwood and fir-studded north coast. These three regions are marked by distinct differences in weather and climate, flora and fauna, and species of fish.

Southern California. San Diego is a fabulous sportfishing center, famous not only for its overnight "albacore specials" to the offshore tuna grounds, but for its all-year around party boats that ply back and forth to the banks and sea-mounts with the regularity of commuter buses, for its long-range luxury sportfishing charter trips to the islands off Baja California and even down around Cabo San Lucas and up into the Sea of Cortez. San Diego is also a major yachting and private boat center, complete with some of the finest marinas in the world.

Yellowtail remains the king of all saltwater sportfishing in these waters, however, and during the peak season from June to September, more than 100,000 anglers will be on the ocean pursuing these superb game fish. The albacore season starts in July and runs through September, with charter trips going as far as 120 miles offshore. Huge white seabass are caught in the early spring around the Coronados Islands. Giant seabass, halibut, barracuda, bonito, calico bass, and ocean whitefish are included in the reef and bottom species. Surf perch, lingcod, sheephead, kelp bass, rockfish, white croakers, rubberlip seaperch, opaleyes, sand bass, sculpins, bocaccio, chilipepper, flounder, jacksmelt, sharks, rays, corbina, grunion, and sargo, are only a few of the dozens of marine species found in the surf, among the kelp beds, and alongshore. The halibut mentioned is, incidentally, the California halibut *(Paralichtyhys californicus)*, or "port-sider," not to be confused with Pacific halibut *(Hippoglossus stenolepis)*.

Two or three companies operate long-range sportfishing charters to Guadalupe Island, Cedros, San Bonito Islands, Magdalene Bay, and Cabo San Lucas. Some go as far up in the Sea of Cortez as La Paz, and are generally around-the-clock fishing expeditions that also hit all the good, known, offshore banks coming and going. The trips last from four to sixteen days, during all the summer months. The boats range in size from eighty-five-footers to 105-foot welded

The "mob" at the mouth of the Klamath River.

aluminum jobs. They are all completely equipped and safe, with the larger boats offering such luxuries as air-conditioned staterooms and television. These are all-expense packaged tours with all details such as Mexican fishing licenses included and taken care of. The only drawback is that they offer no time for leisurely sight-seeing. You are seldom offered an opportunity to get ashore for a break, and almost all your time is occupied with fishing for yellowtail, marlin, sailfish, bonito, tuna, giant sea bass, wahoo, dorado (dolphinfish or *mahi-mahi*), and a couple dozen other tropical and subtropical game fish.

Northward from San Diego, the area around La Jolla (pronounced "La Hoya") is popular with skin divers, surf and rock anglers, and alongshore boats. It is also the home of the famed Scripps Institute of Oceanography. Offshore trips are made to the San Clemente Islands, to the forty-three-fathom and thirty-five-mile banks. The marlin waters extend from La Jolla to the Coronados Islands in the summer and early fall.

Del Mar, Encinitas, and Oceanside are all popular sportfishing centers. There is good corbina and surf fishing around San Mateo Point. Spring and summer and early fall are best for bottom fish from Oceanside north. Marlin are taken close in from Laguna to the "Barn" at this time, as are bluefin tuna.

Newport Bay is a large sportfishing center, with surf and bottom fishing as well as marlin, bluefin tuna, albacore, and other offshore species. Long Beach on San Pedro Bay is another busy area, and the jumping-off point for the Catalina Islands. This offshore group includes Catalina, Santa Barbara, San Nicolas, Santa Rosa, San Clemente, San Miguel, and numerous reefs and rocks. Big-game fishing for tuna, marlin, broadbill swordfish is popular, as is scuba diving. Sport boats come from the San Pedro Bay ports, and from Port Hueneme, Santa Barbara, and other points.

North from Long Beach, sportfishing is done from Santa Monica, Redondo Beach, Hermosa Beach, Manhattan Beach, Malibou, Dume Point, Port Hueneme, and Ventura for reef, surf, and bottom fishes. Anacapa Island is a popular spot for yellowtail, bottom fish, barracuda, sheephead, and red abalone. The Santa Clara River flats and vicinity are popular surf fishing areas.

The Santa Barbara Channel is heavily fished for most marine species, with sport boats going out from several points, but mainly from Santa Barbara. There are yellowtail, an occasional stray coho salmon, bonito, barracuda, white seabass. Carpenteria and Goleta Point are well-known centers as far north as Point Conception.

Middle California. Clamming is popular from Pismo Beach to Guadalupe. Surf and pier fishing are done all year, and there are many outlets where bait, tackle, and clam forks can be obtained.

The Avila area supports a year-round boat fishery, with launching from a public pier. Skin diving is also popular from skiffs. There is some "poke-poling" in the tidal pools for monkey-face eels.

In the Morro Bay area, year-round party boat operations are found, mostly for bottom species, but also an occasional salmon. Bonito, barracuda, and albacore are found here, too. Skiffs can be rented and launched at Embarcadero and Morro Bay State Park. There is clamming for Pismos, gapers, and Washington clams. Pier fishing is good in summer and fall, surf fishing is fair for perch, and an occasional striped bass is taken here.

Cayucos is another popular party boat and skiff base during the spring, summer, and fall. There is also pier and surf fishing in the spring and summer. Grunion spawn occasionally on the Cayucos beach in the spring, but most of the beach areas are privately owned. There is skin diving for abalone and bottom species.

From Piedras Blancas Point to Cambria on both sides of San Simeon is found some of the state's best abalone picking, as well as surf and rock fishing. There are several access points, including a state park. Party boats operate in the summer, but there are no skiff facilities. Some pier fishing is done.

State Highway 1 hugs the beach from Cape San Martin to Yankee Point, but the shoreline is rugged with few access points. There is no skiff launching or party boats, but sev-

Salmon (left) and stripers (right) caught on San Francisco beaches.

eral public campgrounds are found at Pfeiffer-Big Sur State Park and in the national forest areas.

From Carmel to Monterey the fishing ports are less numerous but there is much activity. Carmel, Pacific Grove, Moss Landing, Point Lobos, Pacific Grove, and Monterey Bay are the most popular.

There are numerous kelp beds in the Carmel Beach-Point Lobos area, with some steelhead fishing in the fall. Skiff angling is done around the kelp beds. The Hopkins Marine Station is located here but is not open to the public.

Monterey Bay has numerous charter operations all year around, and for salmon during the season. Skiffs can be rented and launched. Halibut and salmon are caught by trolling off Seaside. Crabbing is done off Cannery Row (made famous by John Steinbeck). There is bottom fishing over rocky reefs and from the breakwater to Point Pinos, and pier fishing at a couple of locations.

Clams, bottom and surf fishing, and some salmon fishing and abalone picking are available in the Capitola area, Santa Cruz, Natural Bridges, Año Nuevo Beach State Park, Pebble Beach, Halfmoon Bay, and Point San Pedro. Most communities have surf rentals, and charter boats operate out of the bigger centers with trips out to the Farallon Islands and trolling offshore for salmon. Skin diving, pier fishing, and poke-poling are popular.

The San Francisco Bay area, its rivers, and the offshore banks out to the Farallons offer a wide variety of fishing. Party boats operate out of San Francisco, Oakland, Alameda, Berkeley, Richmond, and Sausalito. King or chinook salmon and striped bass are taken trolling. There is bottom fishing at the Farallons, Point Bonita, and Bolinas Bay. Skiff rentals are found in most bay area communities, but you should remember that the waters off the Golden Gate get mighty hairy at times and only large, well-founded boats with experienced skippers work outside.

The beaches from Golden Gate to Pillar Point, including Baker Beach, San Francisco Ocean, Sharp Park, and Rockaway are good for striped bass from May through October, with surfperch in the spring. Skin diving is not popular here due to the shark-infested waters.

Muir Beach, just north of the Golden Gate, is almost inaccessible but offers striped bass, surf fish, and poke-poling. Herring spawn here in the winter months.

The Bolinas-Stinson area has small boat harbor facilities, plus surf and bottom fishing. Drakes Bay has clams, surfperch, bottom fish, and a sea lion rookery.

Abbotts Lagoon offers bottom fishing, especially during years of heavy rainfall, which opens the bay to ocean fishes. The Dillon Beach and McClure Beach areas have party boats and resort facilities for bottom fishing and salmon trolling. Skiff rentals and public launch ramps are also available. Tomales Point is accessible only by skiff, and in many places skiffs can only be launched across the beach.

Bodega Bay has year-round charter and party boats, as well as skiff rentals and launching. There is skin diving and jetty fishing, as well as surf netting for smelt and clamming in the bay.

The Russian River area has skiff rentals but the ocean is hazardous for small boats. Surf casting, rock fishing, smelt netting, and jetty fishing are popular. This is about the southern limit for steelhead in the fall. Striped bass, some salmon, and bottom fish are found here.

There is a good deal of private land along this shoreline, especially from Gualala to Salt Point. No party boats operate here, but there is some skiff launching with free access to some of the state's best fishing. A skiff can be launched at Salt Point and Stewarts Point.

Northern California. Surf and bottom fishing, skin diving, poke-poling, and abalone picking are found from the Point Arena area to Fort Bragg. There are skiff rentals and launchings, with party boats at Fort Bragg from April to October out of Noyo and Albion, for salmon trolling and bottom jigging. King or chinook and silver or coho salmon are found here. From September to November the coho moves up the rivers and are accessible to skiff anglers. Ocean trolling is in July and August. Pier fishing is available, as is jetty fishing. Surf netting is popular for smelt at the mouth of creeks.

Shelter Cove has skiff fishing and abalone picking, rock and surf fishing. The Eel River lagoon has good skiff fishing for salmon in September, October, and November. There is redtail perch in the spring and the crabbing is also good.

Humboldt Bay has complete facilities for sport- and commercial fishing all year around, with the spring, summer, and fall best. Salmon are caught by trolling and mooching. Skiff fishing is hazardous on the outgoing tides. There is clam digging on the flats and in the sloughs, jetty fishing at Buhne Point, surf fishing at Mad River and Centerville, plus pier fishing at numerous points.

Trinidad Harbor offers pier fishing, party boats, and skiff rentals, and skin diving for abalone. Coho salmon appear in August and September. There is surf smelt netting at Luffenholz Beach.

The Klamath River area is the site of some of the most intense fishing activity on the West Coast. The lagoon and

Bodega Bay, California, from the air.

river fishery is for kings, coho, and sea-run cutthroat, and steelhead in the fall and winter. Casting or plunking from shore, or anchored in the current with skiffs, are the most popular methods. Best months for king or chinook are August and September; coho, September and October; for cutthroat, winter and early spring. Surf netting for smelt is done on the beach. Candlefish spawn in the lagoon and can be dipped during the spring run. Sturgeon, flounder, and redtail perch are also caught.

Crescent City harbor has party boat and skiff rentals for salmon trolling and bottom fishing, May through September being the best months. Pier fishing, skiff launching, and other facilities can be found here. Razor clam digging, skin diving, and surf netting are popular.

The Smith River lagoon is another large skiff fishery during the salmon and steelhead season. Coho, chinook, steelhead, and sea-run cutts are found here in late summer through the winter. Razor clams are found on the beaches and surf casting for perch is a favorite sport.

Hawaiian Islands

There is an old saying in the Islands that when the mango trees bloom, the bonito will come in great crowds, and the marlin will not be far behind. About the middle of March the mangoes are covered with blossoms. And in July each year, the famed Hawaiian International Billfish Tournament gets underway on the Kona coast.

The fiftieth and most exotic state began as an island kingdom, settled by Polynesians who arrived in canoes after long voyages across thousands of miles of open sea. It was frequented by nineteenth century missionaries and Yankee whalers; became an independent republic in 1894, a U. S. territory in 1900, and a full-fledged "overseas" state on August 1, 1959.

Hawaii is a group of eight large and numerous smaller islands sprawling across 1,400 miles of open Pacific in a general northwest-southeast direction, astraddle the Tropic

of Cancer, and a long way from the "South Seas" of song and story, approximately 2,000 nautical miles west of mainland North America. The land area is 6,424 square miles, with the big island of Hawaii accounting for 63 percent of this. The seven other major islands making up most of the land area are Maui, Oahu, Kauai, Molokai, Lanai, Niihau, and Kahoolawe.

Hawaii. The big island covers 4,021 square miles, and has an unusually good climate. The Konas occur from October through April and provide most of the rainfall and gales. At this time lee anchorages are unsafe. November through April is the rainy season, August and September the warmest months, January and February the coldest. The Kona Coast is Hawaii's most famous fishing ground, and headquarters for the giant blue marlin, some of which weigh over 1,000 pounds. Other species are the *mahi-mahi* or dorado, yellowfin tuna *(ahi)*, bonito *(aku)*, jack crevalle *(ulua)*, barracuda *(kaku)*, bonefish *(oio)*, wahoo *(ono)*, and many other tropical species. Oddly enough, the bottom or reef fishes, which include more than forty species of groupers and snappers from Tahiti to Japan, are absent from Hawaiian waters. This wide gap between the larger and smaller marine species in the normal food chain has long puzzled marine biologists, but is probably due to the underwater geology of the archipelago.

Hilo is the principal port of Hawaii, but most of the game fishing is done out of Kailua-Kona where the Billfish Tournament is held in July. The Kona Coast is sheltered from the northeast trades and is popular for its calm clear waters and excellent fishing which is just offshore. The best area is off Keahole Light.

There are many charter boats available, numerous hotels, and all manner of tourist and fishing facilities. The 1972 prices for charters ranged from $125 to $150 a full day, $75 to $90 a half day, for the boat. Single fisherman rates would vary accordingly. Skin diving and light tackle boats vary from $64 a day to $45 for a half day.

Maui Island. Some twenty-six miles northwest of Hawaii,

An 800-pound blue marlin caught off the Kona coast.

Maui is the second largest island. Marine supplies for small craft are found at Kahului and Wailuku, with fuel and water at Kahului, Maalaea, and Lahaina. The latter is a charming remnant of the old whaling days which has been rediscovered by the well-heeled international yacht set. The island has frequent air service.

The waters off Lahaina were once the ancient breeding and resting grounds for Pacific whales, long since killed or driven off by whaling ships. The water is relatively shallow and the run to the deepwater marlin grounds is a considerable trip, often with rough going. Most of the saltwater charter boat fishing is done in the triangular area touching the islands of Lanai, Kahoolawe, and Maui. The southeast tip of Lanai produces the best marlin fishing in the fall. At other times *mahi-mahi, ono,* and various tunas are found in abundance. Charter rates are approximately $125 a day, or $75 a half day, with a maximum of six anglers and all gear furnished.

Kahoolawe Island. Located six miles across Alalakeiki Channel from Maui, this island is a restricted military area closed to the public.

Lanai Island. Eight miles westward across Auau Channel from Maui, it features extensive pineapple production and cattle raising. Lanai City has about 3,500 people and is in the center of the island. Kaumalapau Harbor is the best port. Fishing craft moor to unlighted buoys in the harbor.

Kauai Island. This area has some of the finest fishing in the Hawaiian chain, although charter facilities are limited. The top fish is the yellowfin or Allison tuna, in late spring. The present world record was caught here. Other game fish include the *mahi-mahi,* marlin, and bonito. The best bone-fishing in the Pacific is found here, along the Hanalei or north shore, where the world record was held for years. Light tackle anglers find excellent sport along the beach for jack crevalle and other species. The boats rent for about $10 an hour for inshore fishing, $125 a day for the big ones.

Niihau Island. Just across the channel, about seventy square miles in size, Niihau is privately owned and operated as a cattle ranch.

Oahu Island. Considered the "main" island, Oahu is the third largest. Pearl Harbor and Honolulu are located here, and many lesser ports. The only shelter on the northeast coast is Kaneohe Bay. The climate is exceptionally pleasant, but with great variations in temperature from one part to another.

A large fleet of deep sea sportfishing boats from forty to sixty-three feet in size is located at Honolulu's Kewalo Basin, about five minutes by taxi from the main hotel district. Parties are limited to five or six lines per boat. Rates

vary from $125 to $90 a day, with half days for $70. The
fishing day begins at 7 a.m. and lasts until 4 p.m.

Boats go out for many different species, and a wide variety
of tackle is used. The giant marlin are taken on heavy gear,
of course, with reels as big as 14/0.

Penguin Banks to the South has large numbers of tuna and
mahi-mahi, and Barber's Point and the Waianae coast have
the big marlin and yellowfin. Trips down the coast overnight
to the banks and outside islands will put the angler over a
wide range of sportfishing. These overnight boats anchor at
night and jig for bottom species, not commonly taken on
charter boats.

Molokai Island. This is the site of the famed Leper Colony.
There are a number of small harbors, the best being Kauna-
kakai. Kamalo Harbor, however, offers the best protection
from Konas.

Of the lesser Hawaiian Islands, only Kure Island is open
to fishermen. About fifty miles west northwest of Midway,
this is an atoll about four and a half miles in diameter with
a lagoon and barrier reef. The best anchorage is on the west
side in eight to twelve fathoms, sand and coral bottom. A
break in the barrier reef provides entrance to the lagoon.
The Outer Islands are part of the National Wildlife Refuge,
and entry is restricted. The Midway Islands comprise a
restricted naval defense area, and unauthorized entry is
prohibited.

Mexico

Pescadores who have yet to make the pilgrimage to the
fishing waters of Mexico's west coast, Sea of Cortez, and
Baja Peninsula have a fabulous adventure awaiting them.
This region is without doubt the finest saltwater sportfishing
water in the world. The variety and fecundity of marine life
is almost beyond belief. The Sea of Cortez has been called
the world's greatest "fish trap," and this is no overstatement.

Add to this a climate during the winter and spring fishing
seasons that is matchless—warm, salubrious temperatures,

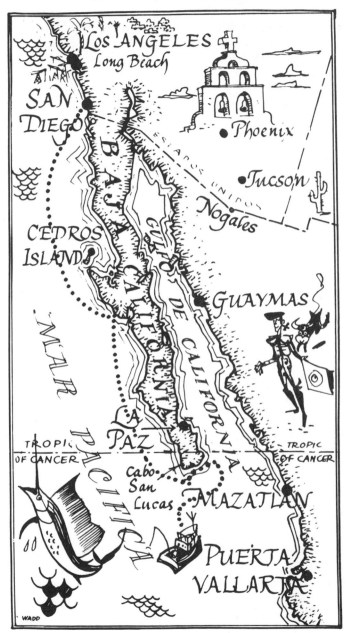

clear blue skies, a turquoise ocean, thousands of miles of white sandy beaches virtually deserted, and flaming sunrises and sunsets—and you have a true South Seas paradise.

Baja California. Also called Lower California, this narrow brown and tan mountainous peninsula hangs like an appendix below the U.S.-Mexican border for about 800 miles, separated from mainland Mexico by the Sea of Cortez (sometimes called the Gulf of California by unromantic mapmakers). With the exception of a few towns, fewer roads, and the modern city of La Paz, the peninsula is a vast primitive region inland from the beaches. The only practical means of transportation for the visitor is by boat or by air. The west coast or Pacific side of the peninsula is the most rugged and difficult to reach, and, of course, is exposed to the open Pacific. The east coast of the peninsula contains all of the towns and luxury fishing resorts, which are mainly reached by air taxi. There is airline service to La Paz, and also ferry ship service to La Paz from Mazatlán on the mainland. The fishing resort hotels all have fleets of modern sportfishing boats and guides, private air strips, and complete facilities. They are located at intervals along the coast as far as the extreme tip at Cabo San Lucas. The visitor can also find excellent guide and boat rental services on his own at the larger towns such as Loreto and Mulege.

The region is a mecca for private yachts making the long run "downhill" from San Diego, or brought overland to mainland ports for launching, and for trailer sailors who tow their boats in by car. Due to the long distances involved in yachting, and the inevitable red tape, there are some problems attendant upon this activity including adequate fuel supplies. Each year, however, more facilities are added and there is gradual improvement.

Oddly enough, private airplane is one of the most practical methods of transportation. There are numerous airstrips, and it is possible to land on the beaches almost anywhere in an emergency. Fuel is available at strategic points, and the flying weather is almost always good.

The long-range sportfishing charter boats from San Diego

make regular trips down the outside of the Baja Peninsula, putting in at offshore islands such as Guadalupe and Cedros, and sometimes calling at Magalena Bay where the gray whales breed, fish the offshore banks and seamounts, and frequently round Cabo San Lucas and run up into the Sea of Cortez to the Gorda Banks and even La Paz.

These trips are run almost continuously in the fall, winter, and spring, and vary from four-day excursions to the long one of sixteen days or more. The boats are modern, well-equipped, safe, and expertly skippered. They range from eighty-five-footers to new 105-footers with air-conditioned staterooms and every luxury. The costs vary considerably, but as a guide, a twelve-day trip would cost about $450 per person at this writing. One can figure that such a vacation would run between $25 and $50 a day, which compares very favorably with domestic vacation trips.

These long-range charter boats have many advantages. They almost always put you on top of the finest billfishing in the "Golden Triangle" that runs from Mazatlán to Cabo San Lucas to Acapulco. They carry live bait for most effective fishing, and they have expert crew members aboard to help the novice and assist with tackle. Nights are usually spent anchored in some cozy cove where you can jig for bait fish, such as the rare *caballita* or "cobbie," a species of mackerel that makes the finest billfish bait of all. These are kept alive in the bait tanks for the next day's fishing.

Sea of Cortez. This is a long gourdlike gulf that separates Baja from the mainland. It was first discovered and settled almost a century before the Pilgrims landed on the east coast of North America. This area is just now being rediscovered by the sportfishermen, and most of the tourist and resort developments at this time are found on the east shore. Modern highways lead south from the U.S. border to large cities such as Mazatlán, Guaymas, Manzanillo and with relatively easy access to Puerto Vallarta and Acapulco. There are numerous boat launching facilities and trailer resorts on the east shore. The modern ferry ship service from Mazatlán to La Paz is a means of taking a car and small boat across to fish the La Paz, Loreto, Mulege, and Rosalia River grounds, but is rather expensive.

The big hotels at places such as Mazatlán offer modern day charter boat service with guides for the offshore bill-fishing, which is found about ten miles from the beach.

The Sea of Cortez is an unbelievable natural marine aqua-rium. At any given time one will see greyhounding dolphin-fish, sharks, porpoises, whales cavorting, seals and sea lions, leaping manta rays, boils of bait fish under attack by forag-ing schools of marlin, sailfish, roosterfish, and other game species. In the rocky caverns under the boat you'll find octopi, endless schools of reef and bottom fishes, lobsters, shrimp.

The prevailing winds are northwesterly from November to May, and southeasterly the rest of the year. Moderate north-west gales occur at the upper or north end of the gulf in December, January, and February. In the lower end, around the mouth, southeasterly gales are common during the rainy season from May to November. A local hurricane called *El Cordonazo* occurs once every few years at the end of the

Sunrise on the Sea of Cortez, off Baja California.

rainy season. A local form of the *williwaw,* called the *chubasco,* occurs about once every five years. For the most part, however, the weather is well nigh perfect and even during the hot season, the nights are cool. Boats can be trailered over a paved road from Mexicali to San Felipe on the Gulf coast.

The Sea of Cortez is noted for its extreme tidal range at the upper end near the mouth of the Colorado River. Boating, however, is considered safe as long as proper attention is paid to prevailing winds and currents. From one end of the gulf to the other there are innumerable small coves, offshore islands, and long stretches of inviting beaches for fishing, skin diving, and swimming. The water is incredibly clear and schools of fish are readily visible from the boat. Lobsters, clams, scallops, and mussels are easily gathered.

Mulege, a tropical oasis on the Rio Rosalia, is a fabulous spot for snook, roosterfish, and grouper fishing. Santa Rosalia, a mining town of some 5,000, is a port of entry further north. A road now being improved leads from La Paz to Loreto and Mulege on the west shore of the gulf. On the mainland coast, Guaymas is one of the best-known towns, with a population of more than 40,000 and a busy wintertime tourist season.

Southward from Guaymas are endless miles of beaches, deserted villages, and groves of palm trees, with an occasional stream such as the Yaqui River. Yavaros, a port of entry, Topolobampo, a village of about 500 and Los Mochis, a city of 12,000, are found along this coast.

Mazatlán, the commercial port of Mexico's west coast, is a modern city of 100,000 with luxury resort hotels, charter fleets, and complete facilities. It is a port of entry, within the jurisdiction of the U. S. consul at Nogales, but the consul at Guadalajara is closer, and more convenient.

The *chubascos* are relatively common here from May to November although not every year. They last from two to four hours and blow with an intensity of Force 8. The gale is usually accompanied by lightning, thunder, and rain, with a rapidly rising sea.

Mainland South. From Mazatlán to the Chamatla River or the Rio del Rosario, the coast is low and sandy. Southward there are long stretches of deserted beach and villages and a small American settlement. Rio Grande de Santiago or Lerma River, also breaks this coast. There are numerous small lagoons, projecting rocky points, and some offshore islands.

San Blas, a busy town of 30,000, port for the cigar-making city of Tepic some thirty miles inland, has been "discovered" by tourists and anglers. The coast here is mountainous with sandy plains, open beaches broken by bluffs.

Puerto Vallarta, once an obscure village and anchorage for cargo barges, became famous when a Hollywood movie company discovered it, and now is a popular tourist mecca.

Southward the coast is backed up by 3,000-foot high mountains, with an occasional remote village. Manzanillo is a major shipping port, where complete facilities are available for the visiting yacht and sportfisherman.

From here on south rocky bluffs, mountains, and breaks

A marlin on the line and fighting hard, off Mexico.

with white beaches mark the coastline, with an occasional lagoon or river mouth such as the Sacatula. The international jet set city of Acapulco is a port of entry for yachts, and has a population of about 100,000 with heavy tourist traffic.

The rainy season here is from June through October, with an annual fall of fifty inches, making it somewhat of a humid tropical environment. In December and January, the temperature seldom exceeds 90°, but inland from the ocean the heat becomes intense at times.

Surprisingly, for a modern city, sanitary conditions are well below standard. Malaria is common through the year, amoebic dystentery and other intestinal diseases are prevalent.

White sandy beaches extend southward for miles, broken by an occasional rocky point, reef or mangrove lagoon. The Gulf of Tehuantepec, a huge indentation in the mainland coast, is relatively shallow and subject to rough seas and heavy surf where currents and tidal effects are confused. Sailing boat skippers know this section as a potentially dangerous lee shore. The *Tehuantepec* is a fierce seasonal gale of hurricane force caused by the venturi effect of the narrow Isthmus of Tehuantepec as the trade winds are forced up and over the mountain passes.

As the coast of Guatemala is reached, the wind veers off to the west and slowly dies. The coastline to the border is a continuous series of high bluffs, rocky beaches, sea stacks, backed by dense undergrowth and broken by an occasional river such as the Tayuta.

CHAPTER THREE

Getting Into Gear

YOU CAN BUY a saltwater fishing outfit for as little as $29.95, but you would have no trouble at all spending $1,000 for just a rod and reel. The serious Pacific saltwater angler doesn't stop with just one outfit, however. Sooner or later he will fish from jetties and reefs, docks and bridges in bays and estuaries, from skiffs, sampans, party boats, and private yachts, and will plunk from beaches and bars.

In these different places he will encounter bottom species, anadromous species, offshore pelagics, tropical fish, and "exotics" (introduced species). He will learn local customs and techniques, which call for a variety of equipment.

So, over the years, his garage will take on the appearance of a sporting goods store. There are ways, nevertheless, of keeping the essentials to a minimum and still be prepared for all kinds of fishing.

Here is how I as one professional fishing editor and columnist, who must go completely equipped for any kind of fishing that might be encountered, cope with this confusion and expense.

When I'm fishing in unfamiliar waters, my first rule is to

rent locally the gear I need. This is almost always possible at any fishing center I have visited, and is simply a routine matter when fishing with a guide or on a charter or party boat. The cost is usually nominal; you don't have to invest in a large inventory. But most important, you don't have to pack it along with you. If you travel by air, the baggage smashers employed by the airlines will quickly convince you that it's better to rent. For those instances where I *must* take tackle—such as for a special story about testing some gear —I pack the rods in a thick-walled aluminum tube, like those used for irrigating crops, and seal the ends with wood and canvas plugs. This has caused no end of frustration and consternation to airline baggage departments, which have yet to devise a way of breaking the rods thus protected.

It should be mentioned right here that the west coast of North America does not have the extensive beach buggy type of fishing found on the east coast. Beaches suitable for this are not as extensive. Much of the seacoast—especially in California and Washington—is privately owned, and in areas where conditions would be favorable, such as Oregon, the use of motor vehicles is often banned.

The freshwater fisherman can often pursue his sport with a single spinning or flycasting outfit. Saltwater angling is complicated by not only a bountiful sea that offers fish from half-pound size to thousand-pound monsters, but by the corrosive action on the metal gear. Another difference is that saltwater species are often many times as ferocious as their freshwater cousins, and many of them have mouths full of razor blades and heads covered with horns and spikes.

The first time I fished offshore in a small boat for albacore, I used one of these so-called saltwater grade spinning reels. The powerful runs of these long-finned lightning bolts shredded the nylon gears into powder.

I have fished over the offshore reefs of the Pacific Northwest with "salmon tackle," where on any given cast one might bring up a lingcod, a red snapper, a greenling, a halibut, or a flounder. Similarly, fishing with a native guide in a *canoa* in a Mexican mangrove lagoon or pass with light

Rigging up gear on the way out to the offshore fishing grounds.

spinning gear at night, I've been smashed by pargo, corvina, and even snook on the same lure.

All of which, over the years, has led me to conclude that it is more practical to outfit for specific *groups* of fishes, rather than to attempt to match tackle to individual species or to organize tackle for different *methods,* such as surf casting, trolling, mooching, or jigging.

When you outfit for specific groups, you can use the same tackle for many different methods and many different species. For example, Lee Wulff fishes for marlin with ordinary flyfishing tackle off Pinas Bay; Al McClane has caught big tyee salmon in British Columbia waters with ultra-light spinning tackle. On the other hand, rigged for marlin and sailfish off Mexico, you are almost sure to hook a dorado or yellowfin tuna sometime during the day. You might be jigging for

ocean whitefish and accidentally hook a 300-pound giant
sea bass or grouper. I have caught shad and striped bass
alternately on light tackle using the same lures (including
flies) on occasions when both species were spawning at the
same time on the surface.

So my method may be of some use to you in outfitting for
your own purposes. It can be as inexpensive as you desire,
and only that part of it that suits your needs, need be ac-
quired. Later, if necessary, the arsenal can be expanded.
Mainly, it will save you hundreds of dollars over the hap-
hazard acquisition of tackle and gear.

I group all saltwater game fish into four basic classes.
There is nothing original in this, and the classes are loose
and flexible, not rigidly closed. Depending upon the region
you fish, you can insert or remove different species. The
primary object is to group species by size and fighting ability
and their tendency to be found in the same waters at the
same time. For example, you might hook a wahoo while
trolling for sailfish, and the wahoo would be in the thirty- to
forty-pound size compared to the 125 to 150 pounds for
the sailfish.

Class I
  giant marlin
  giant shark

Class II
  marlin   wahoo
  sailfish   yellowfin tuna
  dorado   ocean bonito

Class III
  salmon   grouper   yellowtail
  steelhead   barracuda   striped bass
  lingcod   roosterfish   mackerel

Class IV
  sea perches   sculpins   pompano
  sea-run trout   pargo   flounder
  shad   pink salmon   jacks

These are merely examples of how I classify species according to tackle. Naturally, you won't find salmon and steelhead mingling with roosterfish, but at different times and in different places you can use the same gear for all three. The most common group of fishes that you will encounter is, of course, Class III, all of which can be caught on a single outfit, whether it be spincasting, trolling, surf casting, or salmon mooching. If the only saltwater fishing you do is for fishes in this classification, then the same outfit will be practical, no matter what region you fish. For that once-in-a-lifetime trip for Class I or Class II monsters, you can always rent tackle on the spot.

In the Pacific Northwest, I use the same tackle for albacore, chinook salmon, striped bass, and white sturgeon. For Class IV fishes, I use a medium saltwater type spinning gear. Occasionally I use a steelhead and salmon flyrod for streamer fly fishing from rocks and jetties. So you can see how flexible this system can be. At the same time, it keeps one's collection of gear at a minimum, the garage reserved for car and workshop, instead of a tackle warehouse, and your bride in a relatively good mood about the whole thing.

Rods. Almost all saltwater rods in all classes today are made from solid or hollow fiberglass blanks and are far superior to the old-fashioned bamboo and laminated wood. With ordinary care, they are virtually indestructible. Generally they are two-piece, with the tip section about five- to five and one-half feet long. The reels are almost always bolted or screwed on with wing nuts. The better rods, especially for the heavier fish, have roller guides and tips to lessen the friction on the line. In my opinion, all saltwater rods for Class I, II, and II should have roller guides or at least a roller tip, even if you have to get a blank and make your own rod.

Certain tackle combinations are arbitrarily set up by fishing clubs that sponsor contests, so if you plan to enter any of these, keep this in mind in selecting tackle. Most of these competitions take in the size of the line. For example, the Hawaiian International Billfish Tournament rules allow for doubled points if you use a fifty-pound line over a 100-pound line.

For surf casting, which' often requires long pitches with heavy weights against an onshore wind, a special surf casting rod is almost necessary, but this can also be used for other purposes such as pier and jetty fishing, and for bottom jigging. Generally, a lighter more limber tip is needed for Class IV and III fishes, where maximum sinker weight is three or four ounces. Heavier fish and heavier sinkers require a heavier or stiffer tip action.

A light spinning rod will be from seven and one-half to nine feet in length, a medium rod from eight to ten feet, and the heavier surf rod from ten to fourteen feet. Big-game boat

A large "knucklehead" used for marlin and sailfish off Mexico. Note rod and 6/0 reel.

rods are another special breed, and these often are stiff clubs of around six feet.

The trend these days for all-around saltwater use is the spinning or spincasting outfit where any casting is involved. For boat use or trolling, a conventional reel can still be used with a suitable spinning rod.

Ultra-light spinning tackle and flycasting gear for saltwater use also offer a whole new field with tremendous potential.

Reels. Saltwater reels in general use for Pacific fishing are of the conventional freespooling types in various sizes, spinning reels with bail pickup arms, or to a lesser extent the level-wind bait casting or spincasting types.

The size of the reel is governed more by how much line is needed. A 10/0 reel, for example, will hold 500 yards of 36-thread line, or 700 yards of 24-thread line. A 12/0 reel will hold 600 yards of 39-thread line, or 800 yards of 24-thread line. These old tournament classifications are still used today for big-game fishing, but with ordinary saltwater fishing and modern monofilament and braided synthetic lines, they are almost meaningless for the average angler.

The better reels today are precision instruments of the finest noncorrosive materials. The better ones cost from $400 on up. Fortunately, good quality reels that will do the job are available in the average price range. The smaller conventional freespooling reels in sizes 1/0, 2/0, and 3/0 are good for Class III and IV fish, and models in sizes up to 20/0 are built. Most of the big-game fishing is in the Class II category, however, and for this 4/0 and 5/0 reels with a maximum of 12/0 to 14/0 are used with medium and heavy rods. These reels do not have level wind, but do have freespooling and star drags, both of which features are necessary. The best way to select a reel with the capacity you require is to consult the manufacturers' catalogs or instruction sheets.

Reels for fly fishing should be of large capacity, at least one-inch spool width, capable of holding lots of backing plus Number 8 and heavier lines. A reel holding the line and 100 to 150 yards of braided Dacron of eighteen- to twenty-five-pound test is the maximum needed for snook, bonefish, and steelhead.

Lines. This is the age of synthetics, and nowhere has it been more beneficial than in saltwater angling. Anyone who grew up with the old cuttyhunks and silk lines will appreciate the monofilaments, braided Dacron, Nylon, and other synthetics of today.

For big-game fishing braided Dacron is widely used, with braided or mono Nylon for leaders. Nylon has good elastic qualities which take up shock, while Dacron has very little stretch but is easier to handle on the reel. Limp or braided metallic lines are also widely used for big saltwater species, particularly the ones that have lots of sharp teeth. Monofilaments are best for casting. Braided lines should be used for trolling and jigging. Light lines and small diameters are used with small lures and bait, and small reels. For heavier spinning and for rocky areas, monofilaments up to twenty-five-pound test are used.

Fly lines are usually in the weight-forward (WF) class, or with the "saltwater taper" matched to the rod used. The

Hooking up baitfish for bottom species.

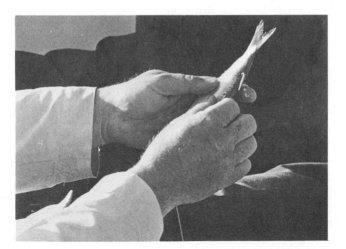

Weighted tuna jigs imitate squid.

floating lines are widely used for general fishing, but sinking lines are necessary to get down quickly to where the fish are when they are not feeding on the surface. The most used saltwater sizes are WF9F, WF10F, and WF11F, but sinking tips or lead core lines are also popular.

Saltwater leaders are usually tapered with twelve-pound tippets tied to the end of the line to take up shock. Shock tippets should be Nylon or stretch and can be anything up to 100-pound test and twelve inches long.

Lures and Bait. Most saltwater flies used are streamers and are supposed to imitate bait fish such as herring, anchovies, candlefish, or sauries. The coho streamer originated in British Columbia, and was later perfected in the Puget Sound area by tank tests which indicated that polar bear hair in red, blue, and green streaks closely simulated these bait fishes.

Streamers with long feathers are excellent producers. Marabou wings are especially good. Tom McNally once gave me a bundle of nameless streamers he had tied up for use in the Caribbean. I found they also worked on salmon in the Pacific Northwest. I have also used Joe Brooks' favorite shrimp flies on west coast shad and striped bass. So it seems that size, action, and color combinations tend to be universal in effectiveness.

Probably the most common fish catcher in any ocean is live or fresh bait, which includes seaworms, clams, pileworms, bloodworms, squid, sand eels, shellfish, sticklebacks, cottids, sculpins, herring, pilchards, anchovies, mullet. Anchovies are widely used in the Pacific for live bait, and can be purchased from bait barges in the major fishing areas. Most big-game boats in areas such as Southern California carry live bait in special circulating tanks, and these are by far the most effective on saltwater species. The live bait is commonly used for tuna, albacore, yellowtail, and billfish in southern waters, but almost never for salmon and northern species. When live bait is used, the game fish are generally scouted by trolling, and when found the boat is stopped amid the school and chummed with the anchovies. This often turns the gamefish school into a frenzied mob that will hit anything thrown at them.

Mackerel, mullet, and similar bait fish are widely used for billfish in special harnesses and hookups that vary from one locality to another. But the most effective method for marlin and sailfish is the use of live bait caught locally and kept in the bait tanks. In Mexican waters a species of mackerel called *caballitas* can be taken easily by jigging at night over deep underwater canyons. These "cobbies" are deadly on all forms of big game fish.

In the Pacific Northwest, the use of frozen herring and anchovies is almost universal. The usual rig is a two-hook harness with the whole fish, or with the head cut off, or "plug cut." Sometimes the bait is cut in strips and fished that way.

Fresh frozen bait is readily available at all sportfishing centers on the west coast, although live bait is harder to come by, unless you catch it yourself. But in all cases, the party and charter boats can supply the bait as well as the tackle.

Artificial lures are available in endless profusion, and generally, all the patterns and styles that have proved successful for freshwater and Atlantic coast fishing work equally as well in Pacific waters from the tropics to the Arctic. This includes plugs, spinners, wobblers, and jigs in metal, plastic, or wood, and in all the usual colors.

There are some special plugs and teasers used for billfish and especially designed for that purpose. One of these, the Knucklehead, and a similar model called the Kona Head, I have found will also work on albacore and even salmon, although even the manufacturer told me they wouldn't. Naturally, he was pleased that I proved him wrong.

Miscellaneous. The saltwater angler usually has the basic clothing needed, as well as equipment, if he is also a freshwater angler. I use several tackle boxes of plastic, (metal rusts out quickly), each supplied with the necessities for a different category or class of fishing. The well-equipped saltwater angler will not forget a good first aid kit, for many marine species have poisonous spines and there seem to be more ways of getting hurt on the ocean than in fresh water. Don't depend on others, especially on charter boats, for such necessities. On one two-week cruise to Mexico, I was on a boat with the latest, most sophisticated electronic gear and other modern refinements. But when I got a case of fish poisoning, the skipper couldn't even find a Bandaid and a bottle of iodine. Seasick pills, aspirin, as well as insect lotion and sunburn creams should be included for any extended trip.

Clothing should fit the climate and season, and it should be remembered that tropics get cold at night, and raingear is useful in all seasons in all regions. And I've never seen a time when a pair of gloves did not come in handy.

Leather rod belts are extremely useful. Some of these have pockets for pliers and knives. Hook removers, sharpners, and other little items are often overlooked.

Little has been said about license fees, which vary widely from region to region. In the Pacific Northwest, for example, no license is needed for marine species and there is usually no bag limit or closed season. This does not apply to salmon, steelhead, and other "managed" fishes. For these a tag or punchcard is also required.

In places like California, even marine species considered "scrap" in other areas, are rigidly regulated as to season and bag limits, and in some instances there is no open season.

Information on license requirements and the licenses themselves can usually be obtained locally, at tackle or sporting goods stores, or from the fish and game department or tourist bureau.

CHAPTER FOUR

The Toothy Critters
and How to Catch Them

BY FAR THE most numerous marine game species fall into the category of "bottom fish," "round fish," "ground fish," or even demersals if you want to get academic. A lot of professional fishermen affectionately call them the "toothy critters," because many have large maws filled with sharp teeth, as well as horns and spines distributed strategically about their heads and bodies.

Many of these species have a bizarre configuration, some look as if they had been put together by a committee, and others, such as the Irish lord of the sculpins, look like monsters out of a horror movie.

These species are disdained by most saltwater anglers, and if caught accidentally, they are either killed and discarded or thrown back. This is a pity, for some of these species such as the snapper (rockfish) and the lingcod are among the world's best eatin' fishes. Some, in spite of their bizarre appearance, have delicate flaky flesh that tastes like crab. The succulent qualities of species such as Pacific halibut defy description.

George Reiger, outdoors and boating writer, is one of the

A nice catch of assorted rockfish.

few saltwater anglers who regularly goes fishing for toothy critters. In fact, he goes farther than even the most dedicated bottom fisherman. He frequently angles exclusively for robinfish and toadfish.

"Once," he told me, "I came upon a fisherman hooking toadfish accidentally in the surf. Instead of simply releasing it, he would attack the fish with a bait knife. I asked him why the sight of a toadfish turned him on like that. You know what he told me? He said it was *evil!* How can a lowly fish be evil? Why, the toadfish is part of the ocean's complex scheme, too. It has its place like the 'beautiful' fishes."

To him, George added, *all* fish were beautiful.

Beautiful or not, the modern sports angler around the Pacific rim is now coming around to an appreciation of what he has been missing all these years. And as sport fishing becomes more crowded each year, with increasing pressure on the most glamorous game species, the bottom or demersal fishes will assume more importance—and in some instances may be the *only* fishing available.

That the bottom fishes are becoming an increasingly valuable resource is indicated by steps taken by fisheries agencies to conserve and protect these heretofore unlimited species from overexploitation in heavily populated areas such as California. California now has a daily limit on rockfish, recently reduced from twenty to fifteen a day. The California and Pacific halibuts are even more severely regulated, presently under a five-a-day bag limit. There is a limit also on most other saltwater species in California, and one species, the garibaldi, is completely protected, with no open season.

In almost all other areas of the North Pacific, fortunately, the marine game species including the bottom dwellers and midwater varieties, are still plentiful and in most instances unrestricted. In Oregon, for example, no license is required, there is no closed season, nor any bag limit on marine game species. This does not include salmon, steelhead, and other anadromous fishes.

There are more than 200 varieties of these "toothy critters" now recognized in the North Pacific, most of which are either good eating or of potential sport value. At this writing, fewer than one-half of these are regularly sought by sportsmen, and only about two dozen are "popular." Most of these species and varieties are found alongshore from the surf line to a depth of fifty fathoms. While they are usually called "bottom" fishes, they will be found feeding or spawning from the surface on down to the sand or mud bottom. Most of them tend to school together for mutual protection and for convenience of reproduction. Anglers fish for them by surf casting, jigging from boats, by trolling and handlining. They use live or fresh bait, metal and wood and bone spinners and wobblers, feathered jigs, and even saltwater streamer flies. Since these fishes feed upon smaller species (including their own kind), upon crustaceans, sea worms, shellfish, and marine life of all kinds, the choice of lure and bait is extensive and easy to duplicate.

The many species of toothy critters are well distributed all along the continental shelf, out in deep water on sea-mounts and around banks and reefs, close in over sand and mud flats, up inside estuaries and bays, in and around kelp beds. The most popular spots are jetties, piers, bridges, breakwaters, beaches, and rocky shorelines, from skiffs, party boats, fishing barges, and private craft. The numerous and confusing varieties and species can be grouped into a few easily understood types: rockfish, sea perches, surf perches, flatfish, and sculpins. Each of these types will be similar in size and characteristics, so that the same gear and bait can be used for all species in the same group.

Size 4/0 to 5/0 O'Shaughnessy hooks are standard for most species. For perch, flounder, halibut, and similar fishes, smaller hooks are needed, often as small as Number 6.

Some specific baits and lures used extensively are weighted metal jigs, feather jigs, conventional casting plugs and spin-ners, fresh or frozen herring, sardines, shrimp, squid, clam chunks, crab, pile worms, kelp worms. Sport and tackle shops in the coastal communities usually stock the most popular baits used locally.

The soles and flounders, including halibut, are technically the true "bottom" fishes, and there are literally dozens of species commonly found on the sand or mud of the ocean floor. Most flatfish are born with eyes on both sides of the head, but as they grow one eye shifts around to join the other on one side, either the left or right (port or starboard) side, and they develop their characteristic of camouflaging their presence by flattening against the bottom. Some of them can even burrow into the sand or mud.

Since some bottoms are more attractive to flatfishes than others, they tend to concentrate in certain areas. These areas are so consistently productive that local anglers depend upon them year after year. By local inquiry, one can usually learn the general whereabouts of these fishes. The angler can also profit from purchase of a large-scale hydrographic or navi-gation chart of the area. These usually indicate what kind of a bottom is found, as well as the contour of the bottom.

LINGCOD
(*Ophiodon elongatus*)

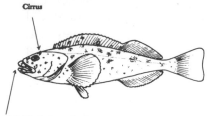

Cirrus

Wide Mouth, Large Teeth

KELP GREENLING
(*Hexagrammos decagrammus*)

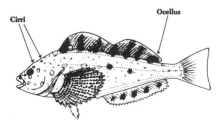

Cirri

Ocellus

RED IRISH LORD
(*Hemilepidotus hemilepidotus*)

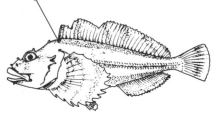

4 Scale Rows

BOCACCIO
(*Sebastodes paucispinis*)

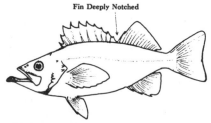

Fin Deeply Notched

REDTAIL SURFPERCH
(*Amphistichus rhodoterus*)

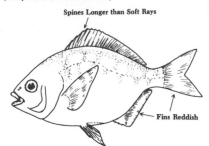

Spines Longer than Soft Rays

Fins Reddish

CHINA ROCKFISH
(*Sebastodes nebulosus*)

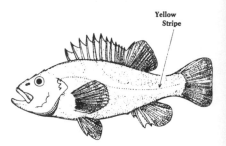

Yellow
Stripe

PACIFIC TOMCOD
(*Microgadus proximus*)

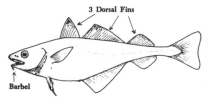

3 Dorsal Fins

Barbel

PACIFIC HAKE
(*Merluccius productus*)

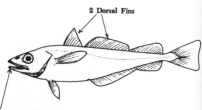

2 Dorsal Fins

Strong Teeth

Ledges, sloping bottoms, and mud instead of sand, are usually more productive. Mud bottoms usually contain more marine life upon which the flatfish feed than do sandy bottoms.

Best baits for flatfishes are pile worms, clam meat, pieces of shrimp, and "ghost shrimp," a soft shrimplike organism found in mud or sand. Small mussels or pieces of mussel, chunks of herring or anchovy, are also highly effective. Small hooks, with light line with a one- or two-ounce sinker, and a short dropper leader attached by a swivel, comprise the usual rig. The bait should be allowed to hit the bottom and bounce along slowly with the current. In a good area, the action is usually "busy" and at first indication of a bite, you should set the hook. Once landed, the fish should be killed immediately and cleaned as soon as possible. In any case, protect against spoilage by keeping it in a suitable container or on ice and out of the sun. This goes for any marine fish. In areas of strong tidal currents, it may be necessary to anchor over a productive spot. In some waters, such as the Pacific Northwest coast, where halibut grow big—sometimes over 200 pounds—one should be prepared with heavier tackle. Most of the flatfishes, however, will be in the one- to five-pound class and make good sport on light spinning gear.

The numerous varieties of perches are caught on the same gear and with the same bait as the flatfishes, but are found at all depths and in the surf, around kelp, and in bays around pilings. Generally, a smaller hook and smaller piece of bait works best for the perches, with no sinker or weight of any kind. I have found that a piece of clam is most satisfactory for perch because it is tough and stays on the hook better, regardless of currents and the length of time it is in the water. Like all school fish, perches are actively feeding at certain hours with periods of inactivity in between. A good time to fish usually is on the ebb tide. This is particularly true of surf perches, which seem to feed on small sand crabs and other marine life washed down by the receding waves. These species also tend to collect in holes just outside the first surf line, and casting into these is often very productive.

The rockfishes include at least fifty varieties commonly found in the popular fishing areas of the North Pacific. Most of these have the ability to feed anywhere from the bottom to the top, having air bladders that allow them to hover. Many of them, hauled up from deep water, will appear to "explode" when landed on deck. Actually, the rapid rise from deep water causes a disgorging of the fishes' "insides."

Most of the rockfishes are voracious and predacious, and will attack anything smaller than themselves. The size and number of teeth in their maws is an indication of this. Frequently, while reeling in a small rockfish, you will find a larger rockfish attached to it, and in some cases a big lingcod hanging onto the larger rockfish that has hold of the smaller rockfish! You will often find several different varieties of rockfish feeding in intermingled schools over underwater reefs. Any kind of an attractor lure, feather jig, or fresh bait will be productive once you find the schools. Fishing from rocks and jetties, even streamer flies are highly effective, as

Cleaning a catch of bottom fish at least offers a certain variety.

are conventional freshwater plugs and spinners. For bottom jigging, the trick is to cast out away from the boat, allow the lure or bait to sink to the bottom, then retrieve with short erratic jerks until the line is straight up and down, then reel in quickly. The strike will usually come at this point.

Needless to say, heavier tackle is called for with all rock-fishes, and in most cases you will want a tough Nylon leader or a flexible wire leader as protection against razor-sharp teeth. Some of the rockfishes will run to fifty pounds or more in size. In subtropical waters, groupers and giant sea bass may run to several hundred pounds. It is best to follow local custom as to size and kind of tackle used.

A word of caution: Most species have either sharp teeth or sharp spines, or both. Great care should be taken in how you handle the fish when caught and still alive. In some cases, a skin puncture will inject a mild poison or at best cause a painful infection. The way to handle a lingcod, for example, is not by the jaw like a freshwater bass, but by grasping it with thumb and forefinger in the eye sockets. On the other hand, don't try this with a red snapper, because this fish has sharp spikes around its eyes! A gaff, not a net, is the best medicine for rockfish.

The sculpins are among the most numerous species encountered in coastal and bay fishing, and in most cases are considered contemptuously as "scrap fish," by sports anglers, but many are highly prized as food fishes by gourmets. Of these, the cabezon is probably the most sought after and best eating (in spite of its flesh, which has a blue hue when caught that turns white upon cooking). The roe of the cabezon, however, is poisonous and should not be used in any way as food. The cabezon as well as the many other sculpins (some of which are prized only as bait) are all small fishes and are caught in the same areas and with the same bait and gear as perches and rockfishes.

The general classification of bottom fishes also includes the many varieties of wrasses, drums such as sheephead, skates, rays, greenlings, sea basses, croakers and groupers, and ocean whitefish. They are all caught on similar gear, bait, and with similar tactics, the only variable being the weight of the line and gear to match the size of the fish.

Variety and fecundity are not only the hope of the future of saltwater sports angling, but a valuable potential source of delicious and nutrious food as well. And their esthetic value, as potential light-tackle sport fishes is a whole new untapped frontier of saltwater angling.

CHAPTER FIVE

Following the Pelagics

Y OU'RE FORTY miles out to sea in a Cape Kiwanda dory off the forested headlands of Oregon, which loom up now out of a thin blue haze to the East. You're skimming along at about eight knots over the long undulating Pacific swells under a bright August sky with a deep, almost indigo blue ocean around you. You slow down and reach over the side. The water feels about right—between 58° and 68°—contrasting sharply with the 40° inshore waters.

You see two porpoises intercept your course and break water alongside—a sign of nearby tuna. Birds are wheeling about 100 yards to starboard. You change course and no sooner are the lines straight out again than wham!—a rod bends and the line screams out against the drag. Almost immediately a second rod bends; then a third; and almost as fast as it takes to say it, you have four hookups on four lines trolling feathered jigs. You are into a fast-moving, roving, voracious school of albacore tuna.

Elsewhere along the northwest coast, ranging from as close as ten to as far as 200 miles offshore, this speedy metallic-blue torpedo will be testing the lines of sports

83

A Kiwanda dory off the Oregon coast at sunrise.

anglers and commercial fishermen alike. The schools first appear off Central America and Mexico in April and May, moving steadily on a counterclockwise course around the rim of the Pacific that brings them into California waters in July, off the Columbia River a few weeks later, and to the waters off Japan a couple of months after that. Later the albacore will appear in the southwest Pacific where they apparently spawn, then in the Humboldt Current off South America, and back up the eastern rim to complete the cycle.

The albacore will average about twelve to fifteen pounds off California, somewhat larger off the northwest coast—to a maximum of thirty-five pounds—and by the time they reach Japan they will weigh in at from fifty to seventy pounds. The Pacific sport record is currently in the fifty-five- to sixty-pound range. Records of early voyages, such as Lord Ansons' round-the-world foray in the early 1700s, reported albacore as large as 130 pounds. Small-boat voyagers such as Captain Harry Pigeon in the *Islander* and Jack London in the *Snark* reported schools of albacore so vast that it took days and weeks to sail through them. The albacore, or long-fin tuna *(Thunnus alalunga),* is no longer so numerous or so large, due probably to the post-World War II exploitation by the world's fishing fleets.

The albacore has been the mainstay of the extensive California saltwater sportfishing "industry," as well as its tuna-packing commercial operations, for decades. Today, along with the fighting yellowtail, it still leads the parade. Off the Pacific Northwest coast, it is a "new" saltwater sport fishery, and a somewhat adventurous one due to the prevailing ocean and weather conditions and the distance the fish are found offshore. As for the commercial fishery, the waters off Oregon now produce the major haul of all U. S. tuna landings.

A pelagic ("of the open sea") sport fish, the albacore is known as *albacora* in Mexican and Central American waters, *ahipalaha* in Hawaii. Others in its class are the yellowfin or Allison tuna (*atun de aleta* in Spanish; *ahi* in Hawaiian); the bluefin (*atun de azul; ahi maguro*); bigeye tuna (*ahi menpachi shibi* in Hawaiian); skipjack tuna (*aku katsuwo*); bonito; mackerel (*sierra* in Spanish); and barracuda (*barracudo* in Spanish; *kaku* in Hawaiian). In the same class, perhaps, are the wahoo or *ono* or *peto*, and the dolphinfish or *mahi-mahi* or *dorado*, but these are most often caught while big-game fishing for marlin and sailfish.

The roving tuna, often found in intermingled schools and often in company with porpoises, seem to prefer the temperature gradients where the warm blue water and the cold continental or coastal waters meet. This area is rich in upwelling nutrients and in forage fish. In the open sea they depend mainly on squid and the Pacific saury for food. Having small stomachs and no air bladders, these species must be moving continuously and feeding frequently, ranging from twenty fathoms or so in depth to the surface.

The tuna seem to appear in annual cycles off the North and South American continents, probably in response to water temperature and climatic cycles. The cycles roughly are six years of good close-in fishing, followed by three years of poor fishing with the schools far offshore. Off the northwest coast, the cycle seems to spread over a decade, the numbers increasing or decreasing, and the schools swing-

ing inshore or far offshore. The availability of forage fish
undoubtedly also affects the numbers. Commercial over-
exploitation of the Pacific sardine before and during World
War II virtually eliminated this important food. Today, the
massive Russian and Japanese factory fleets operating in the
North Pacific are beginning to do the same thing to the
Pacific saury.

A half century ago, Zane Grey wrote of the Pacific tunas:

> But for the other fish—swordfish, white seabass, yel-
> lowtail, albacore—their doom has been spelled, and
> soon they will be no more. . . . The Japs, the Austrians,
> the round-haul (purse-seine) nets, the canneries and the
> fertilizer plants . . . greed and war, have cast their dark
> shadows. . . .

This "bull" dolphin, or dorado, was caught off the coast of
Mexico.

Grey's predictions have not yet come true completely, but the end of the story is not yet written, and even worse dangers threaten these ocean fisheries in the 1970s, namely the new sophisticated space age tuna clippers and the worldwide scramble to harvest the last of the ocean's resources, and the ruthless, laissez-faire attitude of the international fish-packing cartels.

Without immediate international controls and a complete overhauling of the age-old Law of the Sea agreements, the ocean's fisheries and other resources are doomed.

The bluefin are the giant tunas of the Pacific, growing as big as 250 pounds, but still far below their cousins in the Atlantic. Records of the Tuna Club at Avalon on Santa Catalina Island over a half century or more show that the best fishing for them is in July, followed by June, August, and September. They feed on squid, flying fish, mackerel, and all bait species. Trolling with feather or bone jigs, or with fresh bait rigs and 6/0 to 8/0 hooks is generally done until the schools are found. Then they are chummed into the drifting boat with live or chopped bait. Bluefin are extremely wary and are not as easily chummed up as albacore. Like albacore, a lost fish will scatter the entire school, but a hooked fish will often create a feeding frenzy. Bluefin are big and tough, and cannot be horsed in.

Yellowfin will readily smash almost any bait or lure, and I have often caught them while trolling for marlin on teasers, as well as feather jigs and metal squids. They will also hit fresh bait such as squid, mackerel, shrimp, mullet, anchovies, herring, and flying fish. These tuna may get as big as 450 pounds, but the Pacific variety seldom reaches more than 125 pounds. The world sports record is 269 pounds, caught by Henry Nishikawa at Hanalei, Hawaii. The peak of the season in California waters is from June to October. So far there is no record of any yellowfin caught in Pacific Northwest waters. A 9/0 to 14/0 reel is used with suitable line and 8/0 to 10/0 hooks. For record purposes, the last fifteen feet of leader may be doubled (for fifty-pound class), or a stainless braided leader may be used. The yellowfin is a

spectacular fighter, sounding, rolling, sometimes greyhounding. They strike hard and fast, and in seconds can rip off
hundreds of feet of line.

The Pacific yellowtail, a magnificent sport fish similar to
the amberjack in configuration, is the *piece de résistance* of
California and Baja sports anglers. Beginning in April, the
"Yellowtail Specials" lead the offshore parade of charter,
party, and private boats, and occupy all the attention until
the "Albacore Specials" start in July. With the usual California chamber of commerce single-mindedness, the yellowtail is called the California yellowtail, although it is found in
all tropical and subtropical waters, just as the North Pacific
current is called the California current, and the Pacific mackerel the California mackerel, and the Pacific bluefin the
California bluefin. But, in the case of the yellowtail, California is really where all the action is at this writing.

These tough fighters, which average from ten to fifteen
pounds and have a distinctive yellow-bronze body with
metallic-blue or greenish hues on the back, are caught not
only from offshore boats, but frequently while surf casting,
jigging, drifting, trolling, and still fishing for other species.
When the yellowtail are on the bite the action is wild, and
the excitement almost uncontrollable.

Yellowtail feed on sardines, anchovies, squid, herring,
small mackerel, flying fish, and shellfish. Finding the concentrations of these forage species is often the first step in finding the yellowtail. I have caught them on blue and white
"yo-yos" or metal jigs, in fifty fathoms off Mexico along
with sheephead, whitefish, and pinto bass, as well as on
trolled feather jigs, casting plugs, and spoons. Live anchovies, however, are best, and almost all the party and charter
boats carry live bait tanks; 4/0 to 6/0 hooks with suitable
rods and reels are standard.

The world record, incidentally, is 111 pounds in the all-
tackle classification, this one caught by A. F. Plim at Bay
of Islands, New Zealand. An eighty-pounder would be a
huge one in the North Pacific.

Tuna fishing at this time can be characterized as being
done from private and small charter boats, using mostly

trolled lures, off the Pacific Northwest coast; from private sportfishing, charter and party boats off California, Baja, and in Hawaiian waters. Only in California waters has the use of live bait and the chumming technique become highly developed and standardized. It is practiced to some extent elsewhere, but due to less sophisticated operations and the lack of live-bait barges, the old standby method of fast-trolling is used almost exclusively.

Since the bulk of the fishing is done by party boats, and most of this type of operation is carried on in California, this can be considered typical for all practical purposes. Party boat operations are carried on almost continuously year-round out of most ports. The boats are large, sea-going, and designed not only for the purpose of mass fishing, but also for the long runs out to the fishing banks in all kinds of weather. They carry up to 100 anglers, sometimes on day trips and sometimes on overnight or weekend trips, depending on the season and the type of fish sought.

On a party boat trip, you might expect to fish for albacore, yellowtail, giant sea bass, bottom fish, barracuda, or almost anything else that happens to be available, including marlin.

Netting an albacore off the Oregon coast.

There are about 500 individual party boats regularly sailing offshore from California ports, ranging up to 100 feet in length. They carry annually nearly a million anglers, and the annual bag is roughly 5,000,000 fish taken on sport tackle.

Since one is never exactly sure what type of fish will be on the program on any given trip—the skippers play it by ear and try to put their sports onto the best fishing, no matter what it is—the veteran party boat anglers always take along three complete outfits: light, medium, and heavy jigging or trolling tackle.

The light outfit will include a one-piece fast-taper of six and one-half- to seven-foot length (or a two-piece rod) designed for salt water, with a Penn 500 or equivalent reel loaded with spools of twenty-, thirty-, and forty-pound monofilament. The medium will be a two-piece glass rod, with a 6/0 to 9/0 reel with forty- to sixty-pound monofilament for albacore, yellowtail, barracuda, and similar fish. The rod is usually not longer than seven and one-half- to eight-feet. The heavy outfit will include a six- to seven and one-half-foot stiff club for big grouper, tuna, marlin, large yellowtail, and giant sea bass. The reel should be a 6/0 to 9/0 size loaded with eighty- to 100-pound monofilament.

A dozen each tuna-type hooks in sizes 2, 4/0, 8/0 is basic. In addition, size 1 tuna hooks, size 1/0 and even size 6 will be used at times. Sometimes even a 9/0 hook will be needed for giant sea bass. On some boats the skipper will occasionally allow you to use a saltwater fly rod with a large single-action reel holding 200 yards of twenty-pound braided Nylon and a sinking head flyline. Red-and-white and blue-and-white streamers work well on many saltwater species. Green-and-yellow and streamers with Mylar wings are also productive.

Your tackle box will also contain all manner of jigs, metal and wood lures, feathers, and bones. Generally the white and the blue-and-white work best. An assortment of large rubber-core sinkers and seine weights are necessary. Sunglasses, suntan lotion, plastic bags, warm jacket, and rubber deck shoes or boots all add to your comfort.

CHAPTER SIX

Salmon and Steelhead Country

UNIQUE TO the northeast Pacific, the saltwater salmon
fishery without doubt is the world's most valuable, both
in its commercial as well as sport versions. Although ruth-
lessly exploited by a laissez-faire fish-packing industry for
more than 110 years, Pacific salmon have somehow survived
natural and human obstacles to maintain their precarious life
cycle. Paradoxically, as more breakthroughs in the scientific
management of this priceless resource are made, the future
of the species becomes more uncertain. The reason is found
on the high seas, where the nations of the world, in an anachronistic informal set of rules called the Law of the Sea,
still follow the principle that anyone can do anything he
wants to outside established continental fisheries zones or
territorial limits. A current example of this is the Danish
exploitation on the high seas of the Atlantic salmon, which
has doomed this valuable sport and commercial species to
extinction unless it is stopped. The same situation now
looms in the North Pacific where high concentrations of
salmon have been located and are already being exploited
surreptitiously by the Japanese, Russian, and South Korean
commercial fleets.

The situation has been summed up in "The Pacific Salmon Fisheries, A Study of Irrational Conservation" by James A. Crutchfield and Giulio Pontecorvo:

> The stakes in salmon conservation are worthy of careful thought. Even at the depleted levels of the 1960s, the annual gross value of the Pacific salmon catch to American and Canadian fishermen has averaged $60 million. The vicious and continuous political infighting that has plagued the conservation authorities from Alaska to the Columbia River is eloquent testimony to the participants' awareness of economic considerations in fishery management. Yet there is little evidence that the development of scientific research-oriented regulation was accompanied by any substantive awareness of the crucial importance of economic factors.

The reason for this somber preface is to give the newcomer to Pacific salmon fishing a proper perspective and appreciation of this unique fishery.

Salmon leaping the falls at Oregon City.

The Pacific salmons come in six varieties, five anadromous to North American rivers and one Asiatic species called the *masu*, or cherry salmon. The five North American species are chinook (king), coho (silver), sockeye (red), chum (dog), and humpbacked (pink). In addition, but of more importance inside estuaries and on up river, are the steelhead (sea-run rainbow trout), the other sea-run *salmos* such as cutthroat and brown trout, and the char, or dolly varden. All of these sea-runs are distantly related to each other and to the Atlantic salmon, but for the purpose of discussing saltwater techniques for Pacific salmon, we can ignore all but the five anadromous species of North American salmon.

These five species are called anadromous because they run up freshwater rivers to spawn and complete their life cycles. Unlike the Atlantic salmon and the steelhead, the Pacific salmon always die soon after spawning. This inflexible fact offers two unique points to keep in mind: Regardless of other factors, if not enough salmon escape all the dangers of the sea and all the obstructions of the rivers to find the spawning beds of their birth and complete the chain, the run would become extinct within its life cycle; and the *freshwater* phase of the salmon's life cycle is the *only* one at this writing that can be regulated and scientifically managed.

There are few if any restrictions on ocean fishing for salmon, and if there were any, they would be almost impossible to enforce. On the other hand, since the Pacific salmon die after spawning, all those fish not needed to maintain the runs become a wasted resource if not somehow utilized.

Of the five North American salmons, only two are of any importance to sport fishermen—the chinook and the coho. In the future, however, if the Pacific salmon survive, sportsmen can also look forward to regularly fishing for sockeye, chum, and humpback in salt water. The humpies are frequently taken on sports gear while fishing for chinook and coho in certain areas, and they will readily take most salmon lures. Commercial trollers in recent years have learned how to catch sockeye on lures as well as chums. Special lures for both these species are now on the market. Sportsmen, of course, have long taken sockeye on flies in certain places such as the Russian River in Alaska. I have personally caught sockeye in this way, and also have caught chum salmon on small lures and flies in places such as the mouth of the Nestucca River in Oregon. Moreover, sockeye salmon are the same species as the landlocked kokanee, or redfish, that are found in many lakes of the West and readily caught on small lures and flies.

But, for the time being, the saltwater spotlight is on the two stars, chinook and coho, which between them support a 200-million-dollar sportfishing industry in California, Ore-

CHUM

Resembling sockeye, chums have black specks over their silvery sides, and faint grid-like bars. Living three to five years, they weigh up to 10 pounds, are used only for canning.

SOCKEYE

Blue-tinged silver in color, sockeye live four to five years, weigh up to seven pounds. Slimmest and most streamlined of the species, they are used solely for canning.

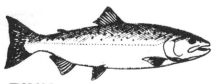

PINK

Living only two years, pinks are smallest of Pacific salmon, weighing up to five pounds. They have heavily-spotted backs over silver bodies, and are also used only for canning.

CHINOOK

Lightly spotted on blue-green back, chinooks live from five to seven years, weigh up to 120 pounds. They are most famous game salmon, are sold commercially mainly in fresh or frozen state.

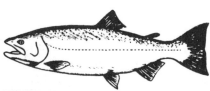

COHO

Bright silver in color, coho live three years, weigh up to 15 pounds. A popular sport fish, they are sold commercially fresh, frozen, canned and smoked.

gon, Washington, British Columbia, and Alaska alongshore waters.

All of the Pacific salmons are superb eating, extremely valuable, and highly prized by gourmets. They are usually of a rich reddish-pink color, delicious to the taste, and loaded with calories. They can be fried like steaks, broiled, baked, minced or chopped, dried, smoked, canned, and even eaten raw. The fish lends itself readily to canning, and this is the version most people outside of "salmon country" have sampled. Most of the world pack of canned salmon is sockeye or humpback. Chum makes up a large percentage of canned salmon, too, but chinook and coho are largely marketed as fresh, fresh-frozen, or "mild-cured" salmon. The ultimate gourmet prize is Columbia River "Royal Chinook" in mild-cured or smoked form, which sells for nearly $4 a pound retail.

Since all Pacific salmons begin to deteriorate rapidly once they leave salt water to travel up their spawning rivers, the finest eating are those that are saltwater-caught. They are at their prime just before starting the spawning runs, after they have been gorging in a feeding frenzy for several months to pack their bodies with energy for the grueling upriver journey, during which they do not feed. In fact, their bodies will not assimilate food once in fresh water. Nature has already triggered their metabolism for the spawning phenomenon.

Thus, it is obvious that salmon angling is not only a superb saltwater sport, but an esthetic one as well. Every salmon fisherman is a meat hunter. He keeps all he is legally allowed. Since a successful sportfishing trip offshore might result in bringing back fifty pounds of meat, worth at least $2 a pound on the retail counter, obviously all salmon anglers are "commercial" fishermen, regardless of what kind of license they hold.

"Salmon country" can be said to be a "river" of fish from the surf line to about ten miles offshore, from San Francisco Bay up past Oregon, Washington, British Columbia, and Alaska, and even into the Bering Sea and the Arctic, as well as out along the Aleutian chain. Salmon prefer water in the

40° to 55° range, and being predacious they go where the food is—food being herring, anchovies, pilchards, candlefish, and other bait species. The sockeye also feeds on plankton and small marine forms. The salmon are school fish, and the individual runs or races seem to stick together during the entire life cycle, although there is much intermingling of species and runs. Salmon travel great distances along the continental shelf following the forage fish, in some instances covering thousands of miles to and from the river of their birth.

The principal salmon-producing rivers are the Sacramento, the Klamath, the Rogue, the Umpqua, the Columbia, the Fraser, the Stikine, the Russian, the Kotzebue, and the Yukon. Almost all rivers tributary to the ocean on the North American continent north of San Francisco, however, have their individual runs. The greatest salmon river of all is the Columbia, followed by the Sacramento, the Fraser, and the Yukon. This river of salmon along the northeast Pacific rim appears to be present almost all year round, although there are periods when the fish seem to disappear and in such instances are probably far offshore or in deep water, following their food.

Downstream migrants, or smolts, in their second or third year of life enter the water when they are approximately six inches long. By the time they return to fresh water on their final spawning run, they will weigh up to ninety pounds for a big chinook, up to thirty pounds for a record coho. The average size of a mature fish nowadays is about ten pounds for a coho and about twenty to twenty-five pounds for a chinook.

Migrants from the Columbia River are found on the high seas as far north as Alaska and as far south as the Golden Gate Bridge. Likewise, Fraser River fish are at times found off Oregon, and Sacramento fish are often caught off Washington. Some salmon tagged off the Columbia have been caught off the tip of the Aleutians, a distance of several thousand miles.

While salmon angling techniques vary from locality to locality, almost all sport-caught fish are taken by boat, that

Landing a 36-pound chinook salmon near the mouth of the
Rogue River in southwestern Oregon.

is, by trolling or mooching with fresh bait, plugs, spoons,
spinners, and streamer flies. There is some casting done from
jetties, rocks, at river bars, and even through the surf, but
so little as to be unimportant. There is considerable salmon
fishing from bank and boat in fresh water during the river
runs, but that cannot be called a saltwater fishery.

The salmon sport fisheries are well developed in most
areas and are concentrated at ports and river mouths from
San Francisco Bay to Alaska. They vary in size and importance from a two- or three-boat charter fleet at Florence on
the Siuslaw, to Westport, Washington, on Grays Harbor,
where a fleet of several hundred charter boats operates daily
offshore from mid-April to September. At times anywhere
from 2,000 to 5,000 boats of all kinds and sizes will be
salmon fishing off the Columbia bar, carrying as many as
25,000 anglers.

While the salmon schools may be present alongshore all

year round, the sportfishing season is usually limited to the summer months by weather, ocean conditions, and feeding patterns of the fish. Off the Columbia, for example, if you fish the last two weeks in August you are almost certain to catch your limit within the first two hours, if you are on a good charter boat with a fair to good skipper.

There is year-round "blackmouth" fishing in Puget Sound and in the Strait of Juan de Fuca. A blackmouth is an immature chinook salmon and averages from five to ten pounds.

This is not to say that only July and August provide good salmon fishing, by any means. The season starts around April 15 at Grays Harbor, for example, and frequently starts with a bang on big chinook.

In addition to the charter boats, which are improving in size, number, and versatility each year, private yachts and even small "offshore" type outboards and I/0 powered seventeen- to twenty-three-footers are practical for sportfishing during the good summer weather. Almost all salmon fishing is now done with fresh bait—herring, anchovies, pilchards— and in a few instances in Canadian waters, with live bait. The latter may have a future, but its obvious disadvantages are lack of ready availability of good live bait, lack of efficient live-bait tanks, and the fact that many boats are based in semifresh or brackish estuaries where the bait does not survive well. Live bait is deadly on salmon, as on any game fish, but the next best thing is fresh or fresh-frozen bait, and this is readily available at any salmon port.

The fresh bait is usually rigged on a two-hook harness for trolling or mooching, in whole condition in a manner that will give it a lifelike spin or darting motion. Often the bait is cut in "cutplug" fashion, its head removed by an angle cut and then rigged with a two-hook harness. Less frequently, the strip bait technique is used, in which fillets of the bait fish are cut and rigged with a harness. In some areas, one method works better than the others, but in truth, this may be due more to local custom than any special preference the fish have.

The fresh bait hook-up is used usually with a Nylon or

monofilament leader of at least ten-pound test and attached behind a crescent sinker, or to a flashing metal dodger. A new innovation in the Pacific Northwest is the diving plane, made of pink or other bright-colored lucite or plexiglass plastic. The principle is simply that the plane takes the bait down to the proper depth by paravane action, without heavy weights. (In the San Francisco area, big cannonballs of lead weighing up to twenty pounds are used to get the lure or bait down through the heavy tidal currents.) When the fish strikes and is hooked, it triggers a change in planing action that brings the fish up to the surface almost immediately. Local names for the diving planes, which originated in Canada among the commercial trollers, are Pink Lady, Oregon Diver, Lady Go-Diver, Chetco Diver, to name a few. A diver rigged salmon tackle at this writing will outfish any other kind by a ratio of ten to one.

Line used for salmon ranges from sixteen-pound monofilament on spinning-type gear, to forty-pound mono or Nylon. A heavy-duty saltwater spinning reel, or a conventional star drag multiplying reel of about 4/0 size, completely filled with monofilament, is ideal for trolling, as well as mooching. Rods should be of good quality, fiberglass with a stiff butt and a fairly limber tip to take up the shock of a strike. A seven- or eight-foot length is about right. In areas where heavy currents and heavy weights are common, a rod with a stiffer tip is recommended. But, since all trolling is done at less than three miles an hour and mooching is little more than drifting, a real heavy club is not needed; in fact, it is a disadvantage.

A rod holder is a necessity for both trolling and mooching, and if the boat does not supply one, equip yourself with a light detachable type. A rod butt apron is also a handy thing, particularly when working on big chinook. One that has pockets for pliers, fillet knife, and hook disgorger is the best kind.

A plastic tackle box with an assortment of swivels, snaps, sinkers, hooks, and two-hook harnesses, reel oil, and other accessories is a necessity. You will also have a wide assortment of metal lures and wooden or plastic plugs, although you will seldom use them when fresh bait is available. The purist who wants to try coho fly or streamer fishing will have a collection of coho streamers of polar bear hair, made up in white-and-red, white-and-blue, white-and-blue-and-red or green. He will also need another rod, a nine- or ten-footer with a fast tip. Streamer fly fishing for coho is mainly trolling at from five to six miles an hour, skipping the streamer on the surface or just under the surface. You will find that few charter boats will allow this, and very few private boats, as it spoils the salmon fishing by any other method. It is widely practiced, however, in Canadian waters, particularly in the Campbell River and Qualicum areas, and to a lesser extent in Puget Sound.

Generally speaking, chinook salmon are found in deep water, often right down on the bottom, and coho on the surface or in "mid-water," but there are many exceptions. When

SILVERY FISH ENTER THE RIVERS ~ HEADED FOR THE SPAWNING AREAS

CHANGE IN FORM BEGINS AS THEY ADVANCE

DETOUR TO HATCHERY

EGGS ARE TAKEN FROM ADULT FEMALES AND FERTILIZED

IN THE FALL ~ SPAWNING SALMON DEPOSIT EGGS IN GRAVEL NESTS ~ AND DIE

EGGS AND YOUNG ARE CARED FOR IN THE HATCHERY

AND GROW TO MATURITY IN THE PACIFIC

Natural Life Cycle
2 TO 5 YEARS

FRY HATCH IN THE SPRING

AND GROW IN THE STREAM

The Hatchery Contribution
UP TO 18 MONTHS OF LIFE CYCLE

FINGERLINGS ARE RELEASED INTO STREAMS

ENTER THE OCEAN

FINGERLINGS MIGRATE DOWNSTREAM

JOIN NATURAL MIGRANTS

LENGTH OF THE LIFE CYCLE AND OF HATCHERY CARE VARY WITH SPECIES AND CONDITIONS the salmon are feeding hot and heavy and the schools are intermingled, you are likely to be catching coho and chinook alternately with often a humpbacked mixed in for good measure. A coho or humpy will fight on the surface, however, while a chinook will try to sound or sulk on the bottom.

Many angling writers credit salmon with a sort of super intelligence, which is absurd when you consider they have a brain smaller than a kernel of wheat. The salmon is a superb example—the ultimate, in fact—of a pure flesh-and-blood machine created by Mother Nature and completely automated by programmed instincts. It has only one purpose, and that is to maintain the species. Thus its entire time in the ocean is spent surviving and putting on weight and storing up strength and energy for the final sexual act. This means that it is feeding almost constantly on whatever is available and wherever it can be found.

The salmon forages for food completely by instinct, striking and eating the same way. Proof of this has been discovered recently in the Columbia River far upstream from the ocean, where the salmon are found with stomachs full of smelt. The salmon continued to eat although the food merely decayed in their stomach because the food assimilation process had already stopped.

Therefore, the salmon will at times strike at anything that is smaller, and that has some sort of attraction by color, motion, or disturbance. Characteristically, a school of salmon will attack a school of bait fish or a herring "ball-up" by charging through, slashing this way and that with their tails to stun the fish, then swinging around to take the wounded or stunned prey in its mouth. For this reason, when mooching, one should give line instead of rearing back when the first sharp strike is felt. Give the salmon a chance to get the bait in its mouth, then set the hook. Salmon will usually hook themselves on trolled bait, but at times you will experience spells of "short striking," and in that case set the rear hook further back.

In any case, the bait must be rigged carefully with the proper action and it must be in fresh and not damaged condition. It should be changed frequently, because even a few scales missing will often turn salmon off. Hooks must be honed razor sharp. If metal lures are used, they must be highly polished. Plugs must be in good repair and freshly painted. Flashers or dodgers should be kept polished, and the proper size used to match the bait and the length of the leader.

I personally do not like to use these heavy pieces of hardware, but they are popular and there is no denying they catch fish. Sometimes the crescent trolling sinker is painted a fluorescent red, and sometimes a plastic skirt of Hootchy-Kootchy is placed over it in lieu of a dodger or flasher. A recent experiment by the Washington Fisheries Department in Puget Sound indicated that a large flasher and Hootchy-Kootchy type lure with clear Mylar or plastic strips, fished deep on the bottom with twenty ounces of lead, was the most effective and consistent salmon catcher. The skirt was attached to the hook with a leader and a short rubber snubber between it and the flasher or dodger. This is known as a "Twinkle Skirt" lure.

Trolling, as mentioned before, is done slowly, at two or three miles an hour. Mooching is merely drifting with the tide or current, generally in the rips, with the lure or bait getting its natural action from the current. Motor mooching is simply a combination of the two, maintaining a slow pace or position with the use of the motor. Another form of salmon fishing, called "strip fishing," is now dying out, but at one time was the most effective. In this method, you are anchored or drifting. You cast your bait out, let it settle to the bottom, and then quickly reel or "strip" it in. Usually a strip of bait is used, rather than a whole or cut herring.

In trolling or mooching, experts have determined that a line angle entering the water should be between twenty and forty degrees for coho, and between forty and fifty degrees for chinook. On charter boats and yachts, it is common to find one angler catching all the fish, while right alongside of him, another is getting skunked. Worse yet, often they change rods and positions, and still the lucky angler gets all the fish. There is a simple explanation for this aggravating and frustrating situation. The lucky angler is using the proper angle for his line, and is placing the lure or bait in a "hot spot" behind the boat. This hot spot is often right up close to the stern alongside the boat on twin screws and directly behind on single screws. The salmon seem to be attracted by the props when they are school feeding. One reason for this is that the screws chop up a lot of bait fish and so in effect the boat has a chumming stream right behind in the wake. The smart angler will remember to experiment a little with best locations to fish on each trip, and not just let the bait drag behind any old way.

Feeding salmon will most often be found in tide rips, in back eddies, and off the mouths of rivers and underwater canyons, sometimes on the surface, and other times deep down, depending on where the food is and the time of day. Generally they will be found close to the surface in early morning and late evening and below thirty to forty feet during the day. Sometimes they go on the bite at the change of

Typical saltwater salmon stream fly patterns.

the tide, sometimes at slack water, sometimes on the ebb and sometimes on the flood, depending on the locality. Without doubt, however, the first two hours after daylight and before dark are most effective times. The fish are almost always caught feeding in tide rips and in currents or eddies.

Coho streamer fishing is best just at daylight and just before dark, at which time they will readily take fast-moving lures, right on the surface.

Bright sunshine will often put the fish down earlier than on cloudy, dull days, or in fog and rain. I have never noticed any wind effect on salmon fishing, but if the sea is rough, of course, it is more difficult to troll or mooch. Around the mouths of rivers, especially during the spring and early summer, you will encounter muddy water from the run-off. This limits visibility for the fish, but often fishing right along the edge of the muddy water, in and out of it, can be effective. On large boats, especially those with twin screws, the surface layer of mud or discolored water is washed aside by the screw action, and in this case directly behind the boat in the wake is a good spot to put the lure or bait. Also, this muddy layer is often merely on the surface and fishing can be good directly underneath it.

In busy salmon waters, one can often spot the schools by the action of the birds and by the herring ball-ups. In the ocean proper, off the northwest states, the salmon can be anywhere from the surf out ten or fifteen miles. In places such as the Strait of Juan de Fuca, around Vancouver Island, up the Inland Passage in British Columbia and Alaska, the salmon runs are often found surprisingly close to shore, especially where the bottom drops off sharply. At river mouths and inlets, of course, the salmon schools become more concentrated as they swim across the bar in narrow channels (usually on the ebb tide).

One should not be misled by seeing salmon leaping, jumping, or rolling on the surface. Actual echo sounder tests made in Puget Sound showed that even when salmon were sighted thus, the main school was below forty feet.

Some anglers tend to use heavier weights in order to go

deeper, such as when blackmouth fishing in the winter. Tests show, however, that a line of thinner diameter and less weight is much more effective than simply adding more metal. Moreover, letting out more line does not increase depth. In fact, more line tends to bring the bait up rather than sink it.

Nothing has been said about steelhead, the habits of which are similar to salmon, and many are caught as "salmon" in the ocean. Primarily, however, the steelhead is a river fish, not for ocean angling.

CHAPTER SEVEN

Hunting the Big Ones

O N THE MORNING of August 25, 1903, between Whites
Landing and Long Point not far off the rocky shore of
Catalina Island, the world heavyweight boxing champion,
Jim Jeffries, worked over a school of bluefin tuna. Suddenly
he hooked into a 200-pounder. The combination of a big fish
and a celebrity in action soon brought a flotilla of other
sportfishing boats circling around to watch the fun.

One of those spectators was a young cornet player in the
Catalina band and part-time boatman for wealthy tuna
anglers, E. H. (Harry) Willey. Watching from his thirty-foot
cruiser, he saw Jeffries break his rod trying to turn the tuna.
The resulting confusion on the champion's boat created side-
splitting hilarity among the audience, including Willey. About
the time he was doubled up with laughter, something big and
tough hit his bait, which had been forgotten.

In a matter of seconds, Willey lost 300 feet of line. Quickly,
he grabbed the rod and set the hook, and in due time landed
the fish. What he had caused him to rush back to Avalon
and the Tuna Club headquarters. Tuna Club officials, however, turned up their sunburned noses at first sight. This was

no tuna, they said; not with that long swordlike bill. Willey then had the fish weighed unofficially, and it came to 182 pounds. Pete Reyes, a photographer at the scene, recorded it for posterity. Willey's father, a sea captain, called the fish a "belaying pin fish," because of the odd bill. Later Captain Willey modified this to the more catchy name, "marlinspike fish." This was subsequently changed to marlin swordfish, and finally to striped marlin or just marlin (Makaira andax).

Three days later, Harry caught a second belaying pin fish, this one weighing 125 pounds, duly recorded by the Tuna Club. After that everyone, including the purist Tuna Club fishermen, got marlin fever. Big-game fishing for marlin, and later swordfish, caught on quickly, and Southern California became the center of Pacific Ocean big-game sport fishing.

Over the years, Harry Willey caught hundreds of marlin, and was identified with the sport to the degree that he became known as "Mr. Marlin." With his father and friends, he pioneered many techniques such as the use of kites and gas-filled balloons to keep the bait skipping over the waves like flying fish. He developed the technique of chumming with a mixture of dog food and fish oil (nowadays chopped fish is widely used in both the Atlantic and Pacific), which attracted the small bait fish and mackerel upon which the big ones foraged. His death on October 14, 1965, ended a long career as the father of big-game fishing in the North Pacific.

In the early part of the century, particularly during the period when he was working in Hollywood on movie versions of his western novels, Zane Grey brought his skill and persistence to the big-game waters of Southern California. In his book, *Tales of Fishing,* the marlin is still referred to as the "marlin swordfish" or just "swordfish." This book reveals the intensity of his approach to fishing. He invested the same intensity in his writing, which brought him the income needed to pursue his hobby. One occasion, fishing with "R.C."—his ever-present brother—and other members of his party in the vicinity of San Clemente Island, in twenty-one days he trolled 1,500 miles around the islands, fishing

Black marlin breaks the surface as it feels the hook dig in.

Hauling in a striped marlin, Bay of Islands.

from dawn to dark. This persistence was probably Grey's secret of successful fishing, and certainly he was one of the greatest anglers produced in America.

Grey's "swordfish" was not the same as the presently designated broadbill swordfish *(Xiphias gladius)*, which was found in the same waters and later became a much sought-after game fish. Its bill extended in a sharp flat sword instead of the round spikelike bill of the marlin and Pacific sailfish *(Istiophorus greyi)*. Later Grey began calling the marlin the "roundbill swordfish, that royal-blue swashbuckler of the Pacific."

Billfishing, as well as tuna fishing, has declined in California waters since those golden years of Avalon and the Tuna Club. The main reason was the ruthless depletion by commercial boats of the sardine or pilchard prior to and during World War II, and the commercial exploitation of swordfish and marlin as well. Swordfish used to be caught as far north as Oregon, but are seldom ever seen in the North Pacific anymore. Longline fishing by roving Japanese commercial boats in Baja and Mexican waters in the 1960s very nearly did the same thing to marlin and sailfish.

The anchovy has been the staple bait fish in the eastern Pacific for years, and its numbers now are seriously diminished. In recent years, the Japanese and Russian commercial fleets have begun to exploit the saury, a bait fish of the open sea and believed to be an important part of the diet of tuna, albacore, and billfish. Without conservation measures, the future of bait fish—the vital link in the food chain—is uncertain.

Today, big-game fishing is still the main attraction for offshore boats along the Southern California coast. The peak of the season is in summer and early fall for marlin and sailfish, and May through September for bluefin tuna, which are most commonly found in the vicinity of the offshore islands and seamounts called "banks." The dorado or dolphin is also found during warm water cycles in the areas off San Diego, particularly the Coronados Islands.

In Hawaiian waters, most big-game fishing is in the channels in and around the islands of Hawaii, Maui, Lanai, Kahoolawe, Molokai, Oahu, Niihau, and Kauai. Marlin, *mahimahi* (dolphinfish), *ono* (wahoo), and tuna provide most of the sport. The blue marlin is king in these waters, and probably the top spot at this time is off the Kona coast of the Big Island, which is sheltered from the northeast trade winds and where fishing conditions are ideal most of the year. About two dozen charter boats operate out of the port of Kailua-Kona, headquarters for the annual Hawaiian International Billfish Tournament. Thousand-pound marlin are not unusual in these waters.

The popularity of the Kona coast in recent years, in spite of its distance from Honolulu, is due partly to the publicity engendered by the star-studded Billfish Tournament, but mainly to the easily accessible fishing waters just offshore. Out of the historic and picturesque village port of Lahaina, for example, it is a long trip over the shallow waters—where once thousands of whales came each year for breeding rites —to the marlin grounds.

The waters around the Islands hold perhaps some of the world's best dolphinfish or *mahi-mahi* angling. A trick used by a friend, Jim Bigelow, who brought the famed sportfisherman, *Marleen,* to Lahaina from New Orleans for *mahi-mahi,* is simple but effective. On the way to the marlin grounds he would drop a wooden box over the side at intervals. On the way back there would be one or two *mahi-mahi* resting in the shade of each box. The *Marleen,* incidentally, was the first boat in the Islands to use the tuna tower.

The third—and some say the greatest—major big-game fishing area of the North Pacific is the west coast of Mexico, including the Sea of Cortez or Gulf of California, and the west side of the Baja Peninsula. The area bounded by lines drawn from the tip of Baja or Cabo San Lucas to Acapulco to Mazatlán is known among big-game fishermen as the "golden triangle" for billfish. It is probably the greatest marlin and sailfish region in the world, although the fish are not as big as those in the waters around Hawaii, South America, New Zealand, and Australia. The billfish are present all year around, but at different times can be found just off the beach or ten to twenty miles out.

Blue and black marlin and swordfish are most plentiful from July to October, with April to June the peak for striped marlin and sailfish. Yellowfin tuna and yellowtail fishing is best in the spring, while the fall is tops for wahoo. During the winter season, the Gorda Banks near Cabo San Lucas are most productive for marlin and sailfish.

All the luxury hotels have fleets of small sportfishing craft, often with guides, as part of the packaged price. At the larger mainland ports such as Mazatlán, Guaymas, and Acapulco, there are also independent charter operations. The mainland coast and the northern area of the Sea of Cortez can also be reached with trailered sport boats launched from the beach. At the other extreme, there are a number of long-range charter boats operating out of San Diego, which make ten-day and two-week trips down the outside of the 1,000-mile-long peninsula. These boats are equipped with live-bait tanks and bring with them a supply of anchovies. They also fish for local bait such as mackerel, which are kept in the tanks until ready to use.

Most of the other boats, however, use the same techniques for marlin, sailfish, and swordfish that are common in other waters. Teasers of mullet, flyingfish, or mackerel are skipped in the wake at a fast clip until a strike is made or fins are sighted, after which the skipper tries to put the bait in front of the fish's nose. Boats using live bait also use this technique, but when a strike is made or a school found, the boat is stopped and chumming is begun with anchovies. At the same time, the live mackerel is hooked on and put over the side. This is probably the deadliest method of all. I have been on a boat when as many as seven marlin and sailfish were hooked up at the same time. At times like this, the sport gets somewhat hectic.

There are several highly effective artificial lures now available, including the famous Knucklehead, which are used in place of or in conjunction with the fresh bait for trolling.

The presence of marlin and other billfish is frequently marked by porpoises, wheeling birds—especially the frigate birds often called "marlin birds"—churning patches of water, and baitfish "ball-ups." Billfish, like all large species,

With the bait still hanging from its mouth, this 8-foot gray
nurse shark is brought to the side of the boat.

range from extreme depths to the surface, depending upon the time of day, currents, water temperature, and salinity. They range over long distances. One marlin tagged in Mexican waters was caught in Hawaii less than sixty days later.

The sight of a dorsal and caudal fin cutting the water on the surface is the classic giveaway, but working over known banks with outriggers and several lines off the stern, trolling teasers, is the usual workaday method. When a fish is struck, the boat is stopped and the extra lines taken in. As mentioned, this is the signal for the crew to start chumming live bait. Tackle is rigged for live mackerel on heavy single hooks of 1/0 to 8/0 size. The hooks are attached in several ways—under the collarbone or in the back with the leader coming out through the mouth or gill opening. Large tough bait such as mackerel is often hooked through the bony eye sockets, which makes them swim in a vigorous but erratic way.

The bait used varies widely from one place to another, depending on what's available. Flyingfish are popular in Mexican waters, and are flown in from California at a cost of about $1.25 each. Anchovies, mackerel, mullet, small *aku* or skipjacks in Hawaiian waters, belly strips of many ocean species such as bonito are widely used, as are feathered jigs and other artificials. A friend of mine owns a battered and chomped-up hand-carved wooden plug which he obtained in Mexico and which is purported to have been a teaser used by Zane Grey. It looks like an oversized Lucky Louie used in Puget Sound for salmon.

Tackle listed for any game fish in the Class II category is satisfactory for most big-game fishing. The giant fish require Class I tackle, although they use the same bait and techniques. Such gear is usually furnished by or available for rent from the charter operation. In Mexican waters, as elsewhere, one should bring his own gear if possible for all but Class I fish. Lines of from twenty- to eighty-pound test with suitable reels are common.

Billfish will often follow the bait or lure at trolling speed for long periods, looking it over, often swinging from one

Landing a large blue marlin often requires good teamwork.

bait to another, then to the outriggers, then back again. Quite frequently the billfish will hit a bait right up under the exhaust pipe. All this action is usually visible to the angler who waits in agony for the fish to hit.

On live or fresh bait, theory says the line should be freespooled immediately with the classic count of ten before striking the fish, but I have never seen this work successfully. You should strike the fish as soon as you are reasonably sure the hook is in position to become securely imbedded. Sometimes the strike of a billfish is almost imperceptible, so one must be alert with just enough tension on the line to feel the first strong pull. In any case, there is almost never a hard strike such as one might get from a wahoo or dorado.

In many billfish areas today, the marlin or sailfish are not killed—in fact, they're not even brought aboard where handling a "hot fish" can be dangerous. They are brought up until the leader can be grasped and the fish released, the sport being the hooking and playing. I'm often asked by readers of my newspaper column what to do with a big fish once you catch it. Usually the angler with his first marlin or sailfish keeps it for mounting or for the meat. Mounting a trophy can run into a lot of money, however. A dollar a pound for small and medium billfish is common. If there are facilities for freezing or canning, by all means keep one for food. Smoked and canned, marlin and swordfish in particular are superb for cocktail snacks or for a smorgasbord. If the fish is to be kept for food, the bill or sword is often removed and mounted as a trophy. I removed the long pectoral fins from the first albacore tuna I ever caught, and mounted them as a memento of the occasion.

Dorado or dolphinfish are superb eating, as are wahoo. Smoked wahoo is especially delicious, but dorado must be eaten fresh as they do not preserve well. Tuna, which are often caught on big-game fishing tackle, are best when canned or smoked and canned.

Of all the big-game fishing areas of the North Pacific, the Mexican waters are probably best suited for small offshore sport craft and light tackle. This is the epitome of all sport fishing.

CHAPTER EIGHT

Fishing the Exotics

BACK IN THE middle nineteenth century, while the West was still being won by Easterners, many a homesick pilgrim found means of bringing across the Rockies his favorite game fish which did not exist on the Pacific slope. It seems incredible that they were able to solve the logistics of moving fragile fingerlings thousands of miles over all kinds of terrain and in all manner of weather, but by the 1870s almost all major streams on the West Coast had received—usually clandestinely—a stocking of smallmouth and largemouth bass, crappie, bluegill, catfish, and other freshwater species. Among the most energetic of these piscatorial Johnny Appleseeds were the dedicated members of the old U. S. Fish Commission, who not only planted the fresh waters but, incredibly, seemed bent on transferring some of the Atlantic's best game fish to the Pacific Ocean.

In 1871, Seth Green, a pioneer fish culturist, brought west eight cans of newly hatched Hudson River fry of *Alosa sapidissima,* the American or white shad, in a railroad baggage car, a trip of seven days which ended at Tehama, California. More than sixty percent of the fry survived the

A huge striped bass is brought in.

arduous trip and were liberated in the Sacramento River. The shad took to their new home and within nine years had spread northward along the coast as far as the Coos and Umpqua rivers in Oregon. Subsequent plantings were made in the Columbia system, and in the early part of this century, as pollution depleted eastern shad fisheries, a commercial nettery developed on the Columbia to supply the eastern gourmet markets. Usually only the roe was shipped and the rest of the fish discarded. Today, not only is there a brisk commercial fishery in the Columbia and other coast streams, but the shad has come into its own as a sport fish. It is now found in almost all rivers as far north as Alaska, although Oregon and California remain the main sportfishing areas.

An anadromous species, the shad returns to its parent stream two or three times to spawn. This happens in the spring, and often coincides with the spring snow runoff from the mountains. Spawning occurs at night on top of the water in a frenzy of activity. The new hatch remains in the river until fall and then heads for the ocean, where the next two to five years are spent, although no one knows where. They have been caught in trawls more than 100 miles offshore, but probably follow the inshore currents where the most feed is located.

The adult fish are from a pound and a half to eight pounds in size, with the females the larger. Except during the actual spawning process, they stick close to the bottom, and the best lures are tiny silver or brass spoons and wobblers with light fast-sinking lines. During high-water periods, deep holes in rivers are most productive. The usual method is to anchor above these holes and let the lure drift down into the deep water with proper weight.

In the evening and early morning, the shad will also take streamer flies in a white or a white-, yellow-, or orange-and-black combination right on the surface. They will also take most common trout wet flies, especially when trolled. One of the most effective shad lures is a local production appropriately called the Shad Killer, which is tied by a marine biologist at Coos Bay, Oregon. It is a white streamer with a red optic and is almost always trolled at a slow rate near the surface.

A flyrod or ultralight spinning outfit is ideal for shad, although the tackle and gear will vary depending upon the water. A big river like the Columbia calls for different methods and techniques than the placid Coos River, but in general the lighter the tackle and the smaller the lures, the better. Shad have a very tender mouth, and since they fight like tigers with much aerial antics, the hook will tear loose if the fish are roughly handled. Bait fishermen will find that small single hooks with seaworms, shrimp, or tiny anchovies or "pinfish" are also effective.

Shad cookery is a culinary art in eastern seaboard areas, but the subject of much confusion on the West Coast. Although the flesh is delicious, the many small bones have most amateur cooks stumped. The best method of preparing this fish seems to be smoking and then canning, a dual process that eliminates the bone problem—and incidentally makes for superb eating. It is excellent boned and broiled. The roe has no "fishy" taste and can be fried or poached or mixed with eggs in omelets.

The greatest run of shad on the West Coast today is found on the Columbia, where nearly half a million fish return annually. Paradoxically, while the series of new dams on the main river and tributaries has threatened to destroy the salmon and steelhead runs, the slack water pools have enhanced the shad, which each year seem to reach a little higher. Currently shad are reported as far inland as the middle Snake River in Idaho, about 400 miles from the ocean.

Another of the West's most famous immigrants is the striped or rock bass, *Roccus saxatilis*. In 1879, a pioneer fish culturist named Livingston Stone transported 132 fingerling stripers across country and released them into San Francisco Bay. These quickly caught on, too, and in a few years were so plentiful that a commercial gillnettery developed. The striper also migrated northward along the coast to the rivers of northern California and Oregon. Unlike the shad, however, the striper has not been found in any numbers north of the Yaquina River in Oregon, and only in rare instances in the Columbia. Currently, the principal striper streams north of the San Francisco Bay area are the Coos, Umpqua, and Smith rivers in Oregon, where the water conditions are apparently best suited for reproduction.

No one knows exactly why, but striped bass will only spawn in brackish tidal waters, usually in bays, where the eggs can be kept in suspension until the fry emerge. The water temperature and velocity of current are key factors. Striped bass have been successfully propagated in freshwater reservoirs on the East Coast and in certain western impoundments such as the lower Colorado River reservoirs, but in each instance the conditions of water velocity and temperature are ideal.

In the San Francisco Bay, Sacramento Delta, and on the Oregon coast, the bass remain in fresh or brackish water most of their lives, although they migrate to the ocean and return frequently, coming back to fresh water to spawn.

The stripers spawn at from two to seven years of age; the males usually spawn for the first time at age three, and the females at four. A bass that survives natural and manmade hazards may live to be more than twenty years old and weigh more than fifty pounds. In one unusual incident, a

Beaching a striper on the Coos River, Oregon.

small striper caught in Coos Bay and tagged by a fishery department worker was caught twenty years later by the same person who had become a commercial gillnetter. The striper had grown from four or five pounds in size to more than forty pounds. A twenty-pound striper is common, and thirty-five-pounders are frequently caught.

Stripers are prolific fish, a large female producing up to five million eggs. Spawning is usually from early May through July, depending on the river. Newly hatched larvae are extremely small and fragile. When they first begin to feed, they eat only tiny organisms such as water fleas. In artificial operations, this sort of feed must be especially cultured for the small fry, which makes their propagation more complicated than that of most species. There is a great demand for the introduction of striped bass in warm water reservoirs, however, where they would become valuable natural predators and excellent sport fish. The future of the striper seems to lie in this direction.

After the first introduction in San Francisco Bay, within

ten years the stripers supported a commercial fishery. This almost eliminated the species from the Sacramento system, along with incidental catches of other species, until 1935, when the California legislature made the striper a game fish and outlawed the nets. Unfortunately, Oregon has not seen fit to follow this example, and gillnetting in the small rivers still prevents what could be a first class sport fishery. As an example of the ruthless disregard for conservation shown by the fish-packing lobby, the main reason the nets are permitted for shad and stripers in these small rivers is merely a means of circumventing the prohibition on netting salmon and steelhead. Under the law, the gillnetters are permitted to keep the "incidental catch," which contains large numbers of salmon and steelhead. Until recent years, the striper catch was simply discarded to rot on the banks. Now it is sold fresh on the local markets for around fifteen cents a pound and used mainly for crab bait.

Stripers, which often confound anglers with their unpredictable ways, seem to like the brackish water of bays and estuaries, making short forays upriver or out to sea and back. They feed on sea worms, crabs, shrimp, squid, eels, and different species of bait fish. There is no scientific basis for the assertion by some that stripers feed on salmon and steelhead to any degree. In fact, the salmon and steelhead feed upon striper fingerlings, too, when they get the chance.

Striper fishing on the West Coast is done from boats, trolling or anchored, from the beach with surf tackle, still fishing from river banks, and from docks and jetties. They are caught casting lures and bait, bait fishing on the bottom, and trolling. In San Francisco Bay, anchoring and bottom fishing is popular and productive. Surf casting on the beach in the vicinity of the Golden Gate Bridge attracts many anglers. When I lived in the bay area, we used to fish for stripers while waiting in a duck blind on the Sacramento Delta during the fall hunting season.

In northern waters such as the Coos and Umpqua rivers, most striper fishing is done trolling with bait or lures, and plunking from the bank at known holes. At certain times, especially during the spawning period, casting surface plugs is also very effective. Although surf casting for stripers is common in California, the excellent and virtually deserted beaches from Coos Bay southward in Oregon await development as a sport fishery. Large stripers have been seen feeding off these sand beaches to the north and south of Coos Bay, and these areas are ideal for surf casting. They are a new sportfishing frontier, awaiting the curious angler.

The striper fishery in Oregon is fair all year around, but is best from early spring through July. Cut bait and whole herring or anchovies are used, as are plastic eels and jointed eel plugs, all of which must be fished on the bottom. Surface plugs such as the Rebel are highly effective during the spawning period, and particularly at night (night fishing for stripers is permitted in Oregon). At this time the bass are frequently observed on the surface in schools, and feeding close inshore on the receding tide.

A recent record forty-pound striper was taken on four-pound test line by a Coos Bay guide, the late Doug Crawford. Another record fish was taken some years ago on the Coos River with a flyrod and popping bug.

In California, a common hookup is a number 1/0 hook baited with shrimp, chunks of herring, fresh sardine, or anchovy. For bottom fishing in the Bay, a fish finder rig with two dropper hooks and a pyramid sinker on the bottom is effective from an anchored boat. This same rig with one dropper hook is used for bank plunking on the Coos and Umpqua rivers.

There is good bait fishing from May to January in the bay area, with late summer and fall best for live bait fishing. In the fall, the stripers move up the rivers in schools and the action is hot until the water cools off in the winter. Then again in March, April, and May the action perks up. Spawning is mainly in April and May.

From the beach, surf casters use the regulation rod, with a six-foot tip and a thirty-inch butt for heavy tackle, or a seven and one-half-foot tip for light squidding. A 2/0 or 3/0 freespooling surf reel or saltwater spinning reel, and up to

300 yards of twenty-pound monofilament line are commonly used. O'Shaughnessy or Sproat hooks in sizes up to 5/0 to 8/0 and a three-ounce pyramid sinker for bait are used; for heavy surf, a six-ounce sinker is used. A wire leader is often used with metal squids.

Other popular striper areas in northern California include the Russian River, Salinas River, Rockaway Beach, Point San Pedro, Half Moon Beach, Double Point, Bolinas, Stinson Beach, and Point Bonito. Bakers Beach, Mussel Rock, and Salada Beach are popular with surf casters.

CHAPTER NINE

How to Identify
and Describe Fishes

TO A LAYMAN used to calling a spade a spade, the curious practice of scientists, who seldom use one word when three will suffice, is puzzling, to say the least. This is especially true in the world of fishes, in which the layman or sports angler finds himself personally involved, and often completely confused.

Why call it an *Oncorhynchus tshawytscha* when everyone knows it's just a common chinook salmon?

Well, the main reason is because the chinook salmon is also known locally and at different times as a king, quinnat, quinault, tyee, spring hog, royal chinook, and a dozen other monikers.

But *Oncorhynchus tshawytscha*, now there's a name everyone the world over can agree on, because scientists—in this case zoologists and ichthyologists—have devised a universal system of identifying, classifying, and naming the world's animals, vegetables, and minerals to avoid confusion. When you consider that there are between 500,000 and 600,000 known kinds of animals alone on the planet Earth, you can readily understand why such a universal system is needed.

Consider this system of naming a sort of roadmap or gazetteer for finding your way around among all these confusing names.

A typical example of how confusing common names can be is the crustacean found in the eastern Pacific. It is locally called a lobster, but does not even belong to the lobster family. The same crustacean is also called a crayfish or saltwater crayfish, which helps describe it as a relative of the freshwater crustacean, but there is no such thing as a saltwater crayfish. Other names of this particular species are spiny lobster, rock lobster, Pacific coast lobster, California lobster, Pacific coast crayfish. The Mexicans down in Baja call it *languaste*, the Germans say it's *Languste*, the French *langouste*, the ancient Romans *locusta*, and Americans rock lobster.

Scientists, however, have identified this succulent little spiny lobster as *Panulirus interruptus,* a name that can be understood in any language. *Panulirus* refers to all spiny lobsters without a median spine on the front margin of the carapace or hard shell covering of the front body. *Interruptus* is the name for this particular kind of lobster to distinguish it from a distant relative in Europe called *Panulirus vulgaris* and a Japanese variety called *Palinurus japanocum.*

In other words, scientific nomenclature is merely a way of bringing order to the identification of species, regardless of national language or customs.

The present method of classifying species is based on the work of the Swedish scientist, Linne, and his monumental work, *Systema Naturae* which by its tenth edition in 1758 included 4,236 species classified and named in Latin. Linne even took for himself a Latin name, Linnaeus, which is still found attached to some Latin names of species. His method was known as binomial nomenclature.

Some species common to the Pacific were known to him even then, but the actual work of classifying Pacific flora and fauna probably began with the naturalist Stellar, who was with Vitus Bering's expeditions to the North Pacific. Other names found in connection with Pacific species are

Jordan, Gilbert, Hubbs, Clemens, Wilby, Ayres, and many others who have been honored by being the first to identify or describe a certain species.

Linnaeus did not, however, use family in his system. Since then, the system has been greatly improved and expanded, and certain rules established. For example, the names of the genus and species are still used to designate a particular kind, and both are given. The genus is a noun and refers to a group of similar forms, such as *Oncorhynchus*. This is always capitalized. When used over again in a series it may also be abbreviated, such as *Onchorhynchus tshawytscha,* *O. nerka, O. kisutch,* and so on. The specific name is an adjective and modifies the noun. This is never capitalized, even when derived from a proper name.

Because scientists in different countries (or even in the sam country) may be working on the same project at the same time, it frequently happens that the same species may be described and named by different persons. When this happens, the rule is that the first published name is adopted,

The author and two striped bass caught pretty close to home.

and the other(s) remain on the record as synonymous. Thus, *Salmo trutta* Linnaeus 1758 indicates that Linnaeus himself named and described the brown trout in 1758. But if the name of the describer is in parenthesis, such as *Alosa sapidissima* (Wilson) 1812, this means it is a species first described by Wilson, but that he did not assign it to the genus in which it is now found, although it is customary to give the source of authority. Another way of showing a change in the generic name is to give the authority followed in making the change, such as *Ophiopholis aculeata* (Linnaeus) Gray.

So, to make it easy to understand this system, one should look at it as a comprehensive system of addressing a letter. Starting with the world, you work your way down to the country, the county, the city, the street and number, and finally to the person to whom the letter is addressed. Translating this analogy to scientific nomenclature we get: Kingdom, subkingdom, phylum, class, subclass, order, suborder, tribe, family, genus and species. Which brings us right back to that rock lobster off the coast of Baja.

Obviously, to give the entire address when referring to a single fish is cumbersome, if not plain silly. The usual practice is to give only the genus and species, sometimes prefaced by the family. As far as the layman or sports angler is concerned, it is enough that he know the genus and species, such as *Salmo salar*, or Atlantic salmon, and then only if there is any reason to question the identification. In a few cases, especially among the numerous rockfishes and perches, this would come in handy. In cases where the common name is descriptive and accepted by everyone, there is no point in worrying about the scientific nomenclature. As Lewis A. McArthur, author of the famed *Oregon Geographic Names*, often said of the five species of Pacific salmon: "as far as I am concerned, there are only *smoked, kippered, broiled, baked,* and *grilled* salmon."

There are, however, several societies and quasi-official agencies and private foundations that attempt to keep catalogs of scientific and common names. Among these are the

International Commission on Zoological Nomenclature, the Fisheries Research Board of Canada, the American Fisheries Society, the California Academy of Sciences, the Scripps Institute of Oceanography, and others.

No one knows how many species exist in the vast Pacific Ocean, but it is certain that only a fraction of the number has been classified or identified. These, of course, would be the most common and most numerous. The famed Canadians, W. A. Clemens and G. V. Wilby, list 272 species belonging to eighty-three families in their work on fishes of the Pacific coast of Canada.

Around the end of World War II, two great California ichthyologists, Dr. Carl L. Hubbs of the Scripps Institute and W. 'I. Follett began an enormous task of bringing order out of chaos in the describing and naming of Pacific fishes. Much of the confusion resulted from promiscuous use of common names by local anglers and commercial fishing interests. Hubbs and Follett also managed to bring some system to

Two effective shad lures.

the common spellings and grammatical construction of the names. For example, the California sheephead is not the same as the Atlantic sheephead, although it is closely related. To make this distinction, the recommended name of the Pacific variety is sheep-head or California sheep-head. In other cases, the word "fish" is sometimes attached and sometimes separated from the prefix, such as rockfish instead of rock fish, and conversely, king fish instead of kingfish.

The Hubbs and Follett system, which is included in their *Manuscript List of the Fishes of California,* is already out of date, according to a personal communication from Dr. Hubbs, and subject to extensive revision. This only illustrates that even the scientific nomenclature is not rigid, but is changing relentlessly as new species are added and old species are reexamined and described. So the young biologist with a fresh degree who arches his brows at the layman's use of a particular name should not be taken too seriously.

This guide to the common marine fishes of the Pacific Ocean includes some 300 separate species. To my knowledge it is the most complete catalog of Pacific fishes available in the popular press today.

The species listed here were selected as those that a sports or commercial fisherman might be apt to encounter, as well as those of interest to amateur naturalists and conservationists. In some cases, lengthy descriptions are given as a matter of lay interest. In a few instances so little is known of the particular species that only its name and general range can be listed. Fishes are indexed alphabetically by their common names.

It is important to remember that fishes, in salt water, vary widely in coloration. Frequently this color changes radically when the fish is removed from water, such as is the case with the beautiful and brilliant *dorado.* Many anadromous fishes, such as salmon and steelhead, change color when they move from the ocean into the freshwater streams, and vice versa. So color is a means of identification, but not a rigid nor a reliable one in all cases.

In identifying a fish, note the color as it comes out of

water, then the general outline of the body, the shape of the head and mouth, the size and arrangement of the fins, and any unique markings. This is usually adequate for a layman. The scientist, of course, goes into more detail such as the number of rays in the fins, the number and position of gill slits, size and construction of scales, and so on.

Finally, it should also be remembered that marine seafood includes species that are toxic, partly toxic, sometimes toxic and sometimes not. Always follow local practice before cooking and eating any ocean species.

GLOSSARY

Abyssal—related to great depths, usually below 1,500 fathoms.

Adipose fin—a fleshy fin on the dorsal median line behind the rayed section of dorsal fin.

Anal—pertaining to the anus.

Anterior—in front.

Barbel—an elongated fleshy projection under snout or around mouth.

Bathypelagic—living freely in the open sea below 200 fathoms.

Bifurcate—divided into two branches.

Canines—doglike conical teeth.

Caudal—pertaining to the tail.

Caudal fin—tail fin.

Caudal peduncle—the juncture between the body and base of tail.

Compressed—flattened from side to side.

Deciduous—falling off, loosely attached.

Decurved—curving downward.

Dorsal—pertaining to the back or upper surface.

Elongate—lengthened, longer than deep.

Furcate—forked, such as tail.

Gill—the opening or structure by which a fish exchanges gases in the water and blood in the body.

Gill arch—arch to which the gill filaments are attached.

Gill rakers—protuberances on the gill arch opposite the gill filaments.

Interspace—space between vertical fins, usual dorsal fins.

Keel—a ridge extending longitudinally on the midline.

Lateral—pertaining to the side, such as lateral line.

Lunate—half moon shaped.

Mandible—main bone of lower jaw.

Maxillary—main bone of the upper jaw.

Median—on the vertical axis of body.

Ocular—pertaining to the eye.

Operculum—gill cover, including bones such as opercle, preopercle, interopercle, and subopercle.

Papilla—small fleshy projection.

Pectoral—pertaining to the chest.

Peduncle—see caudal peduncle.

Pelagic—found freely in the open seas.

Pelvic—pertaining to the basin formed by the pelvic girdle, the sacrum, and sometimes the coccygeal and caudal vertebrae.

Peritoneum—lining of abdominal cavity.

Photophore—specialized organs, on body or head, producing light.

Plankton—minute aquatic plants and animals.

Posterior—behind.

Prickle—a scale reduced to a sharp pointed spine.

Ray—as applied to a fin, refers to segmented support.

Recurved—curved upward and inward.

Redd—a nest in sand or gravel for eggs.

Reticulations—markings in a form of network of lines.

Serrated—like a saw.

Snout—portion of head projecting in front of eyes.

Spine—the unsegmented supports of fin membranes.

Spiracle—opening behind eye of shark or ray.

Stellate—starlike.

Symmetrical—balanced, regular.

Symphyseal knob—a projection or swelling below or in front of the lower jawbones.

Tail—that portion of body aft of the caudal peduncle.

Truncate—ending abruptly or squared-off such as the tail.

Tubercle—a modified scale, sometimes a hard rounded hump.

Ventral—pertaining to the belly or lower parts.

Vomer—the bone in the roof of the mouth, bearing teeth.

FISH IDENTIFICATION

SHARKS AND RAYS

Sharks, skates, and rays belong to the subclass Euselachii of the class selachii (Chonrichthyes), and are among the oldest living things on earth and in the sea. They are found everywhere, in all oceans, under all conditions. There are more than 250 species of sharks alone, ranging from a foot in length to more than sixty feet, and from cowardly prey to vicious predators, including a number extremely dangerous to man.

Feared, misunderstood, and usually avoided by man, the shark has for centuries been regarded as a blackguard and a villain, and just the sight of a dorsal fin sticking out of water is enough to strike fear in many people. But sharks are a great unexploited sport fishery, as well as a food source. The International Game Fish Association compiles records on the white or maneater, the thresher, tiger, mako, porbeagle, and blue species at this time. Although not accepted as a food fish in most civilized countries, the shark has been highly prized in certain areas as a delicacy, and if you have eaten "swordfish" in the gourmet centers of Mexico City and other cosmopolitan places, you probably were eating mako or blue shark. During World War II on the West Coast, hundreds of tons of shark meat were peddled as "swordfish" and as the fish in "fish and chips." For years a brisk commercial shark fishery existed as a source of vitamins, until a synthetic product eliminated the market. Similarly, skates and rays have been, and in some instances still are, marketed in seafood establishments as "scallops" made with circular cookie cutters.

With about thirty common species in the Pacific that can be regarded as game fish, sharks may someday soon come into popular favor among sport anglers.

Sharks will feed upon almost anything, especially anything that moves, but they are also known to eat garbage, marine plants, crustaceans, squid, turtles, sea lions, and each other. They usually feed by following their well developed senses of sound and smell, as well as by sighting prey. They can be caught on any saltwater tackle suitable for their size, and on practically any bait or lure. Most sharks are harmless to man, but a number of species are known to be dangerous including the tiger, bull, lemon, white, and hammerhead. Experts say, however, that all sharks should be regarded as unpredictable and dangerous. Since they are difficult to kill, the most dangerous situation for a sport angler is after the shark has been landed in the boat. They have been known to suddenly "come alive" after several hours out of water and, with a tremendous spasm and snapping of jaws, kill or maim anything within reach. While skates and rays are bottom fish, sharks feed on the bottom, in midwater, and on the surface.

Only a few species of sharks lay eggs. In most cases the young are born alive, and the number is small —seldom more than seventy-five or eighty at a time—compared to egg-laying species that may deposit millions of eggs. At present the economic value is limited to livers, a source of Vitamin A, hide for leather products, fins that are dehydrated for soup stock, especially in the Orient, and flesh for poultry, mink, and livestock food. As mentioned before, in some cases the flesh is sold as swordfish, whitefish, grayfish, scallops, fillet of sole, and even salmon and halibut.

Family: Hexanchidae
Common Name: Cowsharks

The cowsharks have a single dorsal fin far back behind the origin of the pelvic fins, with small gill slits, and no keel on the caudal peduncle. They are bottom-living fishes, favoring warm waters. Only six or seven species exist out of numerous fossil forms.

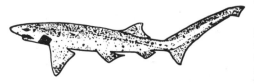

1. Sevengill shark
Notorynchus maculatum
Also: Spotted cowshark, mudshark.
Range: Southern California to northern British Columbia, along the continental shelf.
Size: Length to 8 feet, often larger.
Value: Considered one of the best for food and sport.
Description: Color ranges from sandy gray to reddish-brown with scattered round black spots. Has seven gill slits on each side, a single dorsal fin, and a large scimitar tail. Little is known of habits.

2. Sixgill shark
Hexanchus corinum
Also: Cowshark, mudshark, griset.
Range: Southern California to Gulf of Alaska.
Size: Length to 27 feet.
Value: Has been used in processing of oil and meal; good eating.
Description: Color is dark gray, almost black in some cases, with a pale streak along the sides. Feeds on herring and other fishes. Body elongated, rounded. Large and depressed head; broad blunt snout; ventral mouth. Dorsal fin is 'far back. Scimitar tail. Distinguished by six gill slits on each side and a single dorsal fin.

Family: Alopiidae
Common Name: Threshers

The threshers are pelagic and found world-wide. They are most easily distinguished by the long, scimitarlike tail, and the first dorsal fin behind the pectoral fins. A small anal fin is present also, but there is no keel on the caudal peduncle. The gill slits are small with the fifth located above the pectoral fin. All sharks of this suborder have five gill slits on each side, two dorsal fins, and one anal fin.

3. Thresher shark
Alopias vulpinus
Also: Longtail shark, thrasher.
Range: Southern California to Vancouver Island.
Size: Length to 25 feet, common 10 to 15.

Value: Good food fish, as well as sport species; scrappy fighter.
Description: Color is dark brownish-gray to black on dorsal, white on ventral surface. Elongated body, short caudal peduncle, moderate head, blunt snout, ventral mouth; small, flat, triangular teeth without cusps, small eyes. Easily recognized by very long tail, commonly about half the total length from tip of snout to tip of caudal fin. A fast swimmer, it feeds on herring, pilchards, and other small bait fish. Most abundant and largest in tropical waters, but common off the Pacific Northwest. Not known to be dangerous to humans. Called "thresher" because of its habit of circling bait fish schools, threshing with its tail to stun them. Feeds on the surface mostly. Heavy tackle required. Has been caught on a salmon troll.

Family: Lamnidae
Common Name: Mackerel sharks

Mackerel sharks have some characteristics similar to mackerels, although they are not related. The slender caudal peduncle, for example, and strong keel with a streamlined body makes for a fast swimmer. They have five gill slits, the fifth in front of the pectoral fin. The first dorsal fin is above the pectoral fin. There is a small anal fin. They are pelagic, widely distributed, especially in northern latitudes.

4. Salmon shark   **Lamna ditropis**
Also: Porbeagle, tiger shark, mackerel shark, man-eater.
Range: Northern California to Bering Sea.
Size: Length to 10 feet.
Value: Excellent game fish; has been taken on salmon tackle.

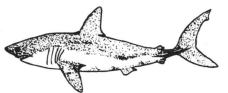

Description: Color is dark, bluish-gray on dorsal, white on ventral surface, usually blotched black. Heavy elongated body, slender caudal peduncle with keel on each side; prominent second keel below and behind caudal fin. Moderate head, prominent snout, pointed and somewhat depressed. Large eyes, high on head; large teeth. Five gill slits, fifth in front of pectoral fin. A fast swimmer and voracious feeder, foraging on salmon and similar fishes. Said to be a man-eater, but there is no recorded instance of human attack.

Family: Cetorhinidae
Common Name: Basking sharks

Basking sharks are so called for their habit of lying motionless on the surface in calm, sunny weather, with the dorsal fin out of water. They grow to large size, up to thirty feet and four tons, but are sluggish plankton feeders. They are the only sharks on the eastern Pacific rim with gill rakers. Feeding is done by swimming with the mouth open, straining small crustaceans through the gill rakers. The dorsal fin is behind the pectoral fin, and a small anal fin is present. The gill slits are large and located in front of the pectoral fins. They were well-known to Indians of the coastal areas, and once were thought to be sea serpents. They are pelagic and world-wide in distribution. In the Pacific Northwest they cause extensive damage to salmon gill nets, and often appear in large schools. They are not considered dangerous.

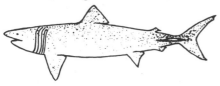

5. Basking shark
Cetorhinus maximus
Also: Oil shark, bone shark, capidoli, pelerin, elephant shark, halsydrus.
Range: Southern California to Gulf of Alaska.
Size: Length to 45 feet maximum.
Value: Considered excellent food fish, rich source of oil.
Description: Color, bluish-gray to brownish-gray on dorsal, paler on ventral surface. Prominent keels; heavy, elongated body; slender caudal peduncle; moderate head; blunt snout; small low eyes; numerous conical teeth. Gill rakers are long, close-set and resemble whalebone.

Family: Scyliorhinidae
Common Name: Cat sharks
With a shape vaguely suggesting a catfish, cat sharks belong to a group having the first dorsal fin above the pelvic fins, a large anal fin, and no keel. The gill slits are moderate, with the fifth and sometimes the fourth on the base of the pectoral fins.

6. Brown cat shark
Apristurus brunneus
Also: Brown shark.
Range: Baja to Vancouver Island.
Size: Length to 2 feet.
Value: Nil at this time.

Description: Color is dark brown, black on fins. An egg-laying shark, it is distinguished by its small size and the two dorsal fins well back toward the tail, which is short and without keel. The body is slender, compressed, head elongated, snout angled up, teeth small, eyes large, five gill slits. Found in deep water, often taken in trawl nets.

Family: Carcharhindae
Common Name: Blue sharks

A widely distributed family, one of which is landlocked in Lake Nicaragua (Charhinus nicaraguensis), they are pelagic, extremely active, and voracious feeders. The first dorsal fin 'is behind the' pectoral fins. There is a small anal fin and no keel. There are five gill slits, the fifth and sometimes the fourth is located on the base of the pectoral fin.

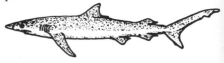

7. Blue shark   **Prionace glauca**
Also: Great blue.
Range: Tropical and temperate waters, from Baja to Gulf of California.
Size: Length to 20 feet, common 8 feet.
Value: An excellent game fish, as well as a .food fish, but usually smoked due to ammonia taint.
Description: Color is bluish-gray, snowy white on ventral surface. Distinguished by cobalt color, long

slender pointed snout, depressed head, short, slender caudal peduncle, no keel, very long pectoral fins, sabre-shape, five gill slits, with the fifth above the pectoral fin. Frequently found with bait fish concentrations and often hooked by salmon trollers. They feed on mackerel, herring, anchovies, and even garbage. They are commonly the sharks that follow ships for scraps, and are believed dangerous to swimmers. Little is known of their habits, except that they give birth to as many as fifty live young at a time.

8. Soupfin shark
Galeorhinus zyopterus
Also: Oil shark, tope.
Range: Found generally in the North Pacific, Baja to Vancouver Island. Similar varieties in the South Pacific.
Size: Length to 6½ feet and 100 pounds.
Value: Famous for its gelatinous rays, which make a much prized Chinese soup. The Vitamin A content is high, and during the pre-World War II days there was a valuable commercial fishery for this species. It is considered a good food fish, and is actually protected by law in some localities.
Description: Color is dark bluish to dusky gray, black on dorsal fins, pale gray underbelly. It has a pointed snout, concave head, large first dorsal fin, small anal fin, short slender caudal peduncle, no keel. There are five gill slits, with the fifth above the pectoral fin. Food consists of herring, anchovies, pilchards, salmon, rockfish, and squid.

They give birth to live young, as many as twenty to thirty at a time. Usually found feeding about six feet above the bottom.

Family: Squalidae
Common Name: Dogfishes

These sharks are plentiful in all oceans, sometimes in large schools that take over an area. They have small gill slits, no keel on the caudal peduncle, and often a large spine in front of each dorsal that is capped with a knob before birth. The females go into shallow water to give birth. It is an important food fish in many areas, and frequently a nuisance to sports anglers.

9. Pacific dogfish **Squalus suckleyi**
Also: Dog shark, grayfish, spiny dogfish.
Range: All oceans, exceedingly abundant in temperate waters of North Pacific.
Size: Length to 5 feet.
Value: Once valuable for oil and meal, the latter having a high nitrogen content, they were much sought for livers by commercial fishermen in the 1940s, until a cheaper synthetic Vitamin A was developed. During the war, tons of dogfish were consumed as "grayfish," and it is a good food fish where accepted.
Description: Color is gray or light brown on dorsal surface, dirty white on the belly. The body is elongated and slender, the caudal peduncle long, slender; head depressed, snout pointed, eyes large, five gill slits. There are two dorsals, no anal fin, and large spine

in front of each dorsal. The female gives birth to as many as fourteen at a time in alternate years. The young have white spots on the back. The dogfish does not travel around much, usually staying in one area with plenty of bait fish such as pilchards, anchovies, smelts, sandlances, squid, crustaceans, and small salmon. They are also scavengers, feeding upon the offal from canneries, reduction plants, and garbage.

Family: Dalatiidae
Common Name: Sleeper sharks

These have no spines, are sluggish of movement, and found worldwide. The first dorsal is behind the pectoral fins, and there is no anal fin.

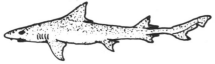

10. Pacific sleeper shark
             Somniosus pacificus
Range: Entire Pacific area.
Size: Length to 25½ feet.
Value: Nil at this time.
Description: Color is gray to sooty black. The body is heavy and elongated, rounded, without anal fin. The snout is blunt, mouth ventral, eyes large. Five gill slits. Fins small, with two dorsals, no spines. A bottom feeder, it feeds voraciously on anything, including carrion. Considered rapacious, and possibly dangerous to humans.

11. Bonito shark   **Isurus glaucut**
Also: Mackerel shark, mako, paloma.
Range: Temperate and tropical waters of the Pacific from the eastern

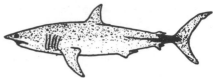

rim to Japan and Hawaii, and Indo-Pacific.
Size: Length to 15 feet, average 8 feet.
Value: An excellent game fish, nearly equal to the marlin, and noted for its out-of-water leaps. During World War II, tons of bonito sharks were sold as rockfish, swordfish, sea bass, and even shark steak.
Description: Color is a dark, metallic blue on the back and a faded gray to white on the underbelly. It differs from its Atlantic relative, the mako, in its shorter head and lower dorsal fin, but has the streamlined shape. It has long, smooth teeth, prominent keels on the sides of the caudal peduncle, prominent front dorsal, small secondary dorsal, and swordlike pectoral fins. It has five gill slits, pointed head, and anal fins. Found close to shore, around islands and bays, and in the open sea where it is a swift and voracious feeder on schools of tuna, bonito, and mackerel, as well as bait fish. The bonito shark is not only prized by sports anglers, but is exceedingly dangerous and has even attacked boats.

12. Maneater shark
             Carcharodon carcharias
Also: Great white, white shark.
Range: Not plentiful, but found in most oceans, usually in temperate waters. It is oceanic and pelagic and roams widely, staying offshore, but sometimes appears in shallow areas around cities, and is definitely dangerous to swimmers.

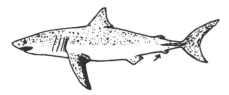

Size: Length to 36 feet, but widely varied. An 8-footer weighs about 600 pounds, while a 13-footer may weigh a ton.

Value: Important to sports anglers as a game fish, mostly because it is so dangerous.

Description: Color is grayish-brown, changing to slate-blue or gray, with dirty white underbelly. The largest specimens are leaden white. The young often have a black spot above the pectoral. Distinguished by its streamlined shape and large size, pointed snout, triangular, serrated teeth, crescent-shaped caudal swordlike pectoral fins. It feeds on anything, including large animals and fish of all kinds, such as sea lions, sturgeon, tuna, turtles, squid. This species has been responsible for several attacks on swimmers on the West Coast and in Australian waters. One specimen was captured which contained a large dog and parts of a horse. Sharks like this have given rise to legends and hairy tales.

13. California swell shark
Cephaloscyllium uter
Range: Found in subtropical waters in eastern Pacific.
Size: Maximum 3 feet, usually smaller.
Value: Nil as a sport fish; slightly toxic as a food fish.

Description: Color is brownish-black, with yellowish underbelly, with entire body covered with round spots. Two dorsals, five gill slits, irregular spots and bars on back. Of academic interest because of ability to inflate its belly with air when threatened. Usually found in kelp beds.

Family: Triakididae
Common Name: Smoothhounds

14. Leopard shark
Triakis semifasciata
Also: Cat shark, spotted shark.
Range: From Baja to Oregon, common in California bays, often taken in the surf.
Size: Length to 5 feet.
Value: Good food fish, as well as sports species; considered dangerous to swimmers.
Description: Distinctive coloring is gray with about twelve cross bands of black, and many dark spots on the sides. Fins are rounded. First dorsal is ahead of pelvic fins. Five gill slits. Two dorsals and anal fin. Females are larger. Feed on crabs, shrimp, clams, small fish.

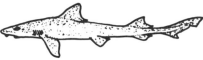

15. Brown smoothhound
Rhinotriacis henlei
Also: Paloma, dogfish, sand shark.
Range: Common along the eastern Pacific rim in temperate waters.
Size: Length to 3 feet.

Value: Excellent food fish, sometimes passed off for soupfin.
Description: One of the requiem sharks. Color is brownish on the back, fading to lighter underbelly, usually whitish. Has four or five rows of razor sharp teeth, five gill slits, slender body, two dorsals, anal fin, slender caudal peduncle. Easily caught, even from piers.

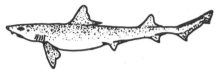

16. Gray smoothhound
Mustelus californicus
Also: Sand shark, gray shark, dogfish, mudshark.
Range: Eastern Pacific from Baja to Oregon.
Size: Length to 3 feet.
Value: Good food fish, often sold as "grayfish."
Description: Color is iridescent dark gray on back, fading to whitish belly. Similar to brown smoothhound, except for rounded blunt teeth and heavier body and color. Has two dorsals, slender caudal peduncle, and anal fins. Found in bays and estuaries, as well as deep water; easily caught.

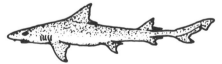

17. Sicklefin smoothhound
Mustelus lunulatus
Also: Dog shark, smoothhound, gato.
Range: Eastern Pacific from Baja to Northern California.
Size: Length to 5 feet.
Value: Often marketed as "grayfish" and considered good food fish.

Description: Gray with lighter belly. Two dorsals, long slender caudal peduncle, pointed lower lobe of caudal, anal fin. Easy to catch on almost any bait.

18. Bay grayshark
Carcharhinus lamiella
Also: Injerto, grayback.
Range: Subtropical waters of eastern Pacific.
Size: Length to 15 feet.
Value: Important as a commercial source of Vitamin A. It is said that one gram of liver oil produces 60,000 U.S.P. units of Vitamin A. Taken on sports tackle usually while fishing for other game fish.
Description: Color is grayish fading to lighter underbelly. Distinguished by large size, long slender scimitarlike caudal peduncle, two dorsal fins, five gill slits, with the fourth and fifth often above base of pectoral fins. Long slender snout, small eyes. Probably dangerous to humans.

19. Tiger shark
Galeocerdo cuvieri
Also: Tigerfish, bayshark.
Range: Subtropical waters in open sea.
Size: Length to 20 feet.
Value: Nil at this time.
Description: Color is grayish-brown, with lighter belly. Long, slender caudal peduncle; large head, short sharp-pointed snout,

heavy body, with many spots. Five gill slits, the fifth over base of pectoral fins. Considered highly dangerous in many areas.

Family: Spyrmidae
Common Name: Hammerheads

Common shark in tropical waters of Atlantic and Pacific, distinguished by its unusual head, high front dorsal, and large size.

20. Common hammerhead
Sphyrna zygaena
Also: Axhead shark.
Range: The open Pacific in tropical and subtropical waters.
Size: Length to 16 feet.
Value: Pursued by sports anglers mainly because of size, unique configuration, and difficulty to catch.
Description: Grayish back with lighter belly. Huge size. Head shaped like double-bitted ax with eyes in front corners; five gill slits, long slender caudal peduncle, high front dorsal, small rear dorsal. Feeds on small bait fish, squid, crustaceans.

21. Scalloped hammerhead
Sphyrna lewini
Range: Found in the open sea in the Atlantic and Pacific, and around the Hawaiian Islands, and other tropical waters.

Description: Similar to common hammerhead, except notched front head.

22. Spanish hammerhead
Sphyrna tiburo
Also: Shovelhead, bonnet shark.
Range: Tropical waters of the North and South Pacific.
Description: Tiburon is Spanish for certain species of sharks. S. tiburo is similar to the common hammerhead, except for a spadelike head, rather than axlike.

Family: Squatinidae
Common Name: Angel sharks

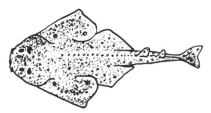

23. California angel shark
Squatina californica
Also: Angel shark, monkfish.
Range: Eastern Pacific from Baja to Alaska.
Size: Length to 5 feet.
Value: Pectoral fins and tail are edible.
Description: Color is dark brown, or reddish-brown, with whitish underbelly. Bears live young. Configuration somewhat like a skate or ray. Has a depressed head, large pectorals almost like wings, short blunt snout, thick elongated tail, pronounced caudal peduncle, and no anal fin.

Family: Rhinobatidae
Common Name: Guitarfishes

The guitarfishes give birth to live young, and are distinguished by prominent configuration, with pectoral fins attached to the snout, forming an angular or circular disk with the head and shoulders in the central part.

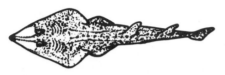

24. Shovelnose guitarfish
Rhinobatos productus
Also: Shovelnose shark, guitarshark.
Range: Subtropical to temperate waters as far north as 40° latitude.
Size: Length to 5 feet.
Value: The tail is said to be edible.
Description: Color is brownish-gray with brownish-tan undersides and disk. It has a long, pointed snout, with the first dorsal fin located about the middle of the tail, pectoral and pelvic fins extend horizontally, thick tail, small spines on back, tail, and around the eyes, skin covered with small close-set tubercles like shagreen leather. Easily taken on sport tackle.

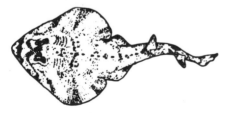

25. Mottled guitarfish
Zapteryx exasperata
Also: Striped guitarfish, brown guitarfish.

Range: Subtropical to temperate waters south of 40° North latitude.
Size: Length to 3 feet.
Value: Of commercial value to Oriental cookery.
Description: Color light olive brown to pale undersides, with bars and spots outlined in black, mixed with yellowish blotches. The first dorsal is forward of the center of the tail, snout slightly rounded, low blunt spikes on middle of back. Skin is covered with tubercles. This species is usually caught incidentally.

Family: Platyrhinidae
Common Name: Thornbacks

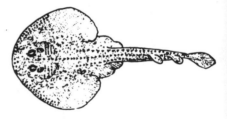

26. California thornback
Platyrhinoides triseriata
Also: Shovelnose, shovelnose shark.
Range: Subtropical waters, common Baja California and Southern California.
Size: Length to 3 feet.
Value: This fish is edible and usually caught in areas of sand bottom.
Description: A light greenish color blending brown to black, light undersides. This species has three rows of strong spines on back and tail, a rounded snout with circular disk. The two dorsal fins are to the rear of the middle of the tail, with small spines on shoulders. Skin is prickled with tubercles. There is a small caudal.

Family: Rajidae
Common Name: Skates

Distinguished by a posterially extended body with a long slender tail, with a longitudinal fold on each side. There are usually two dorsal fins well back on the tail. Skates apparently prefer muddy bottoms, and deep, cool waters, where they lie motionless or gently waving their fins. They are fast swimmers.

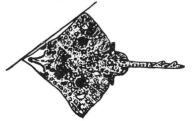

27. Big Skate
                Raja binoculata
Also: Spotted skate, eyespot skate.
Range: From Baja California to Alaska.
Size: Length to 8 feet.
Value: The wings have considerable commercial importance for mink feed; but often sold as "scallops."
Description: Color is dull olive brown or gray to almost black on the dorsal surface, whitish undersides. There is a large dark ringed ocellus or eye-spot on each wing with light spots over the body. The head is depressed, tail slender, body elongated. The snout is long, pointed, mouth ventral, spiracle large and located behind the eyes. There are five gill slits and two dorsal fins far back, no anal fin, broad pectoral fins attached to snout, no caudal fin. The scales are minute, with spines on middorsal line. Easily caught on live bait, or

chunks. "Mermaid's purses" that wash up on the beach are usually egg cases.

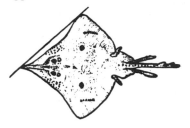

28. Longnose skate   **Raja rhina**
Also: Mottled skate.
Range: found in temperate waters of North Pacific.
Size: Length to 5 feet maximum.
Value: The "wings" are sold commercially, but are less valuable than the big skate, although more common.
Description: Color is brown on dorsal surface, with muddy blue on undersides or ventral, and a black ring at the base of each pectoral, with small white spot posterior to each ring. Distinguished by long pointed snout, angular outline of body, deep notch in each pelvic fin, and bluish undercolor. The head is depressed, mouth ventral, body elongated, tail slender. There are five gill slits, two dorsal fins far back on tail, no anal.

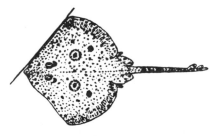

29. Starry skate   **Raja stellulata**
Also: Cheapskate, prickly skate.

Range: Baja to Alaska in the eastern Pacific.
Size: Length to 3 feet maximum, average about 18 inches.
Value: Best eating of the skates.
Description: Color is gray-brown with many black spots and a pair of large eye-spots. The head is depressed, body elongated, tail slender with two dorsals back on tail, no anal, five gill slits, deep notched pelvic fins, broad pectorals attached to snout. The snout is blunt and pointed. There is a middorsal line of spines, and a row on each orbital rim. Prefers deep water, easily caught.

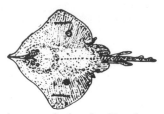

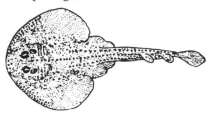

30. Black skate   **Raja kincaidii**
Range: Baja California to Alaska.
Size: Length to 3 feet maximum.
Description: Color is slate black in adults, brown black in young, with small brown or black spots on dorsal surface, whitish undersides, white spot on each side of tail in the young. Has a weak snout, a continuous row of spines, two dorsals far back, no anal, no caudal fin, deep to moderate notched pelvic fins.

31. Deepsea skate **Raja abyssicola**
Range: A rare species, believed common only to offshore British Columbia waters.
Size: Length to 4 feet.
Value: Of no importance to sportsmen at this time, except as a rarity.
Description: Color uniformly brown. The body is elongated, slender, depressed, with a slender tail,

depressed head, bluntly pointed snout, five gill slits, two dorsal fins high and far back, spines on middorsal, large spiracles behind eyes.

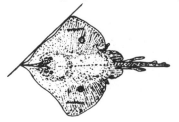

32. California skate   **Raja inornata**
Range: Believed mainly in eastern Pacific from Baja to 42° North.
Size: Length to 2½ feet maximum.
Value: An important commercial fish in California markets.
Description: Color is greenish-brown with small eye-spots, surrounded by dark spots. A single row of spines middorsal, snout is sharp and pointed, pectoral tips are curved slightly, prickles on outer pectorals.

Family: Dasyatidae
Common Name: Stingrays

Stingrays have a posteriorly extended body, with a very long slender tail, whiplike in character, with sharp serrated spine on the dorsal surface. Dorsal and caudal fins are absent, and in some species, particularly in the central and south Pacific, a powerful poison is secreted along the side of the tail spine, which can cause death or serious illness. Some species even ascend coastal rivers, and are numerous in warm waters. If stung, a person should apply first aid treatment at once. Soaking in hot epsom salt solution will ease pain and soreness. Obtain competent medical treatment as soon as possible. At this time, there is no commercial or sports interest in stingrays, and they are generally destroyed before removing from hook as a precaution.

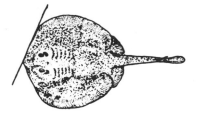

slate brown with spots and blotches. Distinguished by round disk shape, long slender tail, not whiplike, with a small caudal, no dorsal fins, long sharp spine on top of tail. This one is found on the bottom in bays and sloughs, and is abundant in some areas, making it a nuisance and a danger to swimmers and waders.

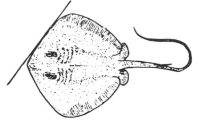

33. Diamond stingray
Dasyatis dipterurus
Also: Rattailed stingray, stingaree.
Range: Baja California to Gulf of Alaska.
Size: Length to 6 feet.
Description: Color bluish-brown. Greatly elongated body, very slender whiplike tail, depressed head, pointed snout, five gill slits, large spine on dorsal surface, sharp and serrated. No caudal or dorsal fins. Eats crabs and mollusks. Much feared by fishermen, the tail is a dangerous weapon.

34. Round stingray
Urolophus halleri
Also: Stingaree, disk stingray.
Range: Tropical and subtropical waters.
Size: Length to 2 feet.
Value: Like other stingrays, this one is important only as a warning to sports anglers.
Description: Color dark brown or

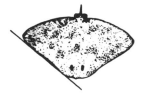

35. California butterfly ray
Gymnura marmorata
Also: Butterfly stingray, bat ray, angel shark, eagle stingray.
Range: Common in subtropical waters of North Pacific.
Size: Length to 5 feet.
Description: Color dark brown or olive, with patterns on wings, and whitish undersides. Distinguished by broad fan shaped body, barely discernible tail, the usual spike or spine.

Family: Torpedinidae
Common Name: Electric rays.
The electric rays have a broad depressed body, short stout tails, two dorsal fins, and large caudal.

They are distinguished by the electric organs on either side of the head and are capable of giving a severe electric shock, although it must be touched at two points to get the full effect. They feed on eels, salmon, flounder, and other fishes. They are most abundant in warm seas.

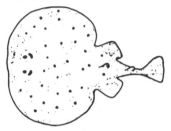

36. Pacific electric ray
Torpedo californica
Range: Subtropical waters of North Pacific.
Size: Length to 3 feet.
Description: Bluish-gray to brownish-gray, dusky gray undersides, small round black spots. The body is elongated, tail short and stout, five gill slits, blunt rounded snout, smooth skin, rounded pectoral fins, broad truncated body, two dorsals, no anal. These have been caught on salmon trolling gear, but food is apparently mostly herring and bait fish.

Family: Chimaeridae
Common Name: Chimaeras

Distinguished by large head, chisellike fins, arrowhead shaped caudal, paddlelike pectorals, prominent teeth, and general weird appearance. The name chimaera suggests the head of a lion, body of goat, and tail of a serpent.

37. Ratfish   Hydrolagus colliei
Also: Rabbitfish, water hare, chi-

maera, king-of-herrings.
Range: North Pacific to Alaska.
Size: Length to 3 feet.
Value: Usually caught incidentally on sport tackle, but of no value. It yields a very fine liver oil, however, that is valuable commercially for lubricating guns and instruments. It is yellowish, not gummy, and has no objectionable odor.
Description: The word Hydrolagus means water hare, indicating the rabbitlike mouth. The color is silvery, with a metallic-gold or brown and similar hues. The body is elongated, stoutish toward the rear, head large, snout blunt, projecting. The mouth is small, with notched upper lip, two nostrils, two dorsal fins, no scales.

Family: Acipenseridae
Common Name: Sturgeons

The sturgeons are primitive fishes, resembling sharks, with a head covered with bony plates, depressed snout, and barbels. They are sluggish, live on the bottom in both fresh and salt water, and eat small fish, worms, crustaceans, and carrion. The marine species are anadromous and enter rivers to spawn.

38. White sturgeon
Acipenser transmontanus
Range: North American waters from Northern California to Alas-

ka, in tidal rivers mainly, but also found landlocked.

Size: Length to 20 feet.

Value: A slow-growing species under much commercial and sport pressure, it is barely making its own way, and could be considered an endangered species because of its value for gourmet processing and roe from which caviar is made.

Description: The color is uniformly gray, the body elongated, head depressed, snout broad, short, bluntly rounded, with four barbels, no teeth, suckerlike mouth, bony shields, prominent caudal. Often found entering rivers at the same time as the eulachon (smelt) runs, but also found all year in upper rivers and behind dams. The largest North American fish, specimens weighing more than 1,800 pounds have been recorded. Little is known of its life and habits, except that it takes as long as fifteen years to mature and reproduce. In many areas only specimens from three to six feet are legal. In some places such as the Snake River all must be returned to the water unharmed. There is a well-developed commercial fishery in the Pacific Northwest and as long as this is important, fisheries biologists will find ways of rationalizing the heavy take.

waters of estuaries and tidal rivers, as well as in the open sea of coastal waters. Little is known of its habits or life cycle. Similar in appearance to the white sturgeon, but has a more cylindrical body, elongated upturned snout, narrow and depressed; no teeth, suckerlike mouth, bony shields, four barbels. Fairly easy to catch in the estuaries of Oregon and British Columbia.

Family: Clupeidae
Common Name: Herrings

The herrings include numerous fishes such as pilchards, shads, and herrings, which occur in large cloudlike schools throughout the Pacific, furnishing bait fish for commercial fishermen, forage for species such as salmon, tuna, cod, lingcod, and other predators. They are packed for sports anglers as frozen bait, as well as canned as "sardines" and food for human consumption. The American shad, introduced on the West Coast in the 1870s, is an anadromous fish, running up the rivers to spawn. Other members of this family are found in the bays and estuaries as well as in the open sea.

39. Green sturgeon
          Acipenser medirostris
Range: Coast of North America north of 42° latitude.
Size: Length to 7 feet.
Value: A food fish, but considerably inferior to the white sturgeon.
Description: Olive green with olive stripes. Found mainly in brackish

40. Pacific herring   **Clupea pallasii**
Range: Most of North Pacific.
Size: Length to 13 inches.
Value: The herring is also the major fishery in tonnage in many areas, and is caught in purse seines and gillnets for reduction plants,

for smoking, canning, pickling, and for bait.

Description: Color is bluish-green with silvery undersides. The body is elongated, head compressed, lower jaw projecting, teeth absent from jaws, scales cycloid, furcated caudal. The herring is abundant in temperate coastal waters, feeding on plankton in the open sea, going into the bays and estuaries to spawn, depositing large numbers of eggs on eelgrass, rocks, wharf pilings. The herring and its eggs are a basic food source for a wide variety of fishes and bird life.

41. Pilchard   **Sardinops sagax**
Also: Sardine, California sardine, firecracker.
Range: North Pacific.
Size: Length to 16 inches.
Value: Harvesting as "sardines" prior to and during World War II demolished the once vast schools. Since then the pilchard fishery has been nonexistent in northern waters, although the fish is found in large numbers along the coast during the summer and fall salmon runs. Pilchard oil is used in the manufacture of paint, soap, shortening, and oleomargarine. The meal is used for livestock feed, and the canned product is sold for human consumption. It is in great demand as a bait by sportsmen during the salmon season.
Description: Color is dark blue on dorsal surface, silvery on ventral, with round black spots on sides and back, black on peritoneum. The body is elongated and deeper than herring, head compressed, teeth absent, single dorsal fin, typi-

cal herring tail. Spawning takes place offshore in the open sea, usually about 100 miles out. The eggs are pelagic and spawned usually in March, April, and May. The food of the pilchard consists mainly of plankton and small crustaceans. This is the same fish previously recorded as **Sardinops caerulea** (Girard), and the name recommended by the American Fisheries Society is Pacific sardine. However, it is more commonly known as pilchard, which is a more descriptive and singular term.

42. California round herring
          Etrumeus acuminatus
Also: Japanese herring.
Range: Found in the North Pacific from 10° to 40° North.
Size: Length to 10 inches.
Value: Like the other herrings, it is a bait and forage fish of great importance.
Description: Color is shiny silver with brown spots on back and sometimes on sides. Similar in configuration to the Pacific herring except for the short base anal fin and the location of the pelvic fin back of the point of the dorsal.

Family: Elopidae
Common Name: Tenpounders

43. Pacific tenpounder **Elops affinis**
Also: Bonefish, mullet, John Marigale, big herring.

Range: An inshore fish, found in bays and estuaries in tropical and subtropical waters, north to San Diego.
Size: Length to 3 feet.
Value: An excellent sport fish, readily taking lures, saltwater flies, live bait.
Description: Color is metallic-blue back and silvery undersides, greenish head. Has deep-forked tail, projecting lower jaw, spineless dorsal, slender body. It is tarponlike in behavior, and often found in shallows like bonefish.

44. Hawaiian tarpon
Elops hawaiensis
Also: Tenpounder, **awaawa, sabalo.**
Range: Tropical and subtropical waters and in Hawaiian waters.
Size: Similar to tenpounder of Mexican coast.
Description: Quite similar to and probably the same fish as the **Elops affinis,** California tenpounder.

Family: Albulidae
Common Name: Bonefishes

45. Bonefish   **Albula vulpes**
Also: O'io, ladyfish, mullet, banana fish, silver shuttle.
Range: World-wide in tropical and subtropical waters, common along Mexican coast and in Hawaiian waters.
Size: Length to 3 feet.

Value: A good game fish readily taking sport lures and live bait.
Description: Color is metallic-blue on back, whitish undersides. Similar to tenpounder in configuration, but with thicker body. Often found with schools of mullet, feeding on crustaceans and other inshore fish.

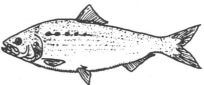

46. American shad
Alosa sapidissima
Range: In the Pacific from San Diego to Alaska and Kamchatka. This is an introduced species, planted in the Sacramento River in the 1870s, and since spread to the entire West Coast.
Size: Length to 2 feet.
Value: The roe is a gourmet prize. The flesh is bony but delicious baked. Best use for human consumption is probably smoked and canned, a superb product. A large and valuable commercial fishery has grown up around the shad, usually harvested by gillnets in the rivers during the spawning season. **Description:** Row of black spots on each side, iridescent silvery to metallic-blue and green on back. Deep, elongated body, loose cycloid scales, soft mouth, compressed head. No scales on head, deep notched tail. An anadromous fish that ascends rivers to spawn, depositing eggs on the surface at night in a frenzy, often in company with striped bass, another introduced species. The fighting qualities of the shad are well known. Surface lures, white flies, small metallic wobblers fished on the bottom, all are effective.

Family: Engraulidae
Common Name: Anchovies

Distinguished by a slender body covered with cycloid scales, large mouth and prominent snout. The origin of the dorsal fin is behind the pelvic fins.

Size: Length to 6 inches.
Value: Not abundant, but useful as a bait fish.
Description: Pale iridescent green, with silvery stripe on sides. Deep body, large mouth, with eyes close to snout.

47. Northern anchovy
                Engraulis mordax
Also: Anchovy, California anchovy.
Range: Temperate waters of North Pacific.
Size: Length to 7 inches.
Value: Main use is for oil and meal processing, canning and pickling, and for fresh frozen bait.
Description: Metallic-blue back, silvery undersides. Eyes located close to end of snout, large subterminal mouth, numerous small teeth. At times this bait fish is found in vast schools. One well-known incident recorded a catch of 200 tons in a single purse seine set. Spawning is during July and August and the eggs are pelagic. The anchovy feeds on plankton crustaceans. At present the schools in the North Pacific are endangered by overexploitation by commercial boats, including large fleets of ships under Asian flags. The future of roving species such as tuna and marlin may be seriously affected by loss of this forage fish.

48. Deepbody anchovy
                Anchoa compressa
Also: Sprat, sardine.
Range: Subtropical waters, mainly found along Mexican coast, and Southern California.

49. Slough anchovy
                Anchoa delicatissima
Also: Southern anchovy.
Range: Inshore waters along Mexican coast.
Size: Length to 6 inches.
Value: Not abundant. Mostly of academic interest.
Description: Greenish sheen with silvery band. General configuration almost identical to other anchovies.

Family: Salmonidae
Common Name: Salmons

This family includes the Atlantic and Pacific salmon, the trouts and chars. The Atlantic salmon are in the genus **Salmo,** as are many of the trouts. The chars are in the genus **Salvelinus** and are commonly called "trout," such as brook trout and dolly varden trout. The European term "char" should be adopted in North America in order to clarify the differences and clear up the confusion. The Pacific salmon are in the genus **Oncorhynchus** and include five eastern Pacific species and at least one Asiatic species. The Atlantic salmon and steelhead, as well as sea-run cutthroat trout, are anadromous like the Pacific salmon; however, the latter always dies on its first spawning run. There are several subspecies of landlocked Pacific salmon, such as the kokanee, that exhibit the same instinct and only spawn once. Some, like the coho or silver salmon, have been introduced into exotic waters such as the Great Lakes, the Atlantic Ocean, New Zealand, and even in impoundments behind dams, with spectacular success. This adaptability is the great hope of the future of sport fishery management.

The Pacific salmon species have similar appearances and life cycles, preferring a salinity of around 33.6 parts per thousand and a temperature of less than 15°C (59°F.). They are generally found in great numbers along the continental shelf from Monterey Bay to the Aleutians, although sometimes farther west than 180° longitude. Once common in all rivers, they are seldom found south of the Sacramento due to pollution, dams, loss of spawning gravels, and overfishing. The principal spawning rivers are the Sacramento, Columbia, Fraser, and Yukon, although most northern coastal rivers and creeks have individual runs.

In the ocean, the salmon feed on bait fish and in some cases on plankton crustaceans, and in turn are preyed on by all manner of large fish and ocean mammals. In salt water they are metallic-blue on the back, silvery underneath. In fresh water during the spawning runs they become progressively red to brown and then turn black and develop elongate hooked snouts. They seldom feed after the start the spawning run.

The Pacific salmons support one of the most valuable fisheries in the world, commercial and sport. Conservation efforts on the high seas are tenuously carried on by the International North Pacific Fisheries Commission, and there are joint treaties between Canada, the United States, and Japan to protect the North American stocks from depletion. Japan reluctantly goes along with the no-fishing rule east of 175° longitude. South Korea and Russia, however, are not parties to the treaty nor to the joint commission and at this writing are raiding the stocks regularly with unrestricted nets and factory fleets. The U. S. State Department and the state and federal fisheries agencies have to this point been ineffective, reluctant, and inactive in protecting these resources.

Although a recently compiled bibliography of books, tracts, reports, and studies on the subject of Pacific salmon listed more than 44,000 entries, very little is really known or understood about these species by fisheries biologists as well as laymen. It is certain that few officials and leaders in Washington understand the full importance and political aspects of this resource.

Management and maintenance of this fragile and extremely valuable resource is today inhibited by ignorance, indifference, lack of funds, anachronistic laissez-faire attitudes and practices of the big fish packing industries, political lobbyists for the big power utilities and the reclamation interests.

Ironically, the greatest share of the financial burden of maintaining this valuable resource falls to the sports anglers and the general public, while the private firms and the foreign interests harvest the profits.

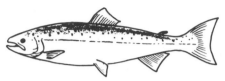

river for one or two years before migrating to the ocean. They return to fresh water between the ages of three to five years.

50. Atlantic salmon   **Salmo salar**
Range: Native to the north Atlantic, but has been introduced with poor results so far in some freshwater lakes of the West Coast, as well as in British Columbia coastal waters.
Size: Length to 4 feet.
Value: Slight at this time.
Description: Color is light brown on dorsal surface, silvery undersides, black spots on body, sometimes X-shaped, no pink or red bands. Body is elongated, moderately compressed; caudal peduncle is slender, with the square tail that readily distinguishes this species from the Pacific salmon. This, with the brownish color and X-spots, helps identify it. Except for the coloring, it is quite similar in appearance to the steelhead or sea-run rainbow trout **(Salmo gairdnerii)**.

First introduced in British Columbia waters in 1905, these plantings have been followed at intervals by provincial and state fish agencies, but it has never caught on to any extent. Occasional specimens are found from north California to Vancouver Island and identified. Without doubt, many others are caught as "steelhead" or one of the Pacific salmons.

Like steelhead and cutthroat trout, they may spawn more than once, returning to the sea in between runs. Spawning is done in the headwaters of streams, with the eggs hatching in the spring, and the young remaining in the

51. Brown trout   **Salmo trutta**
Also: German brown, Loch Leven.
Range: Northern California to Vancouver Island.
Size: Length to 3 feet.
Value: The brown is probably the world's most popular and wily species for fly fishermen. Only one brown trout is caught to every five rainbow or brook trout, because of the brown's wily nature.
Description: Color is a brown to golden-brown on top, silvery on sides, with small black spots and crosses on back and top of head, large black spots on sides, encircled by halos of pink or red.

The brown trout was native to Europe, as the rainbow trout was to northern California, and like the rainbow is now found all over the world. Found in freshwater streams from the Mediterranean to the Arctic, the brown was first brought to North America in 1883, and since to New Zealand, South America, and Africa. Maximum recorded weight is over 30 pounds, but a 10-pounder even in salt water is exceptional. They were introduced to the West Coast in the early 1930s in coastal waters with indifferent results. However, since brown trout eat the same food as do sea-run cutthroats, the lack of interest in them since the first plantings may be largely attributed to lack of knowledge. We used to catch them frequently in Oregon coastal streams along with cutthroat immediately after World War II, but the average angler seldom suspected they were brown trout instead of cutthroat, salmon, or even steelhead. Before they could become popular with the public, the fisheries agencies gave up the initial programs and today the ones that survive the nets and the heavy sport fisheries and the natural hazards are rare indeed. Hopefully, there will be more efforts to reestablish the brown in coastal streams in the future. Browns are well established in the upper regions of western rivers and in many high lakes and reservoirs.

Sea-run browns differ in shape from coastal cutthroat mainly by the pronounced stout caudal peduncle and slightly compressed body, and lack of red slash on jaw, although little color may be present if just in from the ocean. While they feed the same as cutthroat, they are more selective of feeding times, preferring the dark hours.

52. Steelhead trout

Salmo gairdnerii

Also: Sea-run rainbow, ironhead, steelie, salmon-trout.

Range: Southern California to Aleutians.

Size: Length to 4 feet, with record fish in the 40-pound class.

Value: Highly adaptable, like the rainbow trout, the steelhead is a superb sport fish, a worthy equal to the Atlantic salmon in most qualities. Experienced anglers prefer the flesh of Pacific salmon to

either for fresh-cooked steaks. In the Pacific Northwest the steelhead is considered best when smoked or pickled.

Description: Color is metallic-blue on dorsal surface, silvery on sides, black spots on back, caudal fins, adipose, and dorsal fins without halos; no red dash below jaw, with a continuous pink to red band along each side, particularly in males. At sea the color is almost indistinguishable, appearing more pronounced in brackish and fresh water as it makes its spawning run. At the peak of the spawning episode, the steelhead often becomes a sickly dark brownish-red and physically emaciated. Not more than seventy-five percent survive to spawn a second or third time.

The short head, rounded snout, lack of teeth on the back of tongue and square tail help distinguish it from Pacific salmons, but thousands are taken in salt water as "salmon" and commercial fishermen take a heavy toll, especially in those areas such as British Columbia and Oregon where landings of this game fish is legal.

It is now known that the western steelhead is the same fish as the common rainbow trout, but of a race that for unknown reasons migrates to the sea on a spawning cycle similar to the salmon. It enters its home river in its third, fourth, or fifth year after two or more years in the ocean, for the first spawning. Unlike the salmons, the steelhead may enter fresh water practically any month, but generally in two classes known as "summer - run" and "winter - run" fish. Depending upon where its native spawning beds are—some runs travel up the big rivers as far as the Continental Divide—the steelhead will all spawn about the same time, in the spring months. The winter fish are usually heavier and more powerful when they appear in the rivers. The young smolts move down to the sea after one or two years in fresh water, and once in the ocean they travel great distances. Specimens tagged in the Gulf of Alaska have been taken off the mouth of the Columbia. A few stragglers have even been caught off Baja California.

In the sea it feeds on crustaceans, squid, herring, and other fishes. In fresh water it consumes the usual trout fare. The commercial gillnet fishery along the northwest and Alaska coast takes a fearful toll of this fine species. A landlocked variation, the Kamloops rainbow, holds the world record for size and is found in British Columbia lakes, and in Idaho's Priest and Pend Oreille lakes in great numbers. The Kamloops strain has also been tried in smaller lakes and streams and in coastal waters with great success. Strains of steelhead have also been introduced in waters of many other parts of the world with varying success, including the Great Lakes and Atlantic coastal streams.

Lewis and Clark were among the first to take note of this species, calling it a "salmon-trout." It was first identified as a trout in the 1830s.

53. Coastal cutthroat trout
          Salmo clarkii clarkii
Also: Harvest trout, blueback, searun.

Range: Northern California to Alaska.
Size: Length to 30 inches.
Value: A superb game fish, the sea-run cutthroat is also known for its fine eating qualities, with a pink to reddish flesh. When fresh in from the sea, there is no equal to fresh-fried cutthroat and butter sauce.
Description: Color is a greenish-blue on dorsal surface, silvery on sides, black spots on body with no halos, and spotted tail, head, dorsal and anal fins. There is a bright red dash below lower jaw on each side, although not always apparent in salt water. The body is rounded, slightly compressed, with stout caudal peduncle, long head, teeth on head and back of tongue, not as "chunky" looking as the brown.

Subspecies such as the Yellowstone cutthroat **(Salmo clarkii lewisii)** also occur in some river systems with access to the sea. The Montana blackspotted cutthroat is famous in inland waters.

Coastal cutthroat spawn in the spring, sometimes as early as January, and the young descend to the sea in their second or third year, living in a marine environment for one or more years. They seem to remain in the vicinity of the river mouth or estuary, feeding upon small salmon, sandlance, rockfishes, seaperches, sculpins, crustaceans, and other marine foods. In fresh water they feed upon insects, freshwater shrimps, and small fishes.

The late summer period, from July to September and into October, finds most coastal rivers full of cutthroats, and thus the local name "harvest trout," has been applied. During these "dog days" fly fishing for sea-runs is best. They are usually found in the streams close to shore, often under overhanging brush. They are also caught trolling with crawdad tails and worms.

Still considered to be the true native fish of the American West, it has many subspecies and variations. It has been widely transplanted in many places hybridized with golden trout, rainbow, and different strains, until it is unlikely there is a true "native" cutthroat anymore. Because of its tendency to hybridize, early coastal plantings of brown trout may have been absorbed in this way.

54. Dolly varden
Salvelinus malma
Also: Western char, bulls, bull trout.
Range: Northern California to Bering Sea and Japan.
Size: Length to 3 feet.
Value: It is an excellent sport fish in cold water and in salt water, with good eating qualities. It is condemned by many, however, because of its predation on salmon and trout.
Description: Color is olive green to brown on dorsal surface, with pale yellow spots; red to orange spots on sides; in the ocean mostly silver. Distinguished mostly by the color spots on back and sides, and the presence of teeth on the head of the vomer only. The body is elongate, slightly rounded, slightly compressed, with a large head, large mouth, small cycloid scales.

Said to have been named "Dolly Varden" by the wives of a team of fisheries biologists while camped in northern California in the late 1800s, after the popular women's fashions of the day.

It spawns in the fall in streams with gravel beds, the female building a redd like most salmonidae. The sea-run races usually migrate upriver in the fall and seaward in the spring. The young feed on insects, but the adult fish are voracious predators and take a heavy toll of young salmon. It also preys on sticklebacks, herring, and the eggs of spawning fish. It is the native char of the West. At one time Alaska offered a bounty on dolly varden as a conservation measure.

55. Brook trout
Salvelinus fontinalis
Also: Brookie, squaretail, eastern brook.
Range: Northern California to Alaska (in the Pacific).
Size: Length to 3 feet.
Value: Considered an excellent fly-fishing species and good eating.
Description: Color is dark olive green on dorsal surface, without spots; red spots surrounded by blue borders on the sides; dark green vermiculations (wavy lines) on back and dorsal fin; silvery in the salt water.

Best distinguished by the red spots on sides, and dark olive green vermiculations on the back and dorsal fin and teeth on the head of the vomer only. The body is elongate, moderately compressed, head large, mouth large, caudal fin slightly forked and often square.

It is the eastern cousin of the dolly varden and is a char not a trout, sometimes called the speckled char or speckled trout. Introduced to Pacific waters in the early 1900s, it is found in many lakes and coastal streams where it is believed to be anadromous. It has probably often hybridized with the dolly, because north of Vancouver Island the dolly has the characteristic vermiculations on the back. It feeds on crustaceans, insects, and small fishes. Spawning occurs in the autumn months. A nine-pound specimen has been taken from British Columbia waters. Saltwater migrants can seldom be accurately identified by the layman, but are believed to grow to large size in a marine environment. They are cold water fish, thriving best in temperatures below sixty-five degrees. Wild trout are not readily adaptable to transplanting, and most western brook trout now come from hatchery strains. This has resulted in many variations.

56. Humpbacked salmon
Oncorhynchus gorbuscha
Also: Pink, humpy.
Range: Northern California to Bering Sea.
Size: Length to 30 inches.
Value: The flesh is delicately flavored, high in food value. It is most often taken commercially in gill and seine nets, and in reef nets by Indians of Puget Sound. The humpy

is an excellent sport fish, however, and will readily take lures. In the opinion of some it provides the best eating when fresh caught.
Description: Color is metallic-blue on dorsal surface with silvery sides, black blotches of oval shape on back and caudal fin. The males become reddish-yellow on sides at maturity and black blotches become obscured. At maturity the female turns to olive green on the sides with dusky stripes. The young have no parr marks. The flesh is pink, becoming pale pink in older males.

The body is elongated, head compressed somewhat, mouth terminal, teeth small. There are twenty-four to thirty-five rakers on first gill arch; ten to fifteen on dorsal fin, thirteen to seventeen on anal fin which is small, slender, and fleshy. The lateral line is slightly decurved.

The humpbacked is readily recognized by the lack of parr marks in young, by the twenty-four to thirty-five rakers in the first gill arch, and the heavy oval spots on the caudal fin, as well as by the color in salt water.

As indicated by the Russian nomenclature, this is the other species of Pacific salmon first identified by naturalists of Bering's expedition. Through the years they have been discovered, rediscovered, named and renamed by other naturalists, including David Starr Jordan, with varying degrees of accuracy. The early European settlers on the West Coast called the anadromous fish that filled the rivers "salmon" because of their resemblance to the Atlantic salmon. After they were classed in the genus **Oncorhynchus,** the same "salmon" continued to be used commonly.

The pink or humpbacked is the

smallest and most abundant of the five North American species and supplies more than forty percent of the world's canned salmon. It is slender and delicate with small head and large tail. It averages about four pounds and rarely goes past eight pounds.

The humpy is a "two-year fish" which spawns in either the odd or even years depending on its home river, and for that reason never grows large. Ocean movements are relatively unknown. Their food consists mainly of crustaceans, but squid and small fishes are also eaten. Because these fish mature invariably at two years, and about the same time, there is little or no intermingling with runs from different rivers, and even between races in the same river. There is practically no interbreeding between odd-year and even-year runs even in the same river.

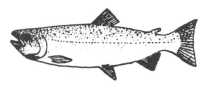

57. Coho salmon
Oncorhynchus kisutch
Also: Silver salmon, medium red, silversides.
Range: Northern California to Bering Sea.
Size: Length to 38 inches.
Value: For the sport fisherman, the coho is the most numerous and most popular of the Pacific salmons, and because of its leaping habits, is the most exciting to catch. Its average size of from six to twelve pounds, however, puts it considerably below the chinook in value. Besides sport tackle, the coho is taken in enormous numbers by commercial purse seines, gillnets, and traps, as well as by trollers. Most of the catch is marketed fresh or fresh-frozen. Some of it is canned as coho or blueback salmon, or as "medium red." It is an excellent fish for mild curing, smoking, baking, broiling, and frying.

The coho is a top sport fish for trolling, for casting in tide waters or lower stretches of rivers when the runs are on, and for saltwater fly fishing. The "coho fly" is a popular saltwater streamer, usually tied with tandem hooks, and using polar bear hair.

Description: Color is a metallic-blue on dorsal surface, silvery on undersides and on caudal peduncle, with numerous black spots on back and on upper lobe of caudal fin. Unlike the chinook salmon, the coho has no black pigment in the mouth along the base of teeth on upper jaw. The flesh is pink to red. The young have well-developed parr marks extending almost completely across the body. There is an orange tinge on pectoral, pelvic, and anal fins, white on anterior margin of anal fin.

The body is elongate, somewhat compressed, with a stout caudal peduncle. The head is conical, mouth terminal, teeth needlelike. There are nineteen to twenty-five rakers on the first gill arch, widely spaced; nine to thirteen on dorsal fin, thirteen to sixteen on anal. The lateral line is slightly decurved, then straight.

The coho is most easily identified by its size, form, habit of feeding and fighting on the surface, leaping when hooked, and by lack of black pigment in mouth. Closer examination of rays in gill rakers and fins gives a more positive identification. The black spotting on the upper lobe of the caudal fin, and the elongated anterior rays in the anal fin, orange tinge on lower fins and elongated parr marks help identify the young.

Most of the young remain in the river of their birth for one year, some migrating to sea in their first or third year (or the end of the third summer). At sea growth is rapid and maturity is reached in the third year, at which time they˙ school up for the return. Some coho return after the second year of life as nonspawning immature "jacks." This is common with hatchery-produced fish. Some runs that are sustained by hatchery plants return as jacks up to ninety percent of the total run. In parts of Puget Sound, some coho in their third year have deep blue backs and bright red flesh. These are called locally, "bluebacks," although blueback is applied elsewhere to the sockeye salmon. The coho feeds in salt water on herring, sandlance, pilchards, anchovies, and other small fish, squid and crustaceans. Like all Pacific salmon, they do not eat once in fresh water on their spawning runs.

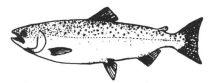

58. Chinook salmon
Oncorhynchus tshawytscha
Also: King, spring, tyee, quinnat, Royal Chinook, Columbia red.
Range: Southern California to Bering Sea.
Size: Length to 5 feet.
Value: The chinook is the most sought after salmon by sportsmen as well as commercial packers. Sports fishing is mostly trolling or "mooching" in salt water, trolling, casting, plunking in the rivers with metallic wobblers and spinners, fresh herring bait, and streamer flies. Commercial fishing is by troll, purse seine, gillnet, and traps. The commercial catch is almost all sold fresh, fresh-frozen, mild-cured, smoked, or salted. Some is canned, but most early fish are sold on the market as fresh spring chinook. The chinook has been commercially packed (salted or mild-cured) since the 1830s, and has long been a gourmet fish in Europe and Asia. Since the middle 1800s, when successful salmon canning methods were developed, the canned variety has been a staple commodity. Fancy pack chinook, sometimes called "Royal Columbia Chinook," brings a premium price. Canned smoked Columbia chinook brings around $4 a pound, packed in seven-ounce tins. This explains why the salmon packing consortiums will do almost anything to maintain the status quo in the big northwest rivers.

Professional salmon charter boat operators call the chinook a "salmon." All other salmon are simply referred to as "fish," which is a further indication of the value the chinook has to both the commercial and sports fisheries. Experienced sport anglers on the Columbia River regard a fresh, ocean-caught chinook steak as the finest eating seafood in the world.
Description: Color is greenish-blue to black on dorsal surface, with faint reddish to rusty hue, numerous black spots on back, dorsal fin, and both upper and lower lobes of caudal fin. Inside the mouth is a line of black pigment along base of teeth. The flesh is red, white, or pink. "White kings" are prized for

smoking and light curing. The young have well developed parr marks, extending across the body.

The body is elongate, somewhat compressed, with stout caudal peduncle, conical head, and terminal mouth. The teeth are conical, moderately sharp, and not rigid. There are eighteen to thirty rakers on first gill arch; ten to fourteen on dorsal fin; thirteen to nineteen on anal fin.

The chinook is readily distinguished by black lining in mouth (in some areas chinook are called "blackmouth"), by the conical teeth, the dark irregular spots on both upper and lower tail lobes, and, of course, by the size of the mature fish.

The spawning runs begin in early spring and continue to late fall, depending on the river. Some rivers such as the Columbia have almost continuous runs during the season. The young may go to sea after the first year, and once in the ocean growth is rapid, with maturity attained after the third to seventh year, but usually in the fourth or fifth. Chinook males that return to the river in the second or third year are nonspawning jacks. Immature fish of both sexes that return are called "grilse" in some areas, mainly Canadian waters.

Chinook salmon travel long distances, not only in the ocean, but also in the streams of their birth. Once a spawning chinook enters the Columbia, for example, it may find its way upstream almost to the Continental Divide, a distance of more than a thousand river miles. This was especially true before mammoth dams were built that blocked the upper Columbia and many of its large tributaries. The grueling, relentless journey of the chinook salmon from the ocean to its spawning bed in the gravelly mountain stream of its birth is one of nature's mysterious and compelling dramas.

In the ocean, the chinook is now known to travel as far as from the mouth of the Columbia to the outer tip of the Aleutians and return, and from the Gulf of Alaska to Baja California. It is interesting to note that the international Pacific salmon treaty between the United States, Canada, and Japan prohibits Japan from fishing for North American salmon east of the 175th meridian. It is now known that even Columbia River chinooks are found far west of 175 degrees.

Food consists of crustaceans, squid, herring, sandlance, candlefish, pilchards, anchovies, and other small fishes. The chinook grows to as large as 125 pounds, but fifty pounds is considered a large fish, with ten to twenty-five pounds most common.

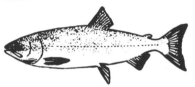

59. Chum salmon
Oncorhynchus keta
Also: Keta, calico, dog salmon.
Range: Northern California to Bering Sea.
Size: Length to 3 feet.
Value: The commercial catch is canned, frozen, mild-cured or salted. In many areas they are called "dog salmon," usually somewhat contemptuously. The name derives from the doglike fangs, and also from the fact that much of the catch has been used for dog food in the past. The flesh varies from light pink to pale yellow. It is sometimes sold as "white salmon."

It is an excellent food fish, and commercially valuable when caught in salt water.

Description: Color is metallic-blue on dorsal surface with irregular, black specklings but not black spots, black tinge on tips of pectoral, anal, and caudal fins. In fresh water the males are reddish to rusty colored with bars across the body, and white-tipped pelvic and anal fins. The flesh is pale pink. The young have narrow parr marks, mostly above the lateral line, and iridescent green backs.

The body is elongate, somewhat compressed, with slender caudal peduncle, conical head, terminal mouth, conical teeth, becoming fanglike in mature males. There are eighteen to twenty-six rakers on the first gill arch, ten to thirteen on dorsal fin, thirteen to seventeen on anal fin. The lateral line is slightly curved, then straight.

The chum is commonly distinguished by the absence of large black spots on body and fins, slender caudal peduncle, the black tinged tips of fins, and series of rusty streaks or bars on the side of adult males in fresh water, and, of course, by counting the gill rakers. The chum is seen mainly by sportsmen when it appears in fresh water, and usually after it has started to deteriorate. It is not sought by sportsmen, but will readily take lures and even flies. No doubt large numbers are caught on the ocean without knowing they are chum. Commercially they are taken by gillnets, purse seines, traps, and reef nets. Their food consists mainly of crustaceans. At maturity the chum reaches a weight of from eight to twenty pounds, but some have been caught weighing more than thirty pounds.

60. Sockeye salmon
Oncorhynchus nerka
Also: Red, blueback, quinault, redfish, kokanee, kickaninny, silver trout, Kennerly's salmon.
Range: Southern Oregon to Bering Sea.
Size: Length to 3 feet.
Value: The Alaska red or sockeye is the mainstay of the legendary Bristol Bay fishery, and was the object of international pirate raids for decades.

Until recent years the sockeye has not been important to the sports angler, although this has mainly been because of lack of knowledge and effort. It was long thought that the sockeye would not take sport lures, even when it was known that the kokanee was an important sport fish. It will, however, readily take lures and flies when properly presented at the right time.

Commercially the sockeye is taken by gillnets and purse seines around the mouths of rivers. Rarely are they caught on trolling gear. It is the most prized fish sought for canning purposes because of its deep red color and rich flavor. It is commercially called red salmon in northern waters, blueback in the Columbia River.

In the big inland lakes such as Pend Oreille, the kokanee is also fished commercially. Usually it is sold as mild-cured or whole smoked fish and is much in demand. There is no finer smoked fish than freshwater kokanee.

Description: Color is greenish-blue on dorsal surface with fine black specks, no black spots, metallic-green on head, brilliant red on body of mature male in fresh water, dark red and green with yellow blotches on body of mature female in fresh water. The flesh is a rich red. The young have parr marks extending below the lateral line, slightly oval in appearance.

The body is elongate, somewhat compressed, head conical, mouth terminal, teeth small and weak, lateral line slightly curved, then straight.

There are twenty-eight to forty rakers on the first gill arch, long, slender, and close set. The dorsal fin has eleven to sixteen rakers, the anal thirteen to eighteen.

The sockeye is commonly identified by the twenty-eight to forty rakers on the first gill arch, the distinguished "blueback" appearance, and its brilliant spawning colors.

The spawning run starts in summer and continues into the autumn, depending upon the river. They traditionally spawn only in rivers which have heads in lakes. The landlocked variety, called kokanee, Kennerly's salmon, small redfish, and silver trout, seem to live deep in the lakes and run up the tributary creeks to spawn in typical salmon fashion. All Pacific salmon, including the landlocked variety, only spawn once.

Upon hatching in the spring, the fry enter the lakes to spend one, two, and sometimes three years. Then they start their migration to the ocean between March and May. Some fry are known to start down to the ocean immediately, however. The sea-run races often stay in fresh water and mature in their second, third, or fourth year. These are called "residual sockeye." The anadromous sockeye mature in the fourth or fifth year, with some going to the sixth and seventh year, and others becoming jacks in their third year.

Sockeye respond exceptionally well to artificial propagation and scientific management. The landlocked variety is the bright hope of freshwater "trout" fishing. It also is a superb forage fish in the big lakes such as Pend Oreille, Priest, and Kootenay where monstrous Kamloops rainbow and dolly varden are found. In some cases, kokanee have been introduced which grow to trophy size.

One of the most dramatic experiments of all time occurred in the case of the Fraser River sockeye run which was once wiped out by a landslide that blocked river passage. This run was later restored artificially and records kept of one 305-acre section of spawning beds in the upper river was credited with producing $30 million worth of mature fish annually.

The sockeye's ocean habits are still much of a mystery to biologists, but they probably range widely over the entire North Pacific. Food in the ocean consists of crustaceans, especially euphausids. They grow to a size of four to eight pounds, but individuals up to sixteen pounds have been recorded.

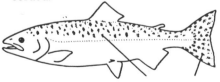

61. Asian masu

Onorhynchus masu
Also: Asian pink, East Kamchatka pink, Japanese humpbacked.

Range: Northwestern Pacific, mainly east of 175° West, from the Sea of Japan to the upper Kamchatka Peninsula.

Size: Length to 30 inches.

Value: Numerous and most important salmon commercially to the Soviets and Japanese.

Description: Similar to the North American pink in size, color, and physical details. It ranges eastward from the Sea of Japan and Sea of Okhotsk as far as the Gulf of Alaska, and may even intermingle with North American stocks, but little more is known of this "sixth species" of Pacific salmon. It is carefully managed on the Asian side of the Pacific in the same way as North American species are managed, but no U. S. or Canadian boats have ever exploited it in the same way as Russian, Japanese, and South Korean factory fleets have "raided" North American stocks.

Family: Osmeridae
Common Name: Smelts

62. Eulachon
                    Thaleichthys pacificus
Also: Candlefish, smelt, ulchen.

Range: Northern California to Bering Sea.

Size: Length to 12 inches.

Value: A principal food of salmon and seals, it is also an excellent and valuable market fish. It is rich and oily, but delicious fried or smoked. Large numbers are processed for animal food. The eulachon was and is used extensively by coastal Indians for cooking oil, and even fitted with wicks and used for candles, hence the name "candlefish." Eulachon oil was once processed in large amounts for export to Europe.

Description: Color is uniform light bluish-brown on dorsal surface, with white silvery sides and bottom, and black stippling on back.

The body is elongate, slender, snout pointed, mouth large and terminal, maxillary not reaching below posterior margin of eye, teeth hooked, jaws small. The lateral line is slightly curved, then straight. The scales are cycloid and moderate.

The eulachon is readily recognized by size, color, and position of dorsal fin, slightly behind the pelvic origins.

Common in northern waters, this member of the smelt family enters the rivers in March, April, and May to spawn, having matured at two to three years of age, and like the salmon probably dies after spawning once. The carcasses are gorged upon by sturgeon and other scavengers. The female produces about 25,000 eggs, which hatch in two to three weeks. The fry are carried by the current to the sea where they develop.

The name is derived from the Chinook jargon and has been variously spelled oulachon, ulchen, oolachon, and oolichan. In southeastern Alaska this is often corrupted to "hooligan."

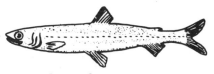

63. Night smelt
                    Spirinchus starksi
Also: Whitefish, nightfish, sand smelt, whitebait.

Range: Northern California to British Columbia.
Size: Length to 10 inches.
Value: Taken in large numbers by dip nets on the high tides, it is an important bait fish.
Description: Color is pale green with silver stripes on sides. Usually recognized by pelvic fin attached about middle, slightly ahead of origin of dorsal, no scales on head, pointed snout, and by color pattern. It makes its spawning runs at night.

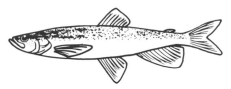

64. Longfin smelt
                    Spirinchus dilatus
Also: Winter smelt, bigfin smelt.
Range: Northern California to Alaska.
Size: Length to 6 inches.
Value: Considered a gourmet delight because of its fine flavor and limited quantity available in markets.
Description: Color is pale olive brown on dorsal surface, silvery on sides and belly with black stippling on head and back, prominent in males during the spawning season. The young have two rows of black spots on each side of midline from head to tail.

The body is moderately elongate, compressed, snout pointed, mouth terminal, teeth hooked, maxillary extending to point below eye, lateral line slightly curved, then straight.

This smelt is easily recognized by the large fins, black stippling, and origin of dorsal fin slightly behind the origin of pelvic fin.

It is found in depths from ten to seventy fathoms and is caught mainly in the winter months, usually accidentally by shrimp trawls. It spawns from October to December and it is not known if it dies after spawning. It feeds mainly on small crustaceans.

65. Surf smelt
                 Hypomesus pretiosus
Also: Surffish, silver smelt, perlin.
Range: Northern California to Alaska.
Size: Length to 10 inches.
Value: This fish is an important forage fish for salmon and other predators, and also finds a ready sale on the fresh fish market. Dipping is done by sportsmen with small nets and rakes, and it is delicious fried or smoked.
Description: Color is light olive green on dorsal surface, silvery to white undersides, bright metallic-silver band along the sides becoming grayish-black out of water. When spawning, the male is light brown on back, golden on ventral surface, while the female is light green on dorsal and silvery white underneath.

This smelt is readily recognized by the silvery-dusky band on each side, and spawning colors.

The spawning takes place in the summer from June to September, on sandy beaches similar to the ·capelin, near the water's edge on the maximum high tide at night. A single female will lay up to 20,000 eggs, which hatch in about two weeks. The fry disappear after hatching, to return in the first, second, or third year.

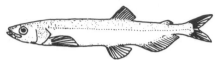

66. Pacific capelin
Mollotus villosus
Also: Silver smelt, sand smelt, northern smelt.
Range: Strait of Juan de Fuca to Bering Sea.
Size: Length to 6 inches.
Value: An important forage fish for salmon, dogfish, water fowl, and highly prized by gourmers. There is no commercial fishery, so it must be caught by amateurs, who must find the right beaches at the right time, in the same way grunion are caught on the southern beaches.
Description: Color is olive green on back, blending into silvery sides and belly, with numerous black dots on opercles. The body is elongate, slender, angular in spawning males, teeth small, scales small and cycloid. Recognized mainly by very small scales, large adipose fin, and villous bands of scales on each side of spawning male.

Inhabiting northern waters to the Arctic, the capelin spawns at night in September and October on sandy beaches during the maximum high tide. The eggs are adhesive and cling to sand grains. Wave action of the ebbing tide buries the eggs up to six inches. A female may deposit up to 6,000 eggs, which hatch in two weeks. The fry disappear and the capelin is seldom seen until the next spawning, three to four years later.

67. Toothed smelt
Osmerus dentex
Also: Needlefish, Arctic smelt.

Range: Vancouver Island to Bering Sea.
Size: Length to 6 inches.
Value: For bait only.
Description: Color is pale olive on dorsal surface, bluish on sides, with a band along lateral line, merging to silvery with gold on belly. The body is elongate, compressed; head elongate with pointed snout and terminal mouth, large with well developed teeth. The lateral line is slightly curved, then straight.

The toothed smelt is recognized by the large mouth and two large teeth on vomer, and origin of dorsal fin above the origin of pelvic fin, as well as by the color.

This is a relatively rare species, and the name Arctic smelt has been recommended by the American Fisheries Society.

Family: Argentinidae
Common Name: Deepsea smelts

Deepsea smelts are usually black or brown, very slender, with large eyes and small teeth. Sometimes the eyes are directed upward. The lateral line may be absent and the adipose fin prominent.

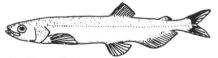

68. Smoothtongue
Leuroglossus stilbius
Also: California smoothtongue.
Range: Southern California to Gulf of Alaska.
Size: Length to 6 inches.

Description: Color is silvery but with black on lining of mouth, gill covers, and dusky on dorsal surface and fins. The body is elongate, with stout caudal peduncle, long snout, large eyes, with projecting lower jaw, and no teeth on the tongue. Spawning specimens have been taken as deep as 220 fathoms.

69. Slender blacksmelt
Bathylagus pacificus
Range: Southern California to Bering Sea.
Size: Length to 8 inches.
Description: Color is black to brownish-black, with bluish-black head and ventral surface and peritoneum. The body is elongate and slender, with slender caudal peduncle, long compressed head, small teeth, no lateral line, moderately large eyes, upward canted, small terminal mouth. Has been taken as deep as 500 fathoms.

70. Stout blacksmelt
Bathylagus milleri
Also: Black-scaled black smelt.
Range: Southern California to Bering Sea.
Size: Length to 6 inches.
Description: Color is black to brownish-black, bluish-black on peritoneum. Body is elongate, caudal peduncle slender. The head is long, deep, and compressed, snout blunt, eyes very large, covering much of head, with large pupils. The mouth is small and terminal. Distinguished readily by the large eyes and blunt head.

Family: Scomberesocidae
Common Name: Sauries

These are pelagic (of the open sea) fishes, occurring in large schools, often seen leaping like their close relatives the flying fishes. Considered a commercial bait fish, at this time not fully exploited.

71. Pacific saury
Cololabis saira
Also: Skipper, garfish, sourbelly, sourfish.
Range: Baja California to Bering Sea.
Size: Length to 14 inches.
Value: The saury is an excellent food fish, presently utilized mainly in Japan.
Description: Color is dark green to blue on dorsal surface, silvery on underbelly, pale on pelvic and anal fins, dusky on other fins. The body is elongate, slender, somewhat compressed, conical flattened snout, mouth terminal, slightly cleft, with lower jaw projecting somewhat. The teeth are small and feeble, snout very pointed. Readily distinguished by pointed snout, single dorsal fin far back on body, and projecting lower jaw.

The saury eat fish eggs and larvae, and occurs in immense schools upon which albacore and other tunas feed. The larvae are pelagic.

Family: Belonidae
Common Name: Needlefishes

72. California needlefish
                    Strongylura exilis
Also: Billfish, garfish.
Range: Southern California to tropics.
Size: Length to 3 feet.
Value: Considered an excellent food and forage fish.
Description: Color is greenish back, silvery underbelly, bluish stripe on sides. The snout and jaws are extremely long, with needlelike beak, slender body, fins located far back on body. The meat is white, the bones greenish. Often taken on small stripbait and feather jigs.

Similar to the California needlefish is the tropical needlefish, **Belone platyura,** found mainly in the tropical western Pacific; and the **Aulorhynchus flavidus,** which has a shorter snout. The latter is an important forage fish, found in large numbers through the North Pacific.

Family: Exocoetidae
Common Name: Flyingfishes

73. California flyingfish
                    Cypselurus californicus
Also: Flying fish.
Range: From Southern California to tropics.
Size: Length to 18 inches.
Value: An excellent food fish, and very common as bait fish for marlin and other game fishes. Used extensively by big game fishermen for kite fishing and trolling for billfish.

Description: Color is bluish on dorsal surface and sides, and silvery on ventral. Body is elongate, slightly compressed, projecting lower jaw, large eyes, large caudal fin, and large spreading pectoral fins. Often seen leaping long distances out of water, especially when pursued by predators. Often lands on decks of small vessels at night.

Similar species are the **Fociator acutus** and the **Exoncutes rondeletii** found in tropical and subtropical waters of the Pacific, both of which are smaller in size than the California flyingfish.

Family: Synodidae
Common Name: Lizardfishes

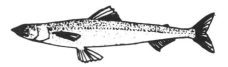

74. California lizardfish
                    Synodus lucioceps
Range: From Baja to northern California.
Size: Length to 2 feet.
Value: Rather rare but sometimes taken by sport anglers, and is considered edible.
Description: Color is greenish-brown, with light gray sides, black stripes on lateral line, sometimes reticulations across back, often gold sheen on back. Body is elongate, slender, lizardlike head, large mouth.

Family: Merlucciidae
Common Name: Hakes

75. Pacific hake
                    Merluccius productus
Also: Whitefish, haddock, butterfish, mellusa.
Range: Baja to Alaska.
Size: Length to 3 feet.

Value: Greatly exploited in Europe and Asia where it is considered a bland food of great medicinal value. North Americans have begun to exploit it for commercial meal and oil, and for reducing to fish protean powder of FPA, the latter being still in the development stage. Since 1966 the hake has been taken by trawls in great numbers off the Northwest coast by Russian fleets, to the point of near extinction. The flesh is soft and lacks flavor, and should be cared for immediately. Readily taken on sport tackle.

Description: Color is dull silvery gray, black speckling on back, brownish pectoral fins, deep black inside mouth. Body is elongate, moderately compressed, head large and mouth large and terminal. The lower jaw projects. The teeth are slender, doglike, and strong. The snout is long, flattened, the eyes large. Easily recognized by color and size, the two dorsal fins, large eyes, black mouth, and projecting lower jaw.

Considered a pest by salmon fishermen and commercial netters, the hake is found on the continental shelf as deep as 500 fathoms. It feeds on squid, small fishes, shrimp. It is also found around the mouths of rivers in relatively shallow water.

Family: Gadidae
Common Name: Cods

A cold water family of fishes of great commercial value, the North Pacific species include the whiting, tomcod, Pacific cod, and longfin cod. These are closely related to the Atlantic haddock, pollock, and several others. There is also a freshwater member of the family on the West Coast, the burbot or ling. These cods should not be confused with a number of other fishes that are miscalled cod such as the rock cods (rockfish), the tommycods, greenlings, black cod (sablefish), cultus cod (lingcod), none of which are related to the true cod, **Gadus**. An effort is being made to eliminate these erroneous names.

76. Whiting
Theragra chalcogrammus
Also: Walleye pollock.
Range: Northern California to Bering Sea.
Size: Length to 3 feet.
Value: At present is not exploited as a market fish or sport species, but is readily caught.
Description: Color is olive green to brown on back, sometimes blotched or mottled, silvery on sides, dusky to black on fins, with two narrow light yellow bands in the young, sometimes a third band. Body is elongate, moderately compressed, head pointed, mouth terminal, lower jaw protrudes slightly, eyes moderately large. Distinguished by barbel on lower jaw.

Large quantities are taken off the West Coast in trawls and sold as mink food. It is abundant at moderate depths, where it feeds on crustaceans, herring, and sandlance.

77. Pacific tomcod
Microgadus proximus
Also: Tomcod, piciata.
Range: Northern California to Alaska.
Size: Length to 12 inches.
Value: Small quantities are found in local fish markets. A bottom feeder, it is taken on sport tackle all year around. Flesh is soft and lacking flavor.
Description: Color is olive green on back, creamy white underbelly, dusky tips of fins. Body is elongate, slender, moderately compressed. The head is elongate, mouth terminal, with teeth on jaws. Eyes are moderate in size, barbel on lower jaw; easily recognized by the three dorsal fins.

Found in moderate depths, often taken in otter and shrimp trawls, but is not as abundant as whiting.

78. Pacific cod
Gadus macrocephalus
Also: Gray cod, true cod, Alaska cod.
Range: California to Bering Sea.
Size: Length to 3 feet.
Value: One of the most important commercial species of the North Pacific, it is taken mainly in trawls and after processing is marketed as fish sticks and fillets. Some is sold fresh or smoked. It is consid-

ered an excellent food fish, but must be handled and processed quickly.
Description: Color is brownish-gray on back, lighter on underbelly, brownish spots on back and sides, dusky fins, white margin on vertical fins, anal and caudal. Body is elongate, stout, moderately compressed. Head is large, snout blunt, mouth terminal, eyes small, barbels on lower jaw are long. Readily recognized by three dorsal fins and long barbel.

It is found in shallow to deep water up to 200 fathoms. It feeds on or near the bottom on crustaceans, herring, and small fishes. Its eggs are spawned in late winter and are pelagic. It is a true cod, closely resembling the Atlantic species. It migrates seasonally from shallow to deep water. An excellent potential sport fish, it is often caught accidentally while fishing for salmon and discarded as a "trash fish."

Family: Lampridae
Common Name: Moonfishes

79. Opah
Lampris regius
Also: Moonfish, mariposa, Jerusalem haddock.
Range: Southern California to Alaska.
Size: Length to 6 feet.
Value: The name is of West Afri-

can origin and the species is valued highly in Europe and Asia as a food fish. The flesh is salmon red rich, and of excellent flavor.

Description: Color is steely blue to dark bluish-gray on dorsal surface, shading to silvery with rose red on sides and underbelly, with white spots on lateral line, golden spots around eyes, vermillion on jaws and fins, white mottling on dorsal and caudal fins. Body is ovate, deep, greatly compressed, with short caudal peduncle, deep compressed head, moderate terminal mouth, no teeth, large eyes. Easily recognized by the large oval-shaped body, coloring and spots.

The fish is found in the open sea, world-wide, usually in the warmer currents, and reaches a size of as much as 600 pounds. Its food consists of crustaceans, small fishes, and squids.

Family: Muraenidae
Common Name: Morays

80. California moray
        Gymnothorax mordax
Also: Moray, conger eel, moray eel, marina, muraena.
Range: Baja to Southern California.
Size: Length to 5 feet.
Value: Can be ferocious and dangerous to swimmers and scuba divers, but is considered an excellent food fish and is taken with long hooked poles and handlines baited with clam, shrimp, and strip-bait.
Description: Color is dark brown

with small light spots, light streaks on ventral surface. Body is long and slender, snakelike, without scales, no pelvic or pectoral fins, slight dorsal and anal fins. Found along rocky coasts, in undersea caverns and kelp beds.

Family: Cyprinodontidae
Common Name: Killifishes

81. California killifish
        Fundulus parvipinnis
Range: Baja California north to Southern California.
Size: Length to 4 inches.
Value: A tiny but important bait fish.
Description: Color is dark greenish back, yellowish ventral surface. Thick caudal peduncle, long dorsal and anal fins, head pointed, mouth small. Usually found in estuaries and brackish water.

Family: Bothidae
Common Name: Sanddabs

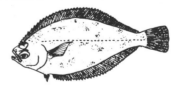

82. Mottled sanddab
        Citharichthys sordidus
Also: Pacific sanddab, megrim, soft flounder, sanddab.
Range: Southern California to Bering Sea.
Size: Length to 14 inches.

Value: One of the common flat-fishes, it is a food fish much in demand by Orientals, who slit and dry it.

Description: Color is dull brown on eyed side, mottled with black, soiled white to light brown on blind side, black on dorsal surface, dull orange spots and blotches on males; young are light olive green on eyed side. The body is elongate, moderately slender, greatly compressed. The head is deep, mouth terminal, lower jaw projecting, snout rounded. Readily recognized by mottled coloration on eyed side; lower eye longer than snout.

It is called megrim in England, and Pacific sanddab by the American Fisheries Society. Abundantly found on sandy bottoms throughout its range, and easily caught on small hooks.

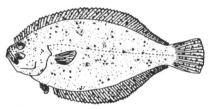

83. Speckled sanddab
Citharichthys stigmaeus
Also: Sand dab.
Range: California to Alaska.
Size: Length to 6 inches.
Value: Similar in size and importance to Pacific sanddab, it is of little commercial importance, but often caught in trawls.
Description: Color is olive brown on eyed side, finely speckled with black, soiled white or creamy on blind side, usually resembles coloring of sandy bottom on which it lives. Body is elongate, moderately slender, much compressed, sinis-

tral. The head is deep, mouth terminal, jaws equal, diameter of lower eye equal in length to snout.

84. Longfin sanddab
Citharichthys xanthostigma
Also: Soft flounder, Catalina sanddab.
Range: Baja to Central California.
Size: Length to 12 inches.
Value: Fair sport.
Description: Color is light olive brown, fading to grayish, with irregular dark spots mingled with yellow spots. Body is sinistral, with long pectoral fins, eyes that are longer than snout, and separated by concave space. Abundant and commonly caught on sport tackle, with small hooks.

85. Bigmouth sole
Hippoglossina stomata
Also: Bigmouth halibut, bigmouth flounder.
Range: Baja to Southern California.
Size: Length to 2 feet.
Value: Fair sport.
Description: Color is brownish with bluish cast, light blue and brown spots. Eye can be sinistral (left) or dextral (right). Mouth is large, eyes large and separated by bony ridge. Taken in shallow water on usual sport tackle.

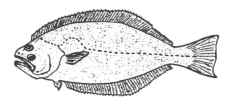

86. California halibut
Paralichthys californicus
Also: Portsider, chicken halibut, southern halibut, alabato, bastard halibut.
Range: South from San Francisco.
Size: Length to 39 inches.
Value: Good family fish.
Description: Color is muddy brown on eyed side, white on blind side, sometimes blotched or white-spotted. Can be sinistral or dextral. Eyes are small, separated by flat space, needlelike teeth, vicious mouth, square jaw. Often found in bays and around piers. A common sport fish in California and will take almost any kind of bait or lure.

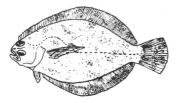

87. Fantail sole
Xystreurys liolepis
Also: Fantail halibut, fantail flounder, longfin sole.
Range: Baja to Central California.
Size: Length to 16 inches.
Value: Family fishing.
Description: Color is brownish, blotched on dorsal, anal, and caudal fins, reddish-brown or rusty on back, with bars and stripes on pectoral fins. Has long pectoral fin, rounded caudal fin, can be sinistral or dextral. Has a blunt snout. Often caught in bays and backwaters on the usual sport gear and bait.

Family: Pleuronectidae
Common Name: Flounders

Flounders usually have eyes on the right side (dextral) which is also colored, symmetrical pelvic fins, one on each side of abdominal ridge. They live in cold water, feed on small fishes and crustaceans. There has been a great deal of confusion over the common names in this family, with much current effort to standardize them for market and statistical purposes.

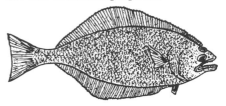

88. Arrowtooth flounder
Atheresthes stomias
Also: Long-jaw flounder, turbot, French sole, English flounder, bastard halibut, arrowtooth halibut.
Range: California to Bering Sea.
Size: Length to 3 feet.
Value: Considerable quantities taken for mink feed by trawlers.
Description: Color is brownish on eyed side, darker on margins, white on blind side, finely spotted with black. Body is elongate, slender, much compressed, dextral, with very large jaws extending behind eyes, and arrow-shaped teeth, left eye on upper margin of head, long slender caudal peduncle.
Found often with halibut on the bottom in deep water, but also in shallow water. Seems to migrate from shallow to deep water and back. Frequently caught on sport tackle. Food consists of herring and shrimp.

89. Pacific halibut
Hippoglossus stenolepis
Also: Northern halibut, right halibut, alabato.
Range: California to Bering Sea.

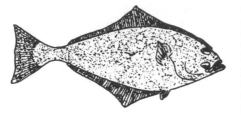

Size: Length to 5 feet, in females often to 9 feet.

Value: The Pacific halibut is one of the most important food fishes in the hemisphere, and one of the finest eating in the world. The meat is a delicate, flaky white, with a succulent flavor. It should be cooked fresh, but can be frozen for later use. The cheeks are a much prized delicacy. Livers and viscera are processed for Vitamin A.

Once found in great abundance in the North Pacific, it was commercially fished from dories in the Grand Banks tradition, to the point of extinction. It has been brought back and is rigidly managed by the International Pacific Halibut Commission. The commercial season is carefully controlled for U. S., Canadian, and Japanese boats, which now use long lines made up in skates with baited hooks run over the banks in depths from ten to 150 fathoms.

Description: Color is dark brown on eyed side, irregularly blotched with lighter color, white on blind side. Body is elongate, rather slender, compressed, dextral, rarely sinistral. Head is elongate, mouth terminal, large and symmetrical, gape wide, teeth well developed on both sides of jaw, eyes large. Large lunate caudal fin, arched lateral line, and narrow smooth scales distinguish this species.

It is found from shallow waters to depths of 600 fathoms and feeds on small fishes, crabs, clams, squid, and other invertebrates. Spawning takes place from November to January in depths from 150 to 225 fathoms. A large female of 140 pounds may have as many as 2.7 million eggs. These drift with the currents, rising to the surface and drifting into shallow water where the hatched fry settle to the bottom on sandy banks and in bays. As they grow bigger they move again into deep water. The females mature in eight to sixteen years, the males somewhat earlier. They live to ripe old age, the female reaching about 470 pounds at age thirty-five, while the male may reach forty pounds at age twenty-five. Tagging operations have shown halibut to remain in the vicinity of spawning grounds, but some have been traced 2,000 miles or more.

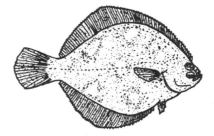

90. Flathead sole

    Hippoglossoides elassodon

Also: Paper sole, cigarette paper, and false halibut.

Range: Strait of Juan de Fuca to Bering Sea.

Size: Length to 18 inches.

Value: Frequently taken in trawls and otter nets, but not considered an important market fish. Readily taken by sport tackle.

Description: Color is uniform gray to olive brown on eyed side, white on blind side, dusky blotches on dorsal and anal fins, sometimes blotched with dusky brown on eyed side. Body is elongate, moderately slender, much compressed, dextral. Head is moderately deep, mouth terminal, gape wide, teeth well developed on both jaws, snout pointed. Food consists mainly of crustaceans and mollusks.

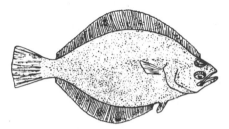

91. Petrale sole **Eopsetta jordani**
Also: Brill, California sole, English sole, Jordan's flounder.
Range: California to Alaska.
Size: Length to 2½ feet.
Value: Good sportfish.
Description: Color is uniform olive brown on eyed side, white on blind side, dusky blotches on dorsal and anal fins. Body elongate, moderately slender, much compressed, dextral. Head is deep, mouth terminal, gape wide, teeth well developed. Has small scales, smooth, completely covering blind side, with teeth in two rows on each side of upper jaw.

Taken in otter trawls to a depth of 200 fathoms. Females reach eighteen years of age. Food consists of crustaceans, anchovies and small fishes, euphausids. Can be taken on sport tackle.

Named for the famed ichthyologist David Starr Jordan, it is known as brill in Canadian waters. Petrale is a Mexican word meaning rocky. Petrale has been adopted by the American Fisheries Society.

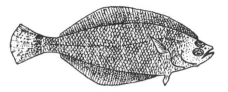

92. Slender sole **Lyopsetta exilis**
Also: Slender flounder, rough sole.
Range: Baja to Alaska.
Size: Length to 12 inches.
Value: Good sportfish.
Description: Color is pale brown on eyed side, minute dark points outline scales, pale orange to white on blind side. Body is elongate, slender, much compressed, dextral. The head is narrow and pointed, teeth moderate on both sides of jaw, snout bluntly pointed, eyes large. Recognized by slender body and rather large mouth, the large rough deciduous scales on both sides of body, and light brown coloration. Commonly caught in trawls, but not common on the fresh fish market. Found frequently in rocky areas, in depths from shallow water to 300 fathoms. Will readily take bait on sport tackle.

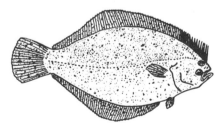

93. Sand sole
Psettichthys melanostictus
Also: Sanddabs, spotted flounder, fringe sole.
Range: San Francisco to Bering Sea.
Size: Length to 2 feet.

Value: Taken over sandy bottoms in trawls, it is a delicious fish much in demand for its delicate flavor.

Description: Color is light green on eyed side with hue of light brown, finely speckled with black, white on blind side, dull yellow on tips of dorsal and anal fins. Usually takes on color of bottom it inhabits. Body is elongate, moderately deep, much compressed, dextral with deep caudal peduncle. The head is deep, mouth terminal, symmetrical, gape wide. The teeth are large and well developed; snout rounded; eyes small. Recognized by the long free rays in the anterior of dorsal fin, the deep caudal peduncle, and coloring.

It feeds on crustaceans, small mollusks, worms, and tiny fishes. Readily takes sport bait with small hooks.

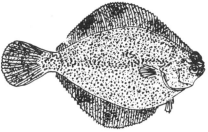

94. Roughscale sole
Clidoderma asperrimum
Also: Japanese sole.
Range: Vancouver Island to Alaska.
Size: Length to 22 inches.
Value: Uncommon now.
Description: Color is brown on eyed side, gray on blind side. Body is elongate, deeply ovate, compressed, dextral. The caudal peduncle is deep, the head is deep, mouth terminal and moderate, gape small on eyed side, teeth strong and conical in two rows on

both jaws, snout moderate, eyes large, somewhat protruding, scales modified to rough bony tubercles on eyed side. Recognized by ovate body, rows of rough tubercles, long maxillary on blind side. The species is relatively rare in the eastern Pacific, common in Japanese waters; generally taken by deep trawls.

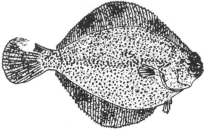

95. Curlfin sole
Pleuronichthys decurrens
Also: Curlfin turbot, sanddab, California turbot.
Range: Baja to Alaska.
Size: Length to 12 inches.
Value: Good sportfish.
Description: Color is brownish to black on eyed side, mottled, finely spotted, no black spot in middle of body, creamy white on blind side, very dark on all fins. Body is elongate, deeply ovate, much compressed, dextral. The caudal peduncle is deep, head deep, mouth small, eyes protruding and large, closely set, snout short. Recognized by deep ovate body, high dorsal and anal fins, and coloring.

More abundant in California waters, not a commercial fish, but readily takes bait on sport tackle. Found in shallow to deep water.

96. Diamond sole
Hypsopsetta guttulata
Also: Diamond turbot, halibut, diamond flounder.
Range: Baja to Oregon.

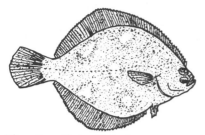

Size: Length to 18 inches.
Value: Good sportfish.
Description: Color is dark brown with light bluish blotches. Body is elongate, dextral, ovate, compressed; mouth very small. Found in shallow bays and estuaries. Takes bait on sport tackle readily.

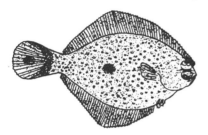

97. C-O sole
Pleuronichthys coenosus
Also: Popeye sole, C-O turbot, mottled turbot.
Range: Baja to Alaska.
Size: Length to 14 inches.
Value: Taken in quantities by deepwater trawls, and some are marketed but tough skin makes filleting difficult. Readily takes sport tackle, with a wide range of bait on small hooks.
Description: Color is dark brown to black on eyed side, black spot about size of eye on lateral line, sometimes on caudal fin, dark bar often found across base of caudal fin, creamy white on blind side, all fins very dark. Body is elongate, deeply ovate, much compressed,

dextral. The caudal peduncle is deep, the head is deep, mouth small and terminal, lips thick, teeth mostly on blind sides of jaws, snout short and blunt, eyes large and protruding. Easily recognized by coloring, deep ovate body with high dorsal and anal fins, embedded scales.

98. English sole
Parophrys vetulus
Also: Lemon sole, common sole, California sole, pointed nose sole, sharpnose sole.
Range: Baja to Alaska.
Size: Length to 22 inches.
Value: Resembles the lemon sole of European waters. It is the most sought of the small flatfishes, with a delectable flavor, and easily filleted. They are taken commercially in deep trawls up to fifty fathoms on sandy bottoms.
Description: Color is yellowish-brown on eyed side, light yellow to white, tinged with reddish-brown on blind side, especially under head. Young are variously colored, often spotted, of sandy hue. The body is elongate, slender, much compressed, dextral. The head is slender, pointed, mouth terminal, eyes large, upper somewhat behind lower, snout bluntly pointed. Recognized by coloring, pointed head. and smooth scales anteriorly.

One female will contain as many as two million eggs. The spawning is from February to April. Young sole spend their time in intertidal zones, moving to deep water later. Food consists of crustaceans, worms, small mollusks. This species roams a good deal and is found over wide areas. English sole is the designation of the American Fisheries Society, but it is called lemon sole in Canada. Readily takes sport bait. When you order fillet of sole in a good restaurant, this is the one you get.

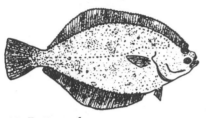

99. Butter sole
Isopsetta isolepis
Also: Rock sole, Bellingham sole, Skidgate sole, scaly-fin flounder.
Range: Baja to Alaska.
Size: Length to 18 inches.
Value: Widely marketed as fillets and also sold as mink food. Readily takes bait on sport gear.
Description: Color is gray, blotched and spotted with yellow and green on eyed side, white on blind side, bright lemon yellow on tips of dorsal and anal fin rays. Body is elongate, slender, much compressed; head is slender, mouth terminal and small, gape narrow; teeth mostly on blind side of jaws; snout bluntly rounded; eyes small. Recognized by rough scales on eyed side, lemon color on tips of fins.

Found in moderate to shallow waters. Large numbers taken in trawls over soft, silty bottoms. Spawning occurs in March to late April in bays and inlets.

100. Spotted sole
Pleuronichthys ritteri

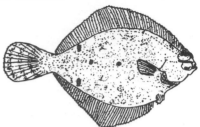

Also: Spotted turbot, spotted flounder.
Range: Baja to Southern California.
Size: Length to 9 inches.
Value: Good sportfish.
Description: Color is grayish-brown, light spots on head and body, several large spots along lateral line. Body is elongate, ovate, dextral, eyes protruding, separated by bony ridge. Not common, except in local areas. Readily taken on sport gear.

101. Forkline sole
Inopsetta ischyra
Also: Bastard sole, forked turbot (may also be hybrid).
Range: Northeast Pacific from Strait of Juan de Fuca north.
Size: Length to 18 inches.
Value: Little is known of this species, but often taken in trawls.
Description: Color is olive brown on eyed side, mottled with light and dark hues, pale on blind side. Body is moderately slender, much compressed, dextral. The head is slender, pointed, mouth small, gape narrow, teeth on both sides of jaws, snout bluntly pointed, eyes moderate. Recognized by low flat curve in lateral line with a short forked accessory branch posterior to eyes, rough scales.

102. Rock sole
Lepidopsetta bilineata

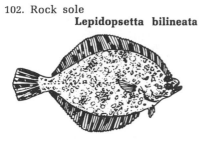

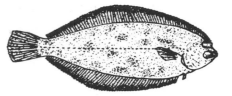

Also: Rough-back sole, gravel sole, double-line sole.
Range: Baja to Bering Sea.
Size: Length to 22 inches.
Value: Excellent eating and much in demand, second only to the English sole.
Description: Color is usually dark brown on eyed side, mottled with darker, sometimes scattered small red spots or pale blotches, reddish-yellow to white on blind side, brown to black streaks on fins. Body is elongate, deeply ovate, much compressed, dextral. The head is deep, mouth small, gape narrow, teeth mainly on blind side. Recognized by deep ovate body, coloring, and prominent arch in lateral line.

Very abundant in most areas in moderate depths. Large numbers taken in trawls and beach seines in sandy areas, or just offshore from eelgrass beds. This sole frequently will take a fly fished wet. Spawning is from late winter to early spring. Eggs are bright yellow-orange. Food consists of crustaceans, small fishes.

Microstomus pacificus
Also: Rubber sole, Chinese sole,
103. Dover sole
smear dab, lemon sole, slippery sole.
Range: California to Arctic.
Size: Length to 24 inches.
Value: Good sportfish.

Description: Color is variable from brown to black and greenish-yellow, often mottled. Body is elongate, dextral, with mucous secretion, small mouth, teeth only on blind side, black or very dark brown fins, short caudal peduncle. Found in shallow to moderate depths and near mouths of streams and in bays in summer months. Readily takes sport bait.

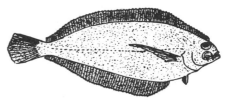

104. Rex sole
Glyptocephalus zachrirus
Also: Longfinned sole, witch sole.
Range: Baja to Bering Sea.
Size: Length to 23 inches.
Value: An excellent eating fish but not found readily in markets. Readily taken on sport gear.
Description: Color is light brown on eyed side, white to faintly dusky on blind side, fins dusky. Body is elongate, slender, much compressed, dextral. The caudal peduncle is very short, head slender, mouth small, gape narrow, snout bluntly rounded, eyes large. Recognized by long pectoral fin on eyed side, nearly straight lateral line.

Common species taken in great numbers by trawlers in depths from ten to 150 fathoms, often in depths to 350 fathoms in northern waters.

105. Starry flounder
Platichthys stellatus
Also: Grindstone flounder, great

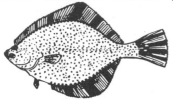

flounder, roughjacket.
Range: Baja to Bering Sea.
Size: Length to 3 feet.
Value: Not common.
Description: Color is dark brown to black on eyed side, creamy on blind side, sometimes blotched, black bands on dorsal and anal fins, white, orange-yellow, or reddish-orange between bands and stripes. Body is elongate, deep, much compressed, dextral or sinistral. The head is deep, gape narrow, lower jaw protruding, teeth on blind side, snout rounded and blunt, eyes small. Easily recognized by black bands on dorsal and anal, black stripes on caudal fin.

Very abundant in most areas of the coast, usually taken in deep water, often on halibut gear. Moderately large trawl catch. Spawning is in late winter and early spring. Eggs are pale orange-yellow. The young often move up into streams. Food consists of crustaceans, worms, small fishes, mollusks. Also known as the grindstone or emerystone because of its extreme roughness. Specimens up to twenty pounds have been recorded.

106. Hornyhead sole
Pleuronichthys verticalis
Also: Sanddab, sharpridge flounder, hornyhead turbot.

Range: Baja to Southern California.
Size: Length to 10 inches.
Value: Good family fish.
Description: Color is chocolate

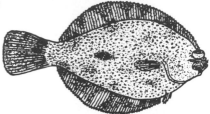

brown with light blotches, fins gray. Body is dextral, with deeply imbedded scales, tough skin, eyes separated by high sharp spine, no teeth on eyed side, deep caudal peduncle. Abundant in southern waters. Easily taken on light sport gear.

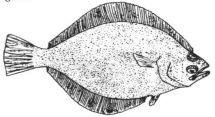

107. Deepsea sole
Embassichthys bathybius
Range: Southern California to Alaska.
Size: Length to 10 inches.
Value: Found mainly in depths as much as 700 fathoms, it is not at this time an important commercial or sport fish.
Description: Color is brown, becoming darker on margins, black on dorsal and anal fin rays, coarsely blotched with pale blue on body and fins, dusky brown on blind side. Body is elongate, slightly compressed, dextral, caudal peduncle is very short and slender.

Head is moderate, mouth small, gape narrow, snout rounded. Recognized by slender body with the upper and lower thirds highly compressed, the high ridge between eyes, and coloring.

Family: Embiotocidae
Common Name: Seaperches

Members of this large family are viviparous, usually elliptical and compressed in shape, and are all marine except for one species which is found in streams of northern California. Because of this, Hubbs and Follett classified them somewhat differently than I have here. They are all of a group, however, that includes surf perches, ocean perches, sea perches. The group generally is divided between marine or ocean perches and the surf and bay perches. To attempt to identify all the local common names would be a hopeless task. The family includes some twenty genera found along the eastern shore of the North Pacific. Most of them give birth to live young which are almost exact miniatures of the mother. This blessed event often occurs in the hands of the angler just after he has caught a female.

108. Walleye seaperch
Hyperprosopon argenteum
Also: Silver perch, China pompano, white perch, surfperch. Walleye surfperch (not hyphenated) is rec-

ommended by the American Fisheries Society.
Range: Baja to southern British Columbia.
Size: Length to 12 inches.
Value: This is an important commercial perch. Can be caught in shallow water along sand beaches and in bays on shrimp, clam pieces, marine worms.
Description: Color is steely blue on dorsal surface, silvery on sides and underbelly, dusky to golden bars on each side, black fin tips. The body is compressed, elliptical; caudal peduncle short, slender; head small and mouth small. Lateral line is high on body anteriorly. Recognition is by high angular spinous portion of dorsal fin, the color and the five faint dusky bars on sides, black margins on pelvic and caudal fins. Mating is in late fall after a five- to six-month gestation period, followed by birth of six to twelve young.

109. Redtail seaperch
Holconotus rhodoterus
Also: Porgy, humpback perch, Oregon porgy.
Range: Baja to Vancouver Island.
Size: Length to 12 inches.
Value: A popular sport fish and excellent eating when filleted and deep fried.
Description: Color light green on dorsal surface, silvery on sides and bottom, reddish bars on each side; about ten, bright rosy red bars on pelvic, anal, and caudal fins. Body is elliptical, compressed, caudal

peduncle short, slender. The head and mouth are small. The lateral line is high on body anteriorly. This one is readily recognized by the rosy tinged fins and reddish bars on side, and the high, angular, spiny portion of the dorsal fin. Redtail perch is the name recommended by the AFS. Found in shallow water along beaches and in surf.

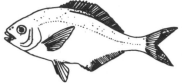

110. White seaperch
Phanerodon furcatus
Also: Shiner, forked tail perch, silver perch.
Range: Southern California to Vancouver Island.
Size: Length to 12 inches.
Value: Fair sportfish.
Description: Color is silvery, somewhat darker on dorsal surface, dark blotches often on anterior of anal fin, dusky on margin of caudal fin. Body is elliptical, compressed, with long slender caudal peduncle. The head and mouth are small. Lateral line is high and curved. Readily recognized by silvery color and configuration.

111. Pile seaperch
Damalichthys vacca
Also: Dusky seaperch, porgie, white perch, silver perch. The AFS recommends pile perch.
Range: Baja to Alaska.

Size: Length to 15 inches.
Value: Family fishing.
Description: Color is brownish-white on dorsal surface, silvery underbelly, blotches of darker color on upper parts, small black spot on preopercle, dusky on dorsal, anal, and caudal fins, pale yellow or orange tip with black on pelvic fins. Body is elliptical, compressed; caudal peduncle short, slender; head and mouth small. The lateral line is high and curved, scales small and cycloid. Recognized by the low spinous portion of dorsal fin with the last spine about half the length of first ray or longer, and the coloration. This species is common in shallow water in summer, going deeper in winter. It is the one most caught by kids on handlines.

112. Striped seaperch
Embiotoca lateralis
Also: Blue perch, crugnoli, rainbow perch, blue seaperch.
Range: Baja to southern Alaska.
Size: Length to 15 inches.
Value: Fair sportfish.
Description: Color is dull red to brown with greenish on dorsal surface, numerous black punctuations, dull orange and bright blue longitudinal stripes along scale rows on sides, bluish-black on dorsal and anal fins, hint of golden yellow on pectoral fins, bluish-black on pelvic fins, dusky on caudal fins. Body is elliptical, compressed, mouth and head small, caudal peduncle short, deep. The spinous portion of dorsal

is low. The lateral line is high and curving. One of the most beautiful ocean fishes, it is readily recognized by its coloration and the usual seaperch configuration. The young are born in early summer and as many as forty are born at a time. Like other seaperches, the food consists of worms, small crustaceans, mussels and herring spawn.

and around docks and wharves, the shiner feeds on crustaceans, herring spawn, and small invertebrates, and especially on barnacles.

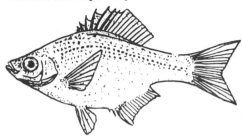

113. Shiner seaperch
Cymatogaster aggregata
Also: Yellow shiner, shiner, shiner perch, bay perch.
Range: Baja to southeastern Alaska.
Size: Length to 8 inches.
Value: Shrimp trawlers take large numbers of the shiner and the catch is readily sold on the fresh market. The Chinese consider it a delicacy.
Description: Color is silvery, dusky on dorsal, dark points in clusters below lateral line, bars on sides, belly silvery, sides yellowish, especially the bars. Body is somewhat elongate and elliptical, compressed. The caudal peduncle is short and slender. The mouth and head are small. The shiner is recognized by the large scales, short slender peduncle, and the vertical light yellow bars on body. This species is abundant, appearing in schools in the shallows during the summer months, going to deeper water in winter. Breeding is from late spring to early summer, and up to thirty-six young are born at once, after ten to twelve months gestation. Frequently found in bays

114. Kelp seaperch
Brachyistius frenatus
Also: Kelp perch, brown seaperch. Kelp perch is recommended by the AFS.
Range: Baja to southern British Columbia.
Size: Length to 8 inches.
Value: Good sportfish.
Description: Color is olive brown on dorsal surface with small dark spot under each scale, light coppery to gold on underbelly, bluish marks in longitudinal rows, pale blue on fins. Body is somewhat elongate, deeply elliptical, caudal peduncle long, deep, mouth and head small. The lateral line is high and curved. Recognized by large scales, stout caudal peduncle, and coloration. Found frequently around kelp beds in depths up to fifteen fathoms. They are carnivorous, and feed on crustaceans mostly.

115. Calico surfperch
Amphistichus koelzi
Also: Humpbacked perch.
Range: Baja to Golden Gate.
Size: Length to 12 inches.
Value: A common sport fish, especially in California.
Description: Color is olive to silvery with brownish to reddish specks and crossbars, with belly

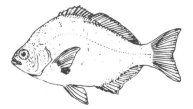

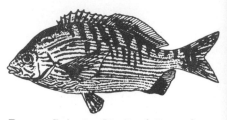

and head sometimes coppery, fins mostly tipped with dusky hues. The body is elliptical, with blunt snout and small head, deep short caudal peduncle. Easily recognized by coloration and more pronounced steepness of body.

116. Black seaperch
Embiotoca jacksoni
Also: Blackperch.
Range: Baja to central California.
Size: Length to 15 inches.
Value: A popular species with rock and jetty anglers.
Description: Color is dark brown, sometimes tan, tinged with red to yellow hues, occasionally dark blue to green. The fins are sometimes red to yellow hued, lips orange, and anal fin striped with blue. Body is typically perchlike, and species is identified mainly by coloration. Found mostly along rugged, rocky coastal beaches, in bays and estuaries. Caught readily on mussels, worms, shrimp, small crab fry.

117. Rainbow seaperch
Hypsurus caryi
Also: Striped perch, bugara, orange seaperch.

Range: Baja to Strait of Juan de Fuca.
Size: Length to 12 inches.
Value: A brilliantly beautiful species, commonly caught on sport tackle along the coasts.
Description: Color is variegated, bright reddish or organ longitudinal stripes, bright blue on body, head and throat, orange bars on dorsal surface, light blue circles around eyes, fins tipped with dusky blue, orange, or mottled. Recognized by the long, straight, underpointed snout, small eyes, and color.

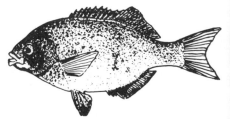

118. Rubbertip seaperch
Rhacochilus toxotes
Also: Porgie, alfione, buttermouth, liverlip surfperch.
Range: Baja to Oregon.
Size: Length to 18 inches.
Value: Readily caught on sport tackle and perch bait.
Description: Color is bluish-black on dorsal surface, silvery on ventral, fins dark tipped, sometimes pale orange or yellow. Easily recognized by thick white or pinkish lips, moderately deep body, and

short anal-pelvic spacing. Common in estuaries, bays, and along rugged coastline in kelp areas. Feeds on mussels, mollusks, spawn.

Family: Phomacentridae
Common Name: Damselfishes

These species are similar to and often mistaken for the seaperches, but are not unimportant to sport anglers. In fact, one of them, the garibaldi, is protected in California.

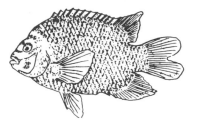

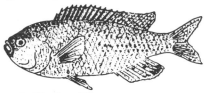

119. Blacksmith
Chromis punctipinnis
Also: Kelp perch, blue perch, pile perch.
Range: Baja to central California.
Size: Length to 10 inches.
Description: Color is slate black or greenish, with blue hues and lighter ventral surface. The fins are dark blue, greenish, or black. The body is elongated, compressed, caudal peduncle short stout, dorsal fin long and continuous, head blunt, snout turned up, scales large and tight. Found in kelp areas. Can be caught on light sport tackle on pieces of clam, mussels and shrimp, but is rather rare.

120. Garibaldi
Hypsypops rubicunda
Also: Garibaldi perch, golden perch, goldfish.
Range: Baja to southern California.
Size: Length to 14 inches.
Value: Good sportfish.
Description: Color is brilliant orange to gold over entire body. Body is steep, elliptical, com-

pressed, caudal fin rounded and notched, head and snout blunt, dorsal continuous. Easily recognized by color and configuration. Protected in California, but abundant over its range.

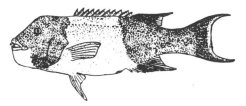

121. Kupipi
Abudefduf sordidus
Also: Damselfish.
Range: Tropical Pacific areas, Hawaiian Islands.
Size: Length to 4 inches.
Description: Color is gray-black with broad vertical bands, black spot on tail. Common in shallows around reefs and in harbors. Popular sport fish for children on light tackle. Good to eat.

122. Maomao
Abudefduf abdominalis
Also: Damselfish.
Range: Tropical Pacific areas, Hawaiian waters.

123. Hilu piliko's
Paracirrhites forsteri
Also: Hawkfish.
Range: Tropical Pacific, Hawaiian Islands.

124. Piliko's
Paracirrhites cinctus
Also: Hawkfish.
Range: Tropical Pacific, Hawaiian Islands.

125. Po'o-paa 'O'opu-kai
Cirrhitus alternatus
Range: Tropical Pacific, Hawaiian Islands.
Size: Length to 9 inches.
Description: Color is barbled bluish-brown with dashes of white, and some red spots. Found in inshore reefs. Feeds on crab, shrimp, and small fish. Easy to catch, but is not an active fish. Food value is doubtful.

Family: Trichodontidae
Common Name: Sandfishes

This family of small Pacific fishes is believed to be abundant, but is not now considered important for commercial or sport fisheries. They get their name from their habit of burying themselves in the sand with only the mouth and eyes showing.

126. Pacific sandfish
Trichodon trichodon
Also: Sandfish.
Range: California to Bering Sea.
Size: Length to 12 inches.
Description: Color is light brown on dorsal surface, silvery on underbelly, light brown along margin of spinous dorsal with dark spots in two series. Body is moderately elongate, much compressed. The head is moderate, mouth large, opening upward, jaws nearly vertical, lips prominently fringed, teeth small, sharp, recurved. Recognized by vertical jaws, fringed lips, broad procurrent pectoral fins and the absence of scales. It is known to be a food taken by Pacific salmon.

Family: Labridae
Common Name: Wrasses

This species is distantly related to the Atlantic sheepshead, but is spelled differently to emphasize the difference. The Pacific variety is generally either "sheep-head" or "sheephead" and is thought related to the freshwater drum.

127. Sheephead
        Pimelometopon pulchrum
Also: California sheephead, fathead, redhead, humpy, redfish.
Range: Cabo San Lucas up into Sea of Cortez, West Coast north to Monterey Bay.
Size: Length to 3 feet.
Value: A popular and abundant game fish, easily taken on mussels, crabs, lobster, shrimp, and metal jigs. Large hook, such as 5/0 generally used.
Description: Color in mature males is reddish-black banded, body and fins between black are red-banded, lighter belly, whitish chin; females and immature males are light to dull red, not banded, but with whitish chin. The body is heavy and deep, with stout caudal peduncle and pointed lobes on caudal fins, spinous dorsal connected to rayed dorsal aft, with pointed lobes. Anal fin lobes pointed. Teeth caninelike in heavy jaws; high, small eyes, sloping forehead, with a pronounced lump in males. A bottom fish, found on sea mounts in deep water, along rocky shores, and among kelp.

128. 'A'awa   **Bodianus bilunulatus**
Range: Tropical Pacific and Hawaiian Islands.

129. Po'ou   **Cheilinus rhodochrous**
Range: Tropical Pacific, Indian Ocean, Hawaiian Islands.

130. Hinalea lauwili
        Thalassoma duperreyi
Range: Tropical Pacific, Indian Ocean, Hawaiian Islands.

131. Hinalea luahine
             Thalassoma ballieui
Range: Tropical Pacific, Hawaiian
Islands.

132. 'Aki-lolo   **Gomphosus varius**
Range: Tropical Pacific, Hawaiian
Islands.

133. 'Omaka   **Stethojulis axillaris**
Range: Tropical Pacific, Hawaiian
Islands.

134. La'O
             Halichoeres ornatissimus
Also: 'Ohua.
Range: Tropical Pacific, Hawaiian
Islands.

135. 'Opule   **Anampses cuvieri**
Also: Hilu.
Range: Tropical Pacific, Hawaiian
Islands.

136. Rock wrasse
             Halichoeres semicinctus
Also: Parrotfish, California wrasse,
rockfish.
Range: California coast.
Size: Length to 15 inches.
Value: Abundant within its range
but seldom caught by sports an-
glers.

Description: Color is dark brown
to greenish on dorsal surface, whitish ventral, several narrow, undulating, bright blue stripes over
opercle; pelvic fins cream-colored,
others red-streaked; black spot on
upper base of pectoral fin. Males
have a wide blue band back of
pectoral and pelvic fins. Eyes are
small, reddish, body is elongate,
dorsal fin long and spinous, snout
pointed, mouth small with protruding teeth.

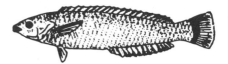

137. Senorita
             Oxyjulis californica

Also: Butterfish, kelp fish, kelp
wrasse.
Range: Cabo San Lucas to Monterey Bay.
Size: Length to 10 inches.
Value: Considered a food fish but
flesh has an exotic taste.
Description: Color is brown on
dorsal surface to whitish ventral,
with brown and bluish streaks on
sides of head, black blotch at base
of caudal fin. Body is long, slender;
snout sharply pointed, teeth small
and sharp, protruding, dorsal fin
long and continuous. A voracious
fish, it harasses anglers in schools
at times, taking all manner of bait.

138. Mudsucker   **Scarus dubius**
Also: Parrotfish.
Range: Tropical Pacific, Hawaiian Islands.

139. Uhu   **Scarus perspicillatus**
Range: Tropical Pacific, Hawaiian Islands.

140. Manini
          Acanthurus sandvicensis
Also: Surgeonfish, convict fish, convict tang.
Range: Tropical Pacific, Hawaiian Islands.
Size: Length to 6 inches.
Value: Hard to catch but delicious when caught.
Description: Color is greenish-yellow with black vertical stripes. A member of the surgeon fish family; has small bony projection at base of tail which can sting. Usually found in schools feeding on seaweed on rock and coral. Small mouth.

141. Paku'iku'i
          Acanthurus achilles
Also: Achilles tang.
Range: Tropical Pacific, Hawaiian Islands.

142. Na'ena'e
          Acanthurus olivaceus
Range: Tropical Pacific, Hawaiian Islands.

143. Palani
          Acanthurus xanthopterus
Range: Tropical and subtropical Pacific and Indian oceans.

Family: Gobiidae
Common Name: Gobies

144. Mudsucker
          Gillichthys mirabilis
Also: Longjaw mudsucker, longjaw goby.
Range: Cabo San Lucas to Vancouver Island.
Size: Length to 8 inches.
Value: A valuable potential bait fish, now coming into much demand in both fresh and salt water areas because it is hardy and inviting to game fish.
Description: Color is dark greenish-black on dorsal surface, with darker mottles, yellowish on ventral, olive green fins. Head large, mouth large with maxillary extending back to base of pectoral fins. Two dorsal fins, eyes placed high, snout long and rounded; caudal peduncle stout, fin rounded. One of a number of small species found in muddy or sandy water in lagoons and bays. It can live out of water for extended periods if kept moist.

Family: Sciaenidae
Common Name: Croakers

There are more than 150 species in this family, most of whom are found in tropical or subtropical seas. The name comes from a common characteristic of humming or grunting and croaking, the sound actually coming from the vibrations of the air bladder. The ear bones (otoliths) of croakers are unusually large and have often been carried by natives as lucky stones. Croakers have a lateral line extending back of the caudal peduncle, a square caudal fin, deeply notched dorsal fin which divides it in two, the spinous or front portion being triangular. Members of this family are usually found over sandy or muddy, rather than rocky bottoms.

145. White seabass
Cynoscion nobilis
Also: White croaker, king croaker, weakfish, shortfin bass.
Range: Baja to Southeast Alaska.
Size: Length to 6 feet.
Value: The white seabass ranks high both as a market and sport fish, and is an excellent food species.
Description: Color is metallic blue to copper on dorsal surface, silvery on underbelly, with fine dark points sprinkled over body, and a prominent black spot on the inner base of pectoral fins. The body is elongate, somewhat compressed, the head pointed, mouth large, lower jaw projecting somewhat. The lateral line is high, curved then straight, extending to caudal fin.

Identification is easily made by color and configuration.

Spawning is from March to August around kelp beds. Food consists of herring, pilchards, anchovies, smelt, crustaceans, squids. A school fish, the white seabass is scarce in some areas due to over-exploitation. Similar or subspecies are found in southern waters, including the gulf corbina, totuava.

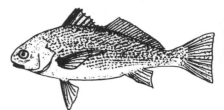

146. White croaker
Genyonemus lineatus
Also: Kingfish, whitefish, tom cod, tommy croaker, carbinetta, chenfish.
Range: Southern California to British Columbia.
Size: Length to 13 inches.
Value: An important market and sport fish, but erroneously disdained by uninformed anglers.
Description: Color is silvery brass on dorsal surface, lighter on underbelly. Body is elongate, somewhat compressed, head blunt and rounded, mouth subterminal, dorsal fin divided. Recognized by color and configuration, short anal fin, and size. Food consists of crustaceans, mollusks, worms, and similar marine life.

147. Black croaker
Cheilotrema saturnum
Also: Black bass, Chinese croaker, blue bass, black perch, surf fish, chinafin.
Range: Cabo San Lucas to central California.

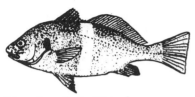

Size: Length to 15 inches.
Value: Fair sportfish.
Description: Color is dusky to blackish, with coppery sheen, ventral surface whitish with dark flecks; a pale band on sides, dusky tips of pelvic and anal fins. Body is elongate, compressed, caudal fin square, dorsal divided, snout moderately pointed, head small with straight sloping forehead. Recognized by dark, prominent spot on upper opercle. Found near sandy beaches and in bays and coves with kelp. Feeds on marine worms, shrimp, mussels, small crabs. Goes into deep water in cold weather.

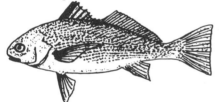

148. Spotfin croaker
                Roncador stearnsi
Also: Surf fish, golden croaker, spotted croaker.
Range: Baja to Central California.
Size: Length to 24 inches.
Value: A favorite of surf fishermen.
Description: Color is metallic gray to coppery on dorsal surface, whitish on ventral. Body is elongate, slightly compressed, head rounded including snout, mouth subterminal, dorsal divided, long pectoral fins which are pointed and have black spots at base. Found in bays and coves over sandy bottoms and in holes outside the surf. Feeds on

marine worms, and small crustaceans. Spawns in summer months.

149. Yellowfin croaker
                Umbrina roncador
Also: Surf fish, golden croaker.
Range: Cabo Sun Lucas, Sea of Cortez, north to California.
Size: Length to 15 inches.
Value: A popular sport fish.
Description: Color is metallic green to gray-black with coppery hues, cheeks white to yellowish, dorsal fins dusky, ventral whitish. Body is elongate, slightly compressed, snout short and rounded, upper jaw projecting, dorsal fin divided, large strong anal fin, no black spot on opercle or pectoral. Recognized by single barbel on tip of lower jaw. Found in bays and estuaries, around docks, in surf, and alongshore. Feeds on mussels, shrimp, marine worms, and clams.

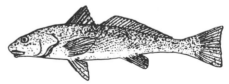

150. California corbina
                Menticirrhus undulatus
Also: Corvina, surf fish, California whiting.
Range: Capo San Lucas to central California.
Size: Length to 18 inches.
Value: Highly prized by surf fishermen.
Description: Color is dark metallic blue, lighter on sides, whitish on ventral surface, dusky fins. Body is

elongate, slender, dorsal divided, fleshy barbel on lower jaw, large pectoral and anal fins, projecting upper jaw, rounded snout. The corbina has no air bladder, is found on the bottom in shallow water, along sandy surf lines. Feeds on marine worms, mussels, clams, shrimp.

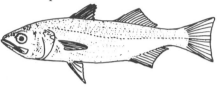

151. Queenfish.　**Seriphus politus**
Also: Herring croaker, bronze back.
Range: Baja California to central California.
Size: Length to 12 inches.
Value: Highly esteemed and in some areas has been over-fished. The flesh is firm and fine flavored, and much prized.
Description: Color is metallic blue to bronze on dorsal surface, silvery ventral, dusky base of pectoral fins, two dorsal fins. Body is elongate, slightly compressed, slender, widely separated dorsal fins, large eyes, pointed pectoral fins, large anal fin, projecting lower jaw, large mouth. Found over sandy bottoms, often with schools of tommy croaker or kingfish.

Family: Haemulidae
Common Name: Grunts

152. California sargo
　　　　Anistotremus davidsoni
Also: China croaker, sea perch, blue seabass.
Range: Baja to central California, and Sea of Cortez.
Size: Length to 15 inches.
Value: Fair sportfish.
Description: Color is silvery, dusky on back, silvery ventral surface, dark blotches on head and back. Large connected dorsal, continuous forked tail, and large black band across back and sides distinguish this species. The body is slightly elliptical, moderately compressed, mouth small, eyes large, head and snout small and mouth thick-lipped. Teeth are small and pointed. Easily caught on pieces of bait in shallow water.

Family: Histiophoridae
Common Name: Boarfishes

There are relatively few members of this family and they inhabit deep water in all oceans.

153. Boarfish
　　　　Pseudopentaceros richardsoni
Range: Generally found in the southern section of Gulf of Alaska.
Size: Length to 2 feet.
Value: At present time not of commercial or sport importance.
Description: Color is brownish-blue on dorsal surface, lighter on underbelly, reddish on head, dark bluish membranes on dorsal fin,

iridescent blue on pectoral fins. Body is stout, compressed, ovate. Head is large, pointed, mouth small, lower jaw projecting. Lateral line is slightly curved then straight, following dorsal line. Caudal peduncle is slender, caudal fin square. Pectoral fins are pointed. Eyes large. Head is slightly depressed above snout.

Common Name: Pomfrets

Little is known of this fish of the open sea, except that it is known to descend to great depths. It is widely distributed in all oceans and often reaches large size. It faintly resembles the freshwater bream.

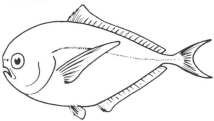

154. Pomfret
Brama raii
Also: Saltwater bream, Ray's bream.
Range: Baja to Alaska.
Size: Length to 4 feet.
Value: The species is abundant but is seldom taken. Sometimes they interfere with salmon trolling operations, being at times so numerous. Believed to be an excellent food fish.
Description: Color is dusky to black with silvery iridescent hues, black snout, and margins of dorsal and caudal fins. Body is moderately elongate, deep, strongly compressed. The caudal peduncle is slender. The caudal fin is deeply

notched, almost elliptical. The profile is rounded, head deep and compressed, mouth moderate and terminal, snout nearly vertical. Readily recognized by size, color and configuration.

Family: Xenichthyidae
Common Name: Salemas

A rare family, the only known member of which is found in California and adjacent waters.

155. California salema
Xenistius californiensis
Also: Striped bass, big-eye bass.
Range: Cabo San Lucas to central California.
Size: Length to 12 inches.
Value: Good sportfish.
Description: Color is bluish back, silvery ventral, with three reddish stripes on sides just above the lateral line, and several more below. Body is bass-shaped, eyes very large, dorsal divided, caudal peduncle slender, tail notched, pectoral fins pointed, lower jaw protruding. Found in bays and lagoons, and along surflines, around kelp. Readily takes bait, either live, or in chunks.

Family: Serranidae
Common Name: Sea basses

The numerous members of this family have classic basslike configurations, with the projecting lower jaw, dual or twin dorsal fins, squarish tail. They are generally voracious and predacious.

156. Striped bass
Roccus saxatilis
Also: Striper, rock bass, rock fish.
Range: Native to Atlantic, but introduced to eastern Pacific in late 1800s; now common from Central California to Central Oregon Coasts,
Size: Length to 4 feet, weight to 80 pounds.
Value: Pollution, netting, and other factors have recently reduced the striped bass in Oregon to secondary importance. It is still considered by many as a "scrap fish" and a predator of salmon, although there is no scientific basis for this.

This fine game fish will take all manner of lures and bait, trolled, cast, or jigged. It is a popular surf fish in most areas. In Oregon it is caught mainly in the brackish coastal rivers and bays on trolled eellike lures.
Description: Color is bronze or brassy-hued, greenish backs, silvery ventral surface and between lateral stripes. Fins are pale to bluish-black, stripes are black. Body is elongate, moderately compressed, eyes small, pectoral fins small, caudal peduncle moderately stout, caudal fin slightly notched, two dorsal fins, snout slightly rounded. An anadromous fish, the striper migrates to fresh water to spawn, but is often found moving in and out of bays and estuaries on the tides. Also found along surf line just offshore. The striper has been successfully introduced into fresh water impoundments such as the Colorado River. The striped bass

was first described by Captain John Smith of Pocahontas fame as ". . . an excellent fish . . . & for daintinesse and diet they excell the Marybones of Beefe. . . ." The striped bass migrated to California courtesy of the United States Fish Commission and a man named Livingston Stone, in July 1879. The fingerlings, along with some eels and lobsters, were shipped from the Navesink River, New Jersey, by rail. About 135 striped bass survived the trip, and these were liberated in the Carquinez Strait at Martinez, California. Another planting was made in 1882 by J. G. Woodbury of the California Fish and Game Commission in Suisun Bay, with fingerlings taken from the Shrewsbury River, New Jersey. The stripers caught on immediately and within a few years specimens weighing up to seventeen pounds were being sold in the San Francisco fish markets. A commercial as well as sport fishery soon developed and in 1935 the striper was declared a game fish in California. Meanwhile the species moved north along the coast. In 1914 the first striped bass was taken in Coos Bay, Oregon. In 1931 the striper was included in the Oregon commercial code, and in 1931 the commercial catch alone was 18,153 pounds in the Coos River. By 1945 the catch totalled 231,005 pounds from the Coos, Umpqua, and Coquille rivers. Oregon anglers have taken stripers up to sixty pounds.

157. Giant sea bass
Stereolepis gigas
Also: California black sea bass, California jewfish, black rockfish, black sea bass.
Range: Sea of Cortez to central California.

Size: Length to 7 feet, weight to 700 pounds.
Value: Good sportfish.
Description: Color is dark brown to black on dorsal surface, with lighter shading on ventral surface. The body is thick, heavy, strong, with large mouth, depressed head, continuous dorsal fin notched between spinous and rayed sections. The caudal fin is slightly notched. Abundant in southern waters and usually found deep in kelp areas, often close to shore. Very heavy tackle is needed and large hooks on the order of 14/0. Bait usually is mackerel, mullet, and similar bait fish, whole or filleted. The liver is believed to be toxic.

158. Hapu'upu'u
        Epinephelus quernus
Range: Tropical Pacific, Hawaiian Islands.

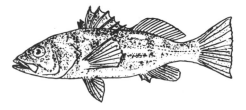

159. Kelp bass
        Paralabrax clathratus
Also: Sand bass, bull bass, cabrilla, rock bass, calico bass.

Range: Baja to central California.
Size: Length to 2 feet.
Value: Good sportfish.
Description: Color is dark gray or brown on dorsal surface, mottled with brown, lighter on ventral surface with yellowish hues, and yellowish fins. Body is basslike with notched dorsal fin, the forward section being prominent and heavily spined, the aft section soft and spinous. Square caudal fin, large rounded anal fin, and large pectoral fin. Abundant around kelp beds in some sections but now scarce in others. Will take all manner of bait, fished on the bottom, as well as jigs handlined.

160. Sand bass
        Paralabrax nebulifer
Also: Rock bass, kelp bass, Johnny Verde.
Range: Baja to central California.
Size: Length to 2 feet.
Value: Good sportfish.
Description: Color is muddy gray with greenish hue on dorsal surface, whitish ventral, dark mottling and vague bars on head, small brownish spots on snout and sides of head. Basslike body, recognized by long third spine on front section of dorsal fin which is divided, square tail, large anal and pectoral fins, and coloration. Fairly abundant over range. A bottom feeder, it will take most bait fish and jigs.

161. Baya grouper
        Mycteroperca jordani
Also: Broomtail.

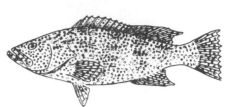

Range: Baja west side and Sea of Cortez.
Value: Fairly common sport fish in southern waters.
Size: Weight to 260 pounds.
Description: Color is dark brown to black or olive gray on dorsal surface, lighter green or olive on ventral. Four rows of olive green markings on sides, and wavy streaks on side of head. Recognized by basslike body, square tail and markings.

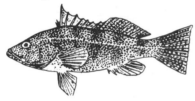

162. Spotted sand bass
Paralabrax maculatofasciatus
Also: Spotted cabrilla, rock bass, spotted bass.
Range: West coast of Mexico and Central America.
Size: Length to 18 inches.
Value: Of minor importance to sportsmen.
Description: Gray-greenish color on dorsal surface, gray-white underbelly, with spots and mottled bars. Probably a variation of the sand bass, both belonging to the seabass family **Serranidae.** Can be identified by brown brownish spots that cover entire body, and large fins. Will take strip bait and live bait on small hooks.

163. Broomtail grouper
Mycteroperca xenarchus
Also: Spotted broomtail, gray

broomtail, garuppa, pinto seabass.
Range: From Baja south along west coast of Mexico and Central America.
Size: Weight to 80 pounds.
Description: Brown to black or blue on dorsal surface, lighter ventral, with fins and body almost entirely covered with small leopardlike spots. Body is typically basslike with square, serrated caudal fin, continuous, slightly notched dorsal fin, large pointed anal fin, large pectoral fins, large mouth, protruding lower jaw. Found over rocky bottoms and reefs in great numbers, and will take live or cut bait, or trolled lures.

164. Aholehole
Kuhlia sandvicensis
Also: Mountain bass.
Range: Tropical Pacific and Hawaiian Islands.
Size: Length to 8 inches.
Value: Excellent food fish.
Description: Color is bright silver. Feeds on shellfish, usually at night in large schools. Shrimp and bread best bait, but they take it slowly and cautiously. Lights are used for night fishing.

165. Kalikali
         Pristipomoides sieboldi
Also: Snapper.
Range: Tropical Pacific and Indian oceans, Hawaii, Japan.

166. 'Opakapaka
         Paralabrax microlepis
Also: Hawaiian sea bass.
Range: Tropical Pacific, Indian Ocean, East Indies, Hawaii.

167. Onaga   **Etelis carbunculus**
Range: Tropical Pacific and Indian oceans, Hawaiian Islands.

168. Uko Gorotsuki
         Aprion virescens
Also: Snapper.
Range: Tropical Pacific and Hawaiian Islands.

169. 'Aweoweo
         Priacanthus cruentatus
Also: Scad, goggle-eye, goggler.
Range: Tropical waters world-wide, Hawaiian Islands.

170. 'Alalaua   **Priacanthus alalaua**
Range: Tropical Pacific, Hawaii.

171. 'Upapalu   **Apogon snyderi**
Range: Tropical Pacific, Hawaiian Islands.

172. 'upapalu   **Apogon menesemus**
Range: Tropical Pacific, Hawaiian Islands.

Family: Branchiostegidae
Common Name: Blanquillos or tile-fishes

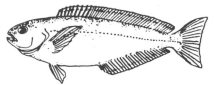

173. Ocean whitefish
         Caulolatilus princeps
Also: Tilefish, whitefish, blanka, blanquillo.
Range: Baja to central California, tropical Pacific.
Size: Length to 4 feet.
Value: Easily taken on strip bait and popular with the party boats.
Description: Color is brown-yellow on dorsal surface, lighter ventral, bluish or yellowish strips on fins. Body is elongate, moderately compressed, head and snout rounded, long, narrow pectoral fins, long, continuous anal and dorsal fins with rays of equal length, slender caudal peduncle, caudal fin slightly lunate. The males display a bulging fatty head during spawning. Found over seamounts and reefs, rocky bottoms, and around kelp. Feeds near the bottom on crustaceans, squid, mussels, abalone.

174. Ala-'ihi
         Holocentrus lacteoguttatus
Also: Squirrelfish.
Range: Tropical Pacific and Hawaii.

175. 'U'u, Menpachi
         Myripristis berndti
Also: Squirrelfish.
Range: Tropical Pacific and Hawaii.

176. 'U'u Menpachi
        Myripristis argyromus
Also: Squirrelfish.
Range: Tropical Pacific, Hawaii.

Family: Belonidae
Common Name: Needlefishes

177. Needlefish   **Belone platyura**
Range: Tropical Pacific, Hawaii.

Family: Girellidae
Common Name: Nibblers

178. Opaleye   **Girella nigricans**
Also: Green fish, blue eye, green
perch, black perch, opaleye perch,
Jack Benny.
Range: Baja to central California.
Size: Weight to 6½ pounds.
Value: Fair sportfish.
Description: Color is greenish-olive
on dorsal surface, grayish-brown to
green on ventral, bright, opalescent
blue eyes. Young have yellowish
spots below dorsal fin. Body is
rounded, snout nearly vertical, head
slightly indented, mouth small.
Caudal peduncle deep, caudal fin
squared, dorsal fin continuous,
large anal fin. Usually found over
rocky bottoms and in surf. Feeds
on small marine life, and will take
small pieces of cut bait. Not a
perch, although often mistaken for
one.

Family: Scorpididae
Common Name: Halfmoons

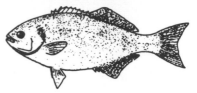

179. California halfmoon
        Medialuna californiensi
Also: Blue perch, Catalina perch,
black perch.
Range: Sea of Cortez, southern
California, Baja.
Size: Length to 12 inches.
Value: Fair sportfish.
Description: Color is slate black or
dark green, lighter sides, whitish
ventral surface. Body is slightly
rounded with small mouth and
small black eyes, single continuous
dorsal fin with small spines in
front portion, large scale-covered
anal fin, small pectoral fins, caudal
fin slightly furcate. Usually found
in kelp areas, often in large numbers feeding on surface. Will take
cut bait readily.

Family: Kyphosidae
Common Name: Rudderfishes

180. Nenue   **Kyphosus cinerascens**
Also: Manaloa.
Range: Tropical Pacific and Hawaii.

181. Zebraperch
Hermosilla azurea
Also: Convict fish, sea perch, Mexican sea perch.
Range: Baja to central California.
Size: Length to 12 inches.
Value: Fair sportfish.
Description: Color is tan to gray-blue, vertical black bars, prominent black spot on opercle, dark fins. Body is perchlike, mainly recognized by the · twelve bars or zebra stripes. Usually found among rocks and kelp in shallow water and readily taken with small cut bait.

182. Weke
Mulloidichthys samoensis
Also: Weke-'a'a.
Range: Tropical Pacific and Hawaii.

183. Weke-'ula
Mulloidichthys auriflamma
Range: Tropical Pacific, Hawaii.
184. Malu
Parupeneus pleurostigma
Range: Tropical Pacific, Hawaii.

185. Kumu
Parupeneus porphyreus
Also: Goatfish.
Range: Tropical Pacific, Hawaii.
Size: Weight to 9 pounds.
Value: An excellent food fish.
Description: Color is red with dark patches on upper body. A night feeder usually, travels in schools, lives on crustaceans. Abundant in shallow and offshore waters of reefs.

186. Moano
Parupeneus mutifasciatus
Also: Goatfish.
Range: Tropical Pacific, Hawaii.
Size: Average weight 3 pounds.
Value: One of the finest eating of Hawaiian fishes.
They have slender streamlined bodies, forked tail and two dorsal fins

188. Mackereljack
Trachurus symmetricus
Also: Horse mackerel, Spanish mackerel, jack mackerel.
Range: Tropical and subtropical waters of eastern Pacific, north to Gulf of Alaska.
Size: Length to 2 feet.
Value: Excellent bait fish.
Description: Color is metallic blue on dorsal surface, dull silver on ventral. Body is elongate, fusiform, head pointed, mouth terminal and moderate, teeth small, eyes large. The caudal peduncle is slender, less than the diameter of the eye. The spinous dorsal is triangular depressible in grove. Identification includes single free finlet behind second dorsal and one behind second anal, and the decurved lateral line. Abundant in warm currents offshore and are often taken in commercial net operations, The **caballita,** found only in certain waters of the Baja Peninsula and prized for live marlin bait, appears to be a rare subspecies.

189. Yellowtail   **Seriola dorsalis**
Also: California yellowtail, amberjack.
Range: Panama north to Oregon, Sea of Cortez.

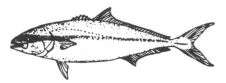

Size: Length to 5 feet.
Value: A highly prized sport fish.
Description: Color is dark red with bands of darker red. A day feeder, caught on bottom on shrimp bait by casting.

187. Mu
                    Montaxis granoculis
Also: Mamau.
Range: Tropical Pacific, Hawaii, Red Sea.

Family: Carangidae
Common Name: Jacks

Jacks are found in warm waters, are pelagic and fast swimmers. Game regulations strictly prohibit commercial exploitation of this superb fish.
Description: They have brilliant brassy and blue coloration with yellow lateral stripe from snout to caudal fin. Body is elongate, moderately compressed, deeply forked caudal fin, caudal peduncle slender, first dorsal low and spinous, second extending to caudal peduncle, anal fin low and extended, pointed snout, short pectoral fin. A gamey, tough fighter, the yellowtail is found in schools mainly in Baja waters north to Catalina. Peak season is May in southern California and June in Catalina waters. Specimens have been caught rarely as far north as the Columbia River. Similar but possibly unrelated species are found off Panama, South

America, and the Galapagos Islands.

190. Kahala   **Seriola dumerilii**
Also: Greater amberjack.
Range: Tropical Pacific, Hawaii, as well as other oceans.
Size: Length to 5 feet.
Value: Good gamefish.
Description: Color is dark body, olivaceous, lighter along sides, with lavender and gold hues and sometimes an amber band from head to tail, silvery ventral surface. Body is somewhat slender, dorsal fin lobe short, caudal peduncle slender, caudal fin deeply forked. It is pelagic and oceanic in spawning and habit, found in most oceans. Can be taken on cutbait near the bottom or on jig lures.

191. Lai **Scomberoides sanctipetri**
Also: Leatherback.
Range: Tropical Pacific, Hawaii, Indian Ocean.

192. 'Opelu **Decapterus pinnulatus**
Also: Mackerel scad, 'Opelu-mama.

193. Akule
              Trachurops crumenopthalmus
Also: Aji, bigeye scad.
Range: Tropical Pacific, Hawaii.

194. Pa'opa'o
              Gnathanodon speciosus
Also: Yellow ulus.
Range: Tropical Pacific, Hawaii, Red Sea.

195. Ulua **Carangoides ferdau**
Range: Tropical Pacific, Hawaii, Red Sea.

196. White ulua
Carangoides ajax
Range: Tropical Pacific, Hawaii.

197. Pa'u'u **Caranx ignobilis**
Also: Ulua.
Range: Tropical Pacific, Hawaii, Red Sea.

198. 'Omilu **Caranx melampygus**
Also: 'Omilumilu, Hoshi ulua.
Range: Tropical Pacific, Hawaii.

199. 'Omaka **Caranx mate**
Also:
Range: Tropical Pacific, Hawaii.

Family: Scombridae
Common Name: Mackerels

The mackerels have slender keeled caudal peduncles, and streamlined bodies with undulating lateral line and a series of finlets. They travel in schools and are swift swimmers. The body is smooth and the main fins are set in grooves, a sure sign of speed. Aerodynamic engineers have said the mackerel body is the most nearly perfect for passage through water. The family includes bonitos, tunas, albacores.

200. Albacore
Thunnus alalunga
Also: Longfin, long-finned tuna, abrego.
Range: Pelagic in warm seas, found over entire tropical and subtropical Pacific.

Size: Length to 4 feet.
Value: An extremely abundant fish at times, it is highly prized by both commercial and sports fishermen. The marketing slogan, "chicken of the sea," refers to the albacore. It is taken with jigs of metal, feathers, and bone, towed at about eight miles an hour, on the surface or submerged, and also by chumming with live bait.
Description: Color is a metallic blue on dorsal surface, silvery-whitish on ventral. The body is elongate, fusiform, caudal peduncle slender with keel on each side. The head is conical, mouth moderate and terminal. The dorsal has a short interspace, long high spinous section, series of finlets top and bottom anteriorly, sabrelike caudal fin, lunate. Easily distinguished by slender caudal peduncle with finlets on top and bottom, and the very long swordlike pectoral fins, from which it gets the name "longfin."

A school fish, the albacore is a voracious and predacious killer, feeding in frenzies at times on school fish like anchovies, sauries, herring, pilchards, and even young mackerel and albacore, squid, zooplankton, and lanternfish.

A tropical fish, the albacore spawns in tropical waters and feeds as it migrates on a counterclockwise course around the Pacific rim, and is almost always found along the 58° to 65° isotherm. In the early 1930s it was discovered off the Oregon, Washington, and British Columbia coasts.

The first important commercial landings in the Northwest were about 1940. The North Pacific is now one of the most prolific producers of this fish. Along the Baja, California, and Northwest coasts, the albacore are apparently young fish in the fifteen- to thirty-five-pound class. By the time they reach Japan's waters they may reach as much as 200 pounds. They appear off the southern coast in March and April, off California in May and June, and off the Northwest coast from July through October. Sports anglers watch the winds and current forecasts, then make the ten mile to 200 mile run offshore to intercept the albacore, a "blue water" fish. Birds and water color are reliable indicators of albacore, as are porpoises. When a school is encountered the action is fantastic.

201. Bluefin tuna   **Thunnus saliens**
Also: Great tuna, leaping tuna, tunny, California bluefin.
Range: Baja to Gulf of Alaska.
Size: Length to 7 feet.
Value: Excellent gamefish.
Description: Color is dark metallic blue on dorsal shading to silvery gray on sides, dusky on spinous dorsal, dusky to reddish-brown on rayed dorsal, silvery gray on pectoral and pelvic fins, large silver spots on underbelly, yellow on dorsal and anal finlets. The body is elongate, fusiform, caudal peduncle slender with keel on each side. The head is conical, mouth moderately terminal. There are series of finlets above and below caudal

peduncle. The caudal fin is sabre-like and lunate. Anal, pelvic, second dorsal, and pectoral fins are pointed. Readily recognized by color and yellow finlets, large silvery spots on underbelly. They feed mainly on small school fish such as anchovies, mackerel, and squid, and are preyed upon by killer whales. Sport fishing for bluefins was begun in the early 1900s by Zane Grey and other pioneers in Catalina waters. Kite fishing is said to have been originated there in 1908 by a man named George Farnsworth, using flying fish as bait. The season is from early spring through December, with midsummer the best. The fishery is not developed yet north of California, but is a potential.

202. Bigeye tuna   **Thunnus obesus**
Range: Found both Atlantic and Pacific in tropical and subtropical waters and in warm currents in high latitudes.
Size: Length to 8 feet; weight to 450 pounds.
Value: They are mainly taken by Japanese longlines in massive numbers.
Description: Color is metallic blue on back, whitish underbelly, yellow fins with black margins. The body is elongate and deep, with typical slender caudal peduncle typical slender caudal peduncle line with rows of finlets top and bottom, scimitar caudal fin, scimitar anal and second dorsal, and moderately long pectoral fins like the albacore. They feed upon school fishes, squids, crustaceans. Spawning is prolific, at any time of year in tropical waters. The largest taken on hook and line is a 435-pound specimen off Cabo Blanco, Peru. They have been discovered off Oregon in recent years.

203. Pacific bonito
Sarda lineolata
Also: Ocean bonito, skipjack, striped tuna.
Range: Baja to Gulf of Alaska.
Size: Length to 3 feet.
Value: Highly prized by commercial and sport fishermen, especially for its superb flavor when baked, and its fighting qualities. It is taken on fast-moving jigs and live bait chummed. It was discovered in northern waters as long ago as 1900, but at this time is an undeveloped fishery north of California.
Description: Color is metallic blue on dorsal shading to silvery on underbelly, with blackish stripes along upper portion slanted anteriorly upward. Body is elongate, fusiform. Slender caudal peduncle has keel on each side and rows of finlets top and bottom. The caudal fin is scimitar-shaped top and bottom. Identified by the slender caudal peduncle and finlets, and the ten or eleven narrow stripes obliquely along body. It is a pelagic fish, occurring in large schools, feeding on squid and other small fishes.

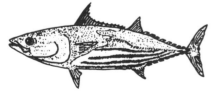

204. Skipjack tuna
Katsuwonus pelamis
Also: Ocean skipjack, ocean bonito, tuna, striped tuna, skippy, aku.

Range: Tropical Pacific, South America to Gulf of Alaska, Hawaii, Japan.
Size: Length to 3 feet.
Value: It is an important commercial and sport fish in California, Hawaii, and Japan. It is caught by fast troll and live bait chumming, and is often found with yellowfin tuna.
Description: Color is dark metallic blue on dorsal surface, silvery on ventral, black to dusky stripes on lower portion. Body is elongate fusiform, with slender caudal peduncle, keel on each side, rows of finlets top and bottom, conical head, long spinous dorsal fin, lunate caudal fin. Distinguished by slender caudal peduncle and finlets, and four to five longitudinal stripes on lower body.
A fish of warm oceanic seas, it occurs in large schools, and travels widely from the south to north Pacific. It was first discovered off British Columbia in 1943. This is probably the same fish as the **aku** in the western Pacific, or **Euthynnus pelamis,** and the Kawakawa or wavyback skipjack, **Euthynnus yaito.**

205. Pacific mackerel
Pneumatophorus japonicus
Also: Greenback, striped mackerel, zebra mackerel, American mackerel.
Range: Tropical and temperate Pacific.
Size: Length to 2 feet.
Value: A superb game fish and especially good food fish with an excellent flavor when baked or

broiled. Can also be smoked.
Description: Often confused with the wavyback skipjack or kawakawa.

206. Yellowfin tuna
Thunnus albacares
Also: Yellowfinned albacore, yellowfin, Allison tuna, 'Ahi.
Range: Oceanic Atlantic and Pacific, tropical and subtropical.
Size: Length to 7 feet, weight to 450 pounds.
Value: They are taken commercially in vast numbers, especially by the wide-ranging Japanese in long line and purse seine operations. They are caught on sport tackle with live bait and trolled feathers. The meat is light, between that of bluefin and albacore and is highly prized for canning. In spite of the huge numbers harvested worldwide, very little is known of the yellowfin tuna.
Description: Color is brilliant yellow stripes on upper body over metallic blue, with bright yellow on fins, white spots and vertical streaks on ventral surface. Body is elongate, fusiform, deep, head conical, eyes large. All yellowtail tuna are now considered the same species. Sometimes individuals with extra long second dorsals and anal fins are called Allison tuna, but are only a variation. The caudal peduncle is typically slender with finlets above and below, and the caudal fin scimitar with upper lobe longer. The pectoral fins are long and swordlike, but not as long as on the albacore. The largest speci-

men taken on handline was said to be six feet ten and one-half inches, weighing 266½ pounds from Hawaiian waters. They spawn in tropical waters and feed on various school fish and crustaceans.

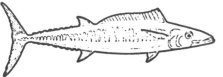

207. Wahoo
Acanthocybium solandri
Also: Ono, Spanish mackerel.
Range: Tropical and subtropical Atlantic, Pacific, and Indian oceans.
Size: Length to 7 feet.
Value: A superb game fish and excellent food fish, too. The flesh is white, tasty, somewhat dry and is best smoked.
Description: Bluish to brownish-back with narrow vertical stripes. Body is elongate, slender, with long tubular snout, strong flattened teeth, low rayed dorsal in front of spinous, with slender caudal peduncle and rows of finlets top and bottom, caudal fin long, thin and crescent. It does not occur in schools like other mackerels, but feeds on a variety of school fish and crustaceans. The female is prolific, releasing several million eggs at a time. The stomach almost always contains the large, leechlike parasites, the giant grematode. They are usually caught while fishing for marlin, dolphinfish, or tuna on trolled jigs and bait. They strike hard and fight furiously. Often they even hit bright swivels or wire lines.

208. Sierra grande
Scomberomorus sierra
Also: Spanish mackerel, Monterey mackerel.

Range: Mainly found in Mexican waters, Central America.
Size: Length to 5 feet.
Value: A good sport fish.
Description: Color is metallic blue back, silvery ventral surface, white anal fin, pectoral fin black with yellowish tips, caudal fin black. Body is slender, snout conical or pointed, first dorsal low, spinous dorsal high triangular, wavy lateral line, rows of orange, blue, yellow spots along sides, teeth large, rows of finlets above and below slender caudal peduncle, scimitar caudal fins. Abundant off Baja and in Sea of Cortez, otherwise rather rare.

209. Monterey sierra
Scomberomorus concolor
Also: Mackerel jack, Spanish mackerel.
Range: Baja and Sea of Cortez, north to southern California.
Size: Length to 2 feet.

Value: An excellent game fish but now quite rare except in Sea of Cortez and west side of Baja. Ranks as one of the most prized food fishes of the world, but harvested to near depletion in cosmopolitan areas.

Family: Syphyraenidae
Common Name: Barracudas

Swift, predaceous fish, these are long and slender, with pointed, pikelike heads and strong sharp teeth. They occasionally attack humans. They are found in tropical and subtropical waters, and occasionally reach eight feet in length.

210. Pacific barracuda
Sypharena argentea
Also: California barracuda, scott, barry, scooter.
Range: Tropical and subtropical Atlantic and Pacific.
Size: Length to 8 feet.
Value: A popular sport fish for light tackle. It it also an important food fish in some areas. The flesh is rich and firm and has a fine flavor.
Description: Color is bluish-brown on dorsal, silvery white on ventral surface. Body is elongate, slender, head very elongate, sharply pointed, lower jaw projecting, teeth fanglike and large, snout acute. Two widely separated dorsal fins. Caudal peduncle slender, caudal fin furcate. Will take feathers, metal lures, bait.

211. Great barracuda
Sphyraena barracuda
Also: Kaku.
Range: Tropical Atlantic and Pacific, Hawaiian Islands.
212. Kawalea **Sphyraena helleri**
Range: Tropical Pacific, Hawaiian Islands, Oceania.
Family: Coryphaenidiae
Common Name: Dolphinfishes

213. Dolphin
Coryphaena hippurus
Also: Dolphinfish, dorado, mahi-mahi, dorade.
Range: Tropical and subtropical seas of the world, sometimes found

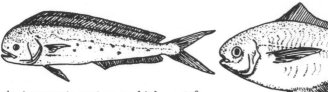

in temperate waters as high as 40° latitude.

Size: Length to 6 feet.

Value: One of the world's most superb and spectacular game fish, often seen greyhounding along on the surface chasing flying fish. A speedy swimmer and voracious feeder, it is caught on fast-trolled lures and bait, often while fishing for billfish or tuna. The flesh is finely flavored and highly prized, but has to be eaten fresh as it cannot be preserved successfully.

Description: Color is brilliant blue or green or gold with bright blue spots, golden or yellow sides and belly, tail and pectoral fins yellow. Body is torpedolike with continuous dorsal fin from head to caudal peduncle, which is slender. Caudal fin is deeply forked. The head is short and blunt; the male forehead bulging more than the female. The anal fin extends half the body length. A characteristic of this species is the rapid change of color once it is out of water, quickly losing its brilliant iridescent hues. It is not related to the mammals called dolphin, members of the porpoise family.

214. Pompano dolphin
                Coryphaena equiselis
Also: Dolphinfish, dorade.
Range: World-wide in warm seas.
Size: Length to 2 feet.
Value: Excellent gamefish.
Description: Color is similar to the dolphinfish or dorado, but the body is deeper and the dorsal fin somewhat higher although the size is

normally smaller. More oceanic than the dorado. Little is known of habits and lifecycles.

Family: Xiphiidae
Common Name: Swordfishes

215. Swordfish   **Xiphias gladius**
Also: Broadbill, broadbill swordfish.
Range: World-wide in temperate and tropical waters.
Size: Weight to 1,000 pounds.
Value: The flesh is highly prized as food and featured on menus of restaurants the world over (although in many cases, the customer gets shark meat instead).
Description: Color is purple-black with silver-gray on ventral surface and crossbars on sides, varying widely in different seas. It is identified readily by the long flat sword, much longer than the head, no pelvic fins, single keel on each side of caudal peduncle, no scales, and high scimitar-shaped dorsal fin just behind the head, smaller scimitar anal fin, and long lobes on deep-notched caudal fin. The swordfish spawns generally in the summer, and is subject to seasonal migrations north and south. They seem to prefer cooler currents, and sometimes even enter

brackish or fresh water. They feed on schooled bait fish, much the same as marlin and sailfish, including dolphin, bluefish, mackerel, and bonito. The sword is used for slashing through schools. Once found in all seas, even in high latitudes, the swordfish has been exploited commercially for centuries and figures in many maritime legends. Once plentiful off California and Oregon, it was brought to near extinction by commercial boats before World War II. Sport angling is done much the same way as for marlin and sailfish, but trolling is slower with the bait or lure under the surface. Large hooks up to 16/0 are needed and strong leaders, up to 450 pounds test for the big ones. In U. S. waters the size is about that of marlin, but specimens up to 1,100 pounds have been taken off South America.

Family: Istiophoridae
Common Name: Sailfishes
216. Striped marlin
Makaira audax
Also: Swordfish, spearfish, sailfish, billfish, kajiki.

Range: Tropical and subtropical Pacific, Indian Ocean, central Atlantic.
Size: Length to 13 feet.
Value: One of the world's most popular and sought after big game fish, the marlin is also an important food fish heavily harvested throughout the Pacific area in tropical and subtropical waters. The marlin meat is highly prized as a food, especially in the Orient.

Smoked and canned marlin is tops for party snacks. Fish kept for trophies are often mounted, which costs approximately a dollar a pound. Many sport anglers keep the bill only for a trophy, and have the rest smoked and canned. **Description:** Color is indigo blue on back, fading to silvery on ventral surface, with light bluish bars on sides, blue-green dorsal fin with blue spots, gray-black on pectoral fins. Body streamlined, extended with hump behind head from white tall dorsal fin, connected with low dorsal fins over rest of back, two small keels each side of caudal peduncle, swordlike caudal fins; the upper jaw extends out into long flat sword, the lower jaw also partly extended.

In spite of much study and investigation, very little is really known about this fish. It is believed to be oceanic, but is also caught close inshore in many areas. It seems to ride the warm currents around the Pacific, and specimens tagged off Mexico have been caught in Hawaii two months later. Others seem to stay around "home waters." The triangular section of ocean between Acapulco, Mazatlan and Cabo San Lucas is considered one of the finest marlin areas in the world. In the late 1960s, Japanese longline boats, however, very nearly depleted this fishery. The marlin caught in Hawaiian and South American waters seem to run to much larger size than those along the Mexican coast. They seem to feed on targets of opportunity, such as schools of saury, mackerel, bonito, squids, crustaceans, octopi, depending on what is available.

The striped marlin is taken on a variety of tackle from twenty-pound test up to heavy gear. Usually bait such as mullet, flyingfish, sardines, and mackerel are trolled at a fast clip with a teaser bouncing in the wake. The skipper on charter boats watches for birds and also for dorsal fins. Hooks used are up to 9/0 with heavy mono leaders. Some charters troll until marlin are hit and then angling is done with live chum and live bait. The thrill of hooking and playing a marlin is hard to beat. Experienced sports anglers usually release their fish, even in tournament competition.

almost always oceanic, although large ones have been caught in Hawaiian and Japanese waters. In the Pacific the blues have been caught from Japan to New Zealand, but in the eastern Pacific seldom north of Mexico. They are found throughout the Indian Ocean and Caribbean. It feeds on all manner of schoolfish up to and including swordfish, and is caught by trolling, handlining, chumming, and spearing. The **M. ampla** classification appears to be the same fish as the Maikaira nigricans.

217. Pacific blue marlin
              Makaira ampla
Also: Kurokajiki.
Range: World-wide in tropical and temperate oceans.
Size: Weight to 2,000 pounds.
Value: Superb big-game fish.
Description: Color similar to striped marlin, including whitish bars, steel blue to indigo back and dorsal fins, shading to silvery white on ventral surface. In death the bars fade out and the fish turns to bronze color, then to dark black-blue. The dorsal is often cobalt with dark spots or blotches. The body is cylindrical forward, not slab-sided, heavier in the body aft than other species. The dorsal fin is relatively low, with a longer anal fin. The spear on the upper jaw is smooth and oval, with a shorter lower jaw. The males grow only to about 300 pounds, the really big fish being females. The blue, largest of the marlins, appears to make regular north-south migrations and the big specimens are

218. White marlin
              Istiompax marlina
Also: Silver marlin, black marlin, shirokajiki.
Range: Tropical Pacific and Indian oceans.
Size: Weight to 2,000 pounds.
Value: The meat is highly prized, and is delicious cooked or raw which makes it a favorite in the Orient.
Description: Color is highly variable from white or silvery to black sometimes with pale blue bars or stripes when alive. Sometimes the fish is milky white, from which comes the Chinese name **pu-pi** and the Japanese **shirokajiki.** All fins are dark. After death the fish usually turns white, or bronze regardless of its former color. The body is torpedo-shaped, with lower dorsal than other istiophorids, and rigid pectoral fins standing straight out from body which cannot be folded. The body is slightly deeper, similar to the blue marlin, with a

more prominent hump and slab sides. This is the same fish as the Atlantic **I. indicus.** The world record sport-caught fish at this writing is 1,560 pounds from Cabo Blanco, Peru. The white spawns in the summer months. The females are larger than the males, like the blues. The young fish are usually darker. Some migration apparently takes place, however the natural distribution is so wide that little is known of its habits. The fish feeds upon all manner of ocean fish including poisonous Portuguese Man of War, large tuna, squid, and other billfish.

Family: Stromateidae
Common Name: Butterfishes

Members of this family are found in the warm open seas, and are highly prized for their rare flavor and brilliant colors.

219. Pacific pompano
Palometa simillima
Also: Pompano, butterfish.
Range: Baja to British Columbia.

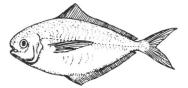

Size: Length to 11 inches.
Value: It is a sought-after market fish because of its fine, rich flesh.
Description: Color is metallic blue on dorsal surface, bright silvery on sides and belly, iridescent, dusky margins on fin lobes. The body is elongate, deep, greatly compressed. The caudal peduncle is short and slender. The head is rounded, mouth small and terminal, teeth

small, jaws small and weak. The pectoral fin is long, connected almost to caudal peduncle. The caudal is deeply furcate. The first species recorded from the North Pacific occurred in 1903. The fish seems to be abundant in some years, scarce in others.

Family: Anoplopomatidae
Common Name: Skilfishes

These are fishes of the north Pacific and include sablefish and skilfishes. They have two well-developed nostrils and head without ridges, and two dorsal fins.

220. Sablefish   **Anoplopoma fibria**
Also: Black cod, coalfish, blue cod, skill fish.
Range: Baja to Bering Sea.
Size: Length to 3 feet.
Value: One of the finest food fishes and is excellent smoked because of its high oil content. The liver is rich in Vitamin A and D, ranking next to lingcod.
Description: Color is slate black to greenish-gray on dorsal surface, light gray on ventral. The fins are pale on outer edges except spinous dorsal which has a black margin. The young are lighter in color, sometimes with dusky bars on dorsal. The body is elongate, slightly compressed, with long slender caudal peduncle. The head is conical, mouth moderate, teeth small. There are two dorsal fins, well separated, large anal fin. Recognized by dorsals, long slender caudal peduncle, and black lining of each operculum. Usually taken in deep water. The

eggs of the sablefish are pelagic and sometimes cover wide distances. Trawls and longlines account for most of the catch. The sablefish is popularly known as black cod, but is not a member of the cod family.

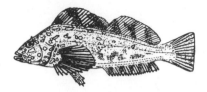

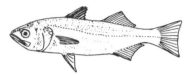

221. Skilfish   **Erilepiis zonfer**
Also: Giant skilfish.
Range: Northern California to Gulf of Alaska.
Size: Length to 6 feet.
Description: Color is very dark, with black dorsal surface and sides, grayish-white on ventral, with gray-white blotches on head of young fish. The body is elongate and stout, head large, mouth moderate, lower jaw projecting. There are two separate dorsal fins, narrow caudal peduncle, solid squarish caudal fin, large anal and pectoral fins. Specimens have been taken in deep as well as shallow water. Little else is known of this fish.

Family: Hexagrammidae
Common Name: Greenlings

Members of this family vary widely in coloration, even among the same species, usually taking on the background of their habitat.

222. Kelp greenling
          Hexagrammos decagrammus
Also: Seatrout, kelp trout, kelp cod, rock trout, bluefish.
Range: Southern California to Gulf of Alaska.

Size: Length to 22 inches.
Value: The flesh is delicious, tender flavored and much in demand. Most of it is caught on handlines or sport tackle and seldom reaches the market. It was a popular food fish of the North Coast Indians. The Aleutians called it the **Idyajuk**, the British Columbia natives, **Tathle-gest,** and the early Russian traders called it **Terpugh**, meaning file. It is most important today as a sport fish for alongshore charter and party boats.
Description: The coloring has been described as a "floating flower bed." At times hues of red, blue, orange, and green are mingled in confusion, in patterns of spots and circles. Coloring varies from male to female. Males are usually brownish-olive tinged with blue or copper, with blue spots on head, surrounded by reddish-brown ring of spots, mottled brown on dorsal fin, dusky blue on pelvic and anal fins, brown to black on pectoral fins. The female is light brown with small red spots to light blue with rows of orange spots, often with pale yellow on fins. The body is elongate, moderately deep. The caudal peduncle is slender, head short, teeth small, single nostril. The dorsal fin is continuous, slightly notched halfway. The anal fin is large and continuous, the pectoral fins butterflylike. A common fish of northern waters, it spawns in the fall discharging pale blue eggs in large masses, upon which salmon and steelhead often feed.

223. Whitespotted greenling
          Hexagrammos stelleri
Also: Sea trout, tommy cod, Atka mackerel, kelp cod, rock trout.
Range: California to Bering Sea.
Size: Length to 16 ınches.
Value: The fish is good eating, with a fine flavor and is popular with young anglers since it can readily be caught from the shore, from jetties and rocks.
Description: Color varies from light brown to green, tinged with pale red, barred with dusky, with conspicuous white spots on body, pale yellow on anal fin with dark bars, light reddish-yellow on pectoral fins with dark bars. The body is elongate, slender, caudal peduncle slender, head short and conical, mouth small, teeth small, single nostril. The dorsal fin is long and continuous with notch in middle, the pectoral fins butterflylike. This species is found in rocky areas, often in shallow water along sandy beaches. The spawn is blue, often deposited on rocks. It feeds on marine worms, small fish, and crustaceans.

224. Rock greenling
          Hexagrammos superciliosus
Also: Rock trout, red greenling, sea trout, fringed greenling, Pacific red rock, kelp cod.
Range: Southern California to Bering Sea.

Size: Length to 2 feet.
Value: Good bottom fish.
Description: Color is bright and variable from dark green, brown, to lighter hues, with red stripes down and back from eyes, pale to bright round spots on sides sometimes red, sometimes brown. The pectoral and anal fins are barred with bands or crescents, sides often blotched, large dark spot on head. The body is elongate, somewhat compressed, caudal peduncle stout, head conical, mouth small, teeth small, single nostril, dorsal fin continuous and notched. There is a fringed cirrus above each eye. Found in rocky areas in shallow waters. Easily caught on cut bait.

225. Painted greenling
          Oxylebius pictus
Also: Convictfish, kelp trout, painted trout.
Range: Southern California to Gulf of Alaska.
Size: Length to 10 inches.
Value: Nil.
Description: Color is light brown to gray, with dark bars, usually seven in number, vertical on body, dorsal and anal fins, as well as tail. The pectoral and pelvic fins have irregular crescent bars. The body is elongate, moderately deep, caudal peduncle stout, head elongate, pointed, mouth small, teeth small, single nostril. This fish is identified by pointed head with two pairs of cirri, notched anal fin, and the vertical bars. It is found along rocky shores and among kelp.

Family: Ophiodontidae
Common Name: Lingcods

Distinguished by large mouth and sharp teeth and coloring, the lingcods are neither cods nor lings. They are important as food and sport fish and highly prized on the fresh market. They are often classified with greenlings, which they resemble in many respects.

226. Lingcod
Ophiodon elongatus
Also: Cultus cod, cultus, skilfish, blue cod, buffalo cod, green cod.
Range: Southern California to Bering Sea.
Size: Length to 5 feet.
Value: Highly prized in fresh markets. It is also a popular and desirable sport fish, available all year around. The liver oil is very rich in Vitamins A and D, probably the richest of all Pacific fishes. The flesh is often green in the young, and white in adults, but always becomes white with cooking.
Description: Color is dark on back from brown to black, blue or green with greenish-gray or cream on belly, often mottled on back with pale blue or orange hues. The females are generally lighter in color with orange instead of blue tracings. The color pattern varies widely between sexes and in different habitat. The body is elongate, moderately deep, caudal peduncle slender, head elongate conical, mouth small, lower jaw projecting, teeth large and fanglike, double nostril. The dorsal fin is long and continuous with slight notch in middle, pectoral fins butterflylike, anal fin

large. There is a large fleshy cirrus above each eye. The lingcod is usually found on the bottom over reefs and among kelp in tidal currents. It is a voracious feeder, eating small fishes, crustaceans, and large fish including hake and whiting. Spawning is in winter or early spring, the eggs being deposited in large masses of adhesive pinkish substance. The male guards them until hatched, fanning the eggs with his pectoral fins to circulate water and driving off predators. They move around at random, and large numbers are taken in trawls. One of the best and most important of all North Pacific demersals. Should be handled only by eye sockets, however, as the mouth is full of knifelike teeth.

Family: Cottidae
Common Name: Sculpins

Sculpins are distinguished by the large head and eyes, often with outsized spines and in grotesque shapes and colors. Most of them are small fish, found in shallow waters. Some cottids are found in fresh water on the eastern Pacific rim and are called mudcats, bullheads, and muddlers. They include many important bait and sport fishes.

227. Cabezon
Scorpaenichthys marmoratus
Also: Giant marbled sculpin, bullhead, blue cod.
Range: Southern California to Gulf of Alaska.

Size: Length to 2 feet.
Value: The flesh is considered a gourmet delight by many. The flesh is white when cooked. The eggs, however, are poisonous. A bottom feeder, it is easily caught on sport tackle.
Description: Color is olive green to brown, mottled with light blotches, margins of darker shades. The color is widely variable from browns to blues and reds. The body is elongate, stout, head large, mouth large, snout blunt, with sharp spines on nose. The dorsal fin is continuous with several notches, the pectoral fins are butterflylike, anal fin long, caudal peduncle stout, caudal fin wide and square. Recognized by stout body, smooth skin, prominent cirrus on snout and configuration of fins. One of the largest of the sculpins, it is found in rocky, sandy, and weedy areas. It spawns prolifically in the winter months. The eggs are greenish, deposited in large masses. The fish feeds on shrimps and crabs, small fish and fish eggs. The word **cabezon** means large head.

228. Brown Irish lord
Hemilepidotus spinosus
Also: Spiny lord.
Range: Southern California to Vancouver Island.
Size: Length to 10 inches.
Value: Nuisance only.
Description: Color is brown, tinged with red, mottled and barred with dark brown, whitish on belly. The body is elongate, stout, head broad and large, mouth large, snout

rounded, teeth strong and sharp. Recognized by the emarginate spinous portion of long dorsal fin, bands of scales on dorsal, many spines on head. Not common, since it inhabits mostly deep water.

229. Red Irish lord
Hemilepidotus hemilepidotus
Also: Spotted Irish lord, bullhead.
Range: Northern California to Bering Sea.
Size: Length to 20 inches.
Value: Nuisance to anglers.
Description: Color is dull to brilliant red, somewhat mottled, barred with brownish-red, with pale red to gray-green on belly, covered with rusty black spots. The body is elongate, stout, head large and broad, mouth large, snout rounded, dorsal continuous and twice notched, pectoral fins large and winglike, anal fin large, spined, caudal peduncle slender. Recognized by color and by dorsal and pectoral fins. A common species of nothern waters often taken by salmon anglers. It spawns in early spring and feeds on crustaceans, mussels, barnacles, and eggs.

230. Staghorn sculpin
Leptocottus armatus
Also: Buffalo sculpin, cabezon, buffalo fish. Pacific staghorn sculpin

is recommended name by AFS.
Range: Southern California to Alaska.
Size: Length to 12 inches.
Value: Good crab bait.
Description: Color is gray olive to green with yellowish dorsal surface, orange-yellow to white on belly, creamy yellow with green or black bars, black spot on spinous dorsal fin. Body is elongate, moderately stout, head depressed, moderately broad, mouth large, snout bluntly rounded, dorsal fin long and notched, continuous anal fin, winglike pectoral fins. All fins are barred except anal. Very abundant in shallow water and tide pools and a favorite with young anglers. It feeds on invertebrates and is fed upon by water fowl.

231. Prickly sculpin
Cottus asper
Also: Bullhead, muddler.
Range: Southern California to British Columbia.
Size: Length to 14 inches.
Value: Crab bait.
Description: Color is gray-olive with black spots and mottling, dark wavy bands on fins, except pelvic and anal. Many prickles over head and body. Has deep shoulders and depressed wedge-shaped head. Found in shallow water and tide pools. Abundant and will take almost any bait.

232. Buffalo sculpin
Enophrys bison
Also: Calico sculpin, horned sculpin.

Range: Southern California to Alaska.
Size: Length to 12 inches.
Value: Family sport.
Description: Color is dark green to brown, yellow-white on belly, black saddles across back, brown, yellow, white bands on sides and back. The body is elongate, very stout with very slender caudal peduncle, continuous divided dorsal fin, large pectoral fin, large anal fin. Recognized by coloring and very long preopercular spines, large raised tubercles on lateral line, no cirri. Easily caught in shallow water where it feeds on small fishes, sea lettuce, crustaceans of all kinds. It can raise its spines when alarmed. A popular "kid fish" but also one that causes frequent injuries with its spines.

233. Great sculpin **Myoxocephalus polyacanthocephalus**
Also: Bull sculpin, barred sculpin
Range: Columbia River to Bering Sea.
Size: Length to 30 inches.
Value: Family sport.
Description: Color is dark olive to black on back, whitish on ventral surface, creamy bands across back, mottled or barred on fins except pelvic. Body is elongate, head large, depressed, mouth large, nasal spines

short and blunt, snout blunt. Dorsal fins separated, caudal peduncle slender. Recognized by color pattern, stout body with scattered papillae. A common species along the coast at moderate depths.

234. Calico sculpin
Clinocottus embryum
Also: Mossy sculpin, rock sculpin, spotted sculpin.
Range: Northern California to Bering Sea.
Size: Length to 3 inches.
Value: Valued by collectors only.
Description: Color is light olive green to pink or maroon on back, light green to dusky on belly, with brownish-green spots or blotches, brown to orange bars on fins except pelvic. Recognized by size and coloring, single blunt spine on each side of head, triangular spot below each eye.

Family: Scorpaenidae
Common Name: Rockfishes

This is a large and important family, including more than fifty species on the eastern rim alone, ranging from rocky and sandy shallows to depths of 800 fathoms and more. Those living in shallow waters usually have brownish color; those in deep water reddish to bright red. All species of the genus **Sebastodes** release live young in large numbers. Local names include names suggesting snappers and cods, but the trend is to discard all but "rockfishes" as there is no close relationship to the true cods, or **Gadidae**. Almost all the rockfishes are highly prized as food, the flesh being white and firm and of excellent flavor. The fresh market trade handles most of the commercial catch as fillets. The family is also extremely important to sports anglers, and probably accounts for the bulk of the "toothy critters" taken by the party boats.

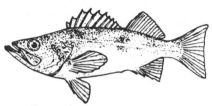

235. Bocaccio
Sebastodes paucipinis
Also: Rock cod, grouper, spotted rockfish.
Range: Southern California to Gulf of Alaska.
Size: Length to 3 feet.
Value: It is a popular sport and commercial fish over most of its range.
Description: Color is light green to dark brown on back, elsewhere clear pale red, frequently with very black spots on body, red on lower jaw, white to silvery on peritoneum. The body is elongate, somewhat slender, head pointed, lower jaw projecting. There are two dorsals, the spinous one in front, connected by deep notch to large rayed portion. Anal fin large and rayed, large pectoral fin. Recognition is by the dorsal fin configuration, the large mouth and projecting lower jaw and coloration. The bocaccio is a fast swimmer, feeds upon small fishes, and is best caught trolling or jigging in deep water. A herring skin makes a good lure, but cut bait and metal jigs also work. Bocaccio means "bigmouth."

236. California scorpionfish
Scorpaena guttata
Also: Scorpionfish, sculpin.
Range: Cabo San Lucas to central California.
Size: Length to 3 feet.
Value: A highly esteemed food fish, easily caught on cut bait or live bait.
Description: Color is reddish-brown with small round brown or green spots, pink ventral surface, with dark bars, but color pattern varies widely. The body is covered with scales and several small cirri on head, body, and snout, especially above the eyes. The dorsal is divided with the spinous portion in front. The anal fin is large with two spines or sometimes three. The eyes are high set, snout blunt. Usually found in shallow water, in bays and over reefs. The fin spines can cause severe infection so care must be used in handling. A recommended remedy is the application of ammonia.

237. Blue rockfish
Sebastodes mystinus
Also: Priest fish, black bass, rock cod, blue cod, black snapper, bluefish, neri.
Range: Baja to Bering Sea.
Size: Length to 20 inches.

Value: Fair bottom fish.
Description: Color is blue-black on back, pale below, dappled or blotched with lighter and darker shades on dorsal surface and sides. Black streaks radiate from eyes; fins are dusky black. The body is elongate and deep, with evenly curved dorsal and ventral profiles. The head is short, blunt, mouth large, lower paw projecting. Recognition is by color and configuration, especially the dorsal fin, which is continuous with no space between frontal spinous section and squarish aft section. This fish matures at from five to seven years. It is usually taken in deep water along the coast from forty to fifty fathoms. It is abundant but not taken as often as the black rockfish.

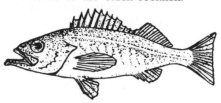

238. Chilipepper
Sebastodes goodei
Also: Red rockcod, red snapper.
Range: Baja to Oregon.
Size: Length to 20 inches.
Value: Excellent food fish.
Description: Color is dark red to pink on dorsal surface, fading to lighter color on sides, with pink ventral surface, and a dark pink stripe along the sides. The body is elongate, moderately slender, slender caudal peduncle, projecting lower jaw.

239. Yellowtail rockfish
Sebastodes flavidus
Also: Yellow rockfish, gialota.
Range: Baja to British Columbia.
Size: Length to 2 feet.

Value: An excellent food fish.
Description: Color is dark gray with streaked or mottled black and dusky green on dorsal surface and fading on sides, lighter on ventral. Fins are dusky green with faint yellow, dusky yellow on tip of caudal fin, white on peritoneum. Body is elongate, moderately deep, lower jaw projecting, head steep in profile. Dorsal fin is continuous, not notched between frontal spinous section and aft section. Large pectoral fins, anal fin has spinous section in front. Found in moderate depths of thirty to forty fathoms.

240. Black rockfish
Sebastodes melanops
Also: black cod, black sea bass, black snapper, sea bass.
Range: California to Gulf of Alaska.
Size: Length to 20 inches.
Value: A popular sport fish, readily taken on most gear, most often taken fishing for salmon and other species. It is an excellent food fish.
Description: Color is olive brown to black on back, fading on sides, soiled white on belly, dusky black on head, dark streak from eye to cheek, dark stream on maxillary, black on fins, white on peritoneum, and occasional red on mandible and fins except dorsal. Body is elongate, deep, head steep in profile, mouth large, lower jaw slightly

projecting. Caudal peduncle is slender, caudal fin slightly notched and rounded on tips; eyes large. Dorsal fin continuous between frontal spinous section and aft section. Feeds on small fishes, crustaceans.

Usually found in rocky shore areas and generally referred to, like all dark rockfish, as "black bass."

241. Bass rockfish
Sebastodes serrandoides
Also: Sugar bass, olive rockfish.
Range: Baja to northern California.
Size: Length to 18 inches.
Value: Good family sport.
Description: Color is gray shading, light ventral surface, white blotches on back, yellowish tinted fins, greenish caudal. Body is moderately slender, eyes small, dorsal fin continuous between spinous portion and aft section, lower jaw projecting. Large anal fin with spines on front edge. Taken on usual bait and tackle in shallow waters along shore.

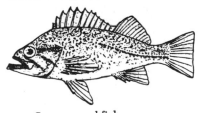

242. Orange rockfish
Sebastodes pinniger
Also: Red snapper, red rockcod, canary, filione, bosco, codalarga. Canary rockfish recommended by AFS.
Range: Baja to British Columbia.

Size: Length to 36 inches.
Value: An excellent food fish, usually called "red snapper" along Northwest coast.
Description: Color is light olive-gray with clear orange-red or yellow-orange, red predominating on back, becoming pale and nearly white on belly. There is a reddish-orange streak along upper body below dorsal, orange blotches above pectoral fin, orange saddle over caudal peduncle, golden blotches on sides of caudal peduncle. Body is elongate, moderately deep, upper profile of head curved, lower jaw projecting. Caudal peduncle slender. Dorsal fin large, continuous, spinous in front section. Anal fin rounded, with spines on fore part. Sharp spines above eyes, short sharp spines on head and gill covers. Very common species alongshore, in moderately deep water up to 100 fathoms. Easily caught with sport gear and live or fresh bait. Specimens caught in deep water will appear bloated when brought to the surface quickly. A prolific fish, females contain up to 600,000 young. Anglers should handle this one by the lower jaw, not the eyes.

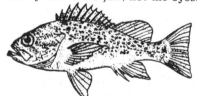

243. Vermilion rockfish
Sebastodes miniatus
Also: Rasher, red snapper, red rockcod, barracho.
Range: Baja to British Columbia.
Size: Length to 3 feet.
Value: Good sport fish.
Description: Color is deep vermilion on back, pink mottled on sides, light red on belly, with black dots clustered over back and sides. Lips are red, maxillary mottled dark red, with orange streaks from eyes, crossed blotches on head, black on fin margins, olive-gray spots on base of spinous portion of dorsal fin, red lining in mouth. Body is elongate, head straight in profile, lower jaw not projecting. Head and eyes covered with short sharp spines. Often called "red snapper" by local anglers and fish markets, it is not closely related to the Atlantic species. Taken easily on sport gear and bait in deep water.

244. Blackmouth rockfish
Sebastodes crameri
Also: Blackblotched rockfish, barred rockfish.
Range: California to Bering Sea.
Size: Length to 20 inches.
Value: Good sport fish.
Description: Color is varied red, pink, or orange with dusky black patches on back, caudal peduncle, rayed dorsal, brown to black on peritoneum. Body is elongate, head straight in profile, lower jaw does not project below upper. Head has many short spines, dorsal fin is continuous between spinous and rayed portions, eyes are large. Recognized by creamy yellow to orange or pink color, the five blotches on back and the brown to black on peritoneum. Found in deep water, small specimens have been found in the stomach of albacore, which is an indication of its range. It will take the usual bait on sport tackle.

245. Kelp rockfish
             Sebastodes atrovinens
Also: Gopher rockfish.
Range: Baja to southern California.
Size: Length to 16 inches.
Value: Good sport fish.
Description: Color varies from olive-brown in hue, with mottled brown and bright yellow fading to cream on belly, dark specks on body and head. The body is elongate, head straight in profile, eyes large, dorsal fin continuous between frontal spinous and rayed sections, anal fin rounded with spines on front edge. Sharp spines on head and gill covers. Abundant in southern temperate waters around kelp and in shallows. Will take the usual strip and cut baits on sport tackle.

246. Redstripe rockfish
             Sebastodes proiger
Also: Little red rock cod, redstripe cod.

Range: Baja to Gulf of Alaska.
Size: Length to 24 inches.
Value: Uncommon for sports.
Description: Color is bright light red, mottled with dusky green on dorsal surface, light red stripe along lateral line, olive stripes radiating from eyes, purple crosses on head, dusky to black on lips,

bright red on fins, black on spinous portion of dorsal fin, olive on rayed section, olive speckling on caudal fin. Body is elongate, slender, head straight in upper profile, lower jaw does not project, dorsal fin continuous between spinous and rayed section, caudal peduncle slender, anal fin spinous. Found in water up to 100 fathoms.

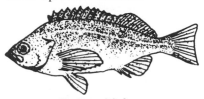

247. Speckled rockfish
             Sebastodes ovalis
Also: Zipola, viuva, speckled cod.
Range: Baja to central California.
Size: Length to 15 inches.
Value: Fair sportfish.
Description: Color is olive-green on reddish hues, dark to black spots on dorsal surface, sides and dorsal fin, other fins yellowish. Body is elongate, moderately deep, head and mouth small, eyes large, spines on head and snout. Dorsal fin continuous between spinous and rayed sections, anal fin large with spines on front edge. Found in shallow to moderately deep water, abundant in warm waters, easily caught on sport tackle.

248. Blackthroat rockfish
             Sebastodes aleutianus
Also: Rougheye rockfish.
Range: California to Gulf of Alaska.

Size: Length to 22 inches.
Value: Fair sportfish.
Description: Color is red on back, shading to pink on sides, dusky bars on body, dusky spot on pectoral fins, reddish on other fins with black outer margins, white or pink lining in mouth. Body is elongate, head straight in upper profile, mouth moderate, lower jaw slightly projecting, dorsal fin continuous from spinous to rayed section, spines over head, snout, around eyes, gill covers. Found in moderately deep water.

249. Red snapper
                Sebastodes ruberrimus
Also: Tambor rockfish, red rockfish, potbelly, cowfish, turkey rockfish. Rasphead rockfish preferred by AFS.
Range: Baja to Bering Sea.
Size: Length to 36 inches.
Value: An excellent food fish, found in fresh markets as fillets and in the round under names such as red cod, red rockfish, turkey rockfish, rasphead rockfish.
Description: Color is deep vermilion, paler on belly, whitish streak along lateral line, body and head dotted and blotched with black, reddish fins, black margins on rayed fins, white with scattered black dots on peritoneum. Body is elongate, deep, head profile slightly curved, mouth large, lower jaw projects slightly, dorsal fin continuous from spinous to rayed section, caudal peduncle slender, caudal fin

slightly rounded. Other fins large and with covered spines. Found in moderate depths up to 150 fathoms. Little is known of life cycle, but some females have contained as many as 2.5 million eggs.

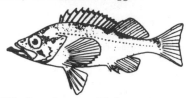

250. Longjaw rockfish
                Sebatodes alutus
Also: Pacific ocean perch (preferred by the AFS), ocean perch, rose fish.
Range: Baja to Bering Sea.
Size: Length to 18 inches.
Value: Once abundant in the trawl fishery, exploitation by foreign fishing fleets in the North Pacific has now depleted the species.
Description: Color is bright carmine red, becoming lighter on sides and belly, olive-brown blotches on back, black lower lip and tip of mandible, red on all fins, black margins, dusky to black on peritoneum. Body is elongate, slender, head profile nearly straight, with prominent knob on lower jaw, large eyes, many small spines on head, around eyes and gill covers. Dorsal fin continuous between spinous and rayed section, covered spines in rayed portion. Caudal peduncle small, all spines covered on fins. It is normally found on the high seas, in water from thirty-eight to 350 fathoms. It is an important food for halibut and albacore.

251. Blackmouth rockfish
                Sebastodes melanostomus
Also: Red rockfish.
Range: Baja to Southern California.

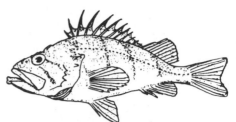

Size: Length to 20 inches.
Value: Relatively rare.
Description: Color is dark reddish to dusky on dorsal surface, scarlet sides, rose ventral surface, often with greenish dusky blotches on head and back. Spinous dorsal usually is light scarlet tipped with black. Other fins bright red, with black tips. Mouth is black appearing. Usually found in deep water.

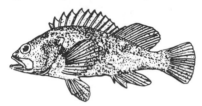

252. Pigmy rockfish
                Sebastodes wilsoni
Also: Wilson's rockfish, spiny rockfish.
Range: California to Gulf of Alaska.
Size: Length to 7½ inches.
Value: Rare for sport.
Description: Color is light brown, tinged with clear red, dark blotches in series along base of dorsal fin, brownish-red stripe below lateral line, silver on belly. The body is elongate, deep, mouth moderate, lower jaw projecting slightly, dorsal fin continuous between spinous and rayed sections, caudal peduncle slender, caudal fin squarish, large pectoral and anal fins, large eyes, short spines on head around eyes and on gill covers. This is an offshore species, taken in moderate depths.

253. Cow rockfish
                Sebastodes levis
Also: Gallo, roosterfish, chefra, cowfish.
Range: Common from central California south.
Size: Length to 36 inches.
Value: Fair sportfish.
Description: Color is pale red to pink, dusky to black crosses or blotches. Body is elongate, deep; caudal peduncle very slender, caudal fin slightly notched; dorsal fin has long sharp spines on spinous section; head sloping in profile, snout blunt, eyes high. Spines on snout and around eyes; lower jaw lipped.

254. Flag rockfish
                Sebastodes rubrivinctus
Also: Spanishflag, barber snapper.
Range: Southern California to southeast Alaska.
Size: Length to 24 inches.

Value: Fair sportfish.
Description: Color is light pink to white with four bright red cross bars, and indistinct band of red from eye to base of pelvic fin, silvery with black dots on peritoneum. Body is elongate, head nearly straight in profile, moderate

mouth, lower jaw slightly projecting. The spinous portion of dorsal fin is high and rounded, notched between rayed section. Spines on anal, pectoral fins, gill covers, and head. Usually found in moderately deep water.

255. Greenstripe rockfish
Sebastodes elongatus
Also: Strawberry rockfish, poinsetta, serena, renia rockfish.
Range: Baja to British Columbia.
Size: Length to 15 inches.
Value: A common rockfish caught by commercial trawlers, usually found in deep water to 500 fathoms. Not common in markets, however.
Description: Color is clear pale red with white on belly, irregular olive-green stripes on sides, olive head, blotched on back, pink under head, black chin tip, pale red on fins with olive on dorsal, pectoral, and caudal fins, dusky peritoneum. Body is elongate, slender, upper head straight in profile, mouth moderate, lower jaw projecting, symphyseal knob small, moderate eyes.

256. Brown rockfish
Sebastodes auriculatus
Also: Bolina, sandbass.
Range: Baja to Alaska.
Size: Length to 18 inches.

Value: Good sportfish.
Description: Color is light brown, mottled with dark brown, and dark brown blotches on upper operculum and under side, dusky pink on fins, silvery white on peritoneum. Body is elongate, moderately deep, straight head in profile, lower jaw projecting slightly, high spinous dorsal, rounded finned section; spines on anal and head; large eyes. Found along rocky shores, covers and inlets. Will take small cut or whole bait.

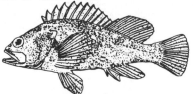

257. Grass rockfish
Sebastodes rastrelliger
Also: Kelp rockfish, schmo, scomoda.
Range: Baja to Oregon.
Size: Length to 18 inches.
Value: Much in demand in Jewish cooking.
Description: Color is black-green, with lighter mottles, olive-green fins, tipped with dusky red. Body is elongate, moderately deep, snout blunt, dorsal fin continuous, small spines on head, opercle, snout, spines on anal fin. Often caught on cut and whole bait in and around kelp.

258. Whitebelly rockfish
Sebastodes vexillaris
Also: Sailfin cod, palermotana, white cod.
Range: Baja to Oregon.
Size: Length to 25 inches.
Value: Good sportfish.
Description: Color is bright vermilion, fading to yellowish and brownish dorsal surface, with large

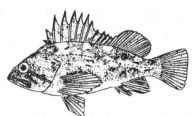

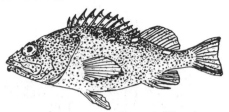

light blotches, fading to offwhite on ventral surface, green stripes on head, fins tipped with orange or dull yellow. Found in moderately deep water.

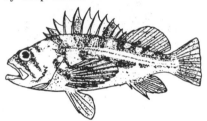

Range: Baja to northern California.
Size: Length to 16 inches.
Value: Good sportfish.
Description: Color is reddish-orange on dorsal surface with green mottlings fading to dull yellowish sides and light ventral surface. Light red fins, with large spots on back. A common species in southern temperate waters, easily caught on cut or strip bait.

259. Copper rockfish
      Sebastodes caurinus
Also: Copper cod, northern rockfish, branca, gopher, barriga.
Range: Baja to Alaska.
Size: Length to 20 inches.
Value: Caught in large numbers by trawlers. Sold to markets as fillets.
Description: Color is dark brown or green, tinged with copper or dusky yellow, or black with copper or yellow faded out, with green to brown stripes radiating from eyes, copper black on fins, white on peritoneum. Body is elongate, moderately deep, head slightly curved in upper profile, lower jaw projecting slightly, very small symphyseal knob. Spinous dorsal is high, spines on anal and pectoral fins, small spines on head. Found in shallow water.

260. Starry rockfish
      Sebastodes constellatus
Also: Spotted rock cod, scacciatale.

261. China rockfish
      Sebastodes nebulosus
Also: Yellowstripe rockfish, black and yellow cod, cefalutano.
Range: Northern California to Alaska.
Size: Length to 12 inches.
Value: Good sportfish.
Description: Color is bluish-black, bright yellow stripe starting on spinous dorsal fin and running obliquely down to caudal fin; yellow and white speckling, sometimes tinged with blue over body, blue-black on fins, white on peritoneum. Body is elongate, deep, head nearly straight in profile, mouth moderate, jaws equal. Easily recognized by unusual broad stripe on back. Found in moderately deep water, often caught on halibut gear. Will take most sport baits.

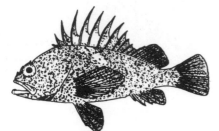

262. Quillback rockfish
Sebastodes maliger
Also: Orange-spotted rockfish, yel-low-back rockcod.
Range: Baja to Gulf of Alaska.
Size: Length to 24 inches.
Value: An excellent game fish, often caught in moderate depths, and puts up a good fight.
Description: Color is yellowish to brownish, often yellow or orange on forward portion, dark brown to black aft, pale brownish stripes radiating from eyes, yellowish area starting on spinous dorsal extend-ing wedge-shaped to lateral line, often absent. Silver-white on peri-toneum, slate-black on rayed fins. Body is elongate, stout and deep, eyes large, jaws nearly equal, head slightly curved in profile, high spines on dorsal, spines on anal fin and on head.

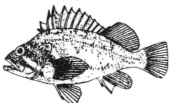

263. Gopher rockfish
Sebastodes carnatus
Also: Butter bass, butter cod, but-terball.
Range: Baja to northern California.
Size: Length to 15 inches.
Value: Fair sportfish.
Description: Color is pale brown

on back and sides, lighter on ven-tral surface, several irregular pink-ish spots on back, darker stripes radiating from eyes, dorsal and caudal fins brown, pelvic and anal fins flesh-colored, pectoral light brown or mottled with pink. Body is elongate, stout, snout short, head steep, jaws equal with no symphy-seal knob. Spinous dorsal high, spines on anal fin, small spines on head. Caught in moderately shal-low water on the usual bait.

264. Calico rockfish
Sebastodes chrysomelas
Also: Brown rockfish, brown rock-cod.
Range: Southern California.
Size: Length to 10 inches.
Value: Popular bottom fish.
Description: Color is light brown with darker streaks on dorsal sur-face, crossing lateral line, lighter ventral surface, brownish streaks radiating from eyes, two dark bars on pectoral fins, pale stripe on lat-eral line. Body is elongate, moder-ately slender, eyes large, head straight in profile, jaws equal, spin-ous dorsals high, spines on anal, pectoral fins, small spines on head. Caught in moderately shallow wa-ter.

265. Blackbanded rockfish
Sebastodes nigrocintus
Also: Barred rockfish, banded rock-

fish, tiger rockfish (preferred by the AFS).
Range: California to Alaska.
Size: Length to 24 inches.
Value: Popular bottom fish.
Description: Color is pink to gray or pale rose with five carmine vertical bars, or bright orange-red with five black vertical bars on each side, no bar on caudal peduncle, dark stripes downward from eye, white on peritoneum. Body is elongate, deep, head nearly straight in profile, lower jaw slightly projecting, small symphyseal knob. Spines on spinous dorsal, anal fin, small spines on head. Abundant in deep water and not found frequently close to shore.

266. Treefish
        Sebastodes serriceps
Also: Barber pole, convict fish.
Range: Baja to southern California.
Size: Length to 14 inches.
Value: Easily caught and generally used for bait.
Description: Color is dark olive on dorsal surface, yellowish ventral, copper-red mouth, two black bands radiating from eyes, five dark vertical bars on sides and dorsal membrane, and wide bar on caudal peduncle. Body is elongate, moderately deep, caudal peduncle slender, jaws equal, blunt spines on snout and head. Common in southern waters.

267. Slim thornhead
        Sebastolobus alascanus
Also: Thornhead, bonehead, channel rockfish, gurnard, gurnet.
Range: Baja to Alaska in water up to 800 fathoms.
Size: Length to 24 inches.
Value: A superior food fish but infrequently taken by sports anglers.
Description: Color is bright red with darkish irregular markings on fins and dorsal. Body is elongate, moderately slender, spinous ridge on cheek, spines on snout, head and preopercle.

268. Widow rockfish
        Sebastodes entomelas
Also: Widowcod, widowfish, becaccfico.
Range: Baja to southern California.
Size: Length to 14 inches.
Value: Fair sportfish.
Description: Color is dusky gray and green blotched, black spot on opercle. Body is elongate, moderate, slender caudal peduncle, head sloping in profile, large eyes, projecting lower jaw; low spinous dorsal fin. Common in southern waters.

269. Smallmouth rockfish
        Sebastodes hopkinsi
Also: Rockcod, widow rockcod.

Range: Southern California to Columbia River.
Size: Length to 16 inches.
Value: Common family fish.
Description: Color is creamy, dark blotches on back and sides. Body is elongate, head slightly depressed in profile, mouth small, spines not so prominent. Usually found in shallow water.

270. Halfbanded rockfish
        Sebastodes semicinctus
Also: Striped rockcod, banded cod.
Range: Baja to San Francisco Bay.
Size: Length to 12 inches.
Value: Fair sportfish.
Description: Color is brownish-black on dorsal, silvery ventral with reddish tinge, black spots anteriorly extending to caudal peduncle, fins whitish. Body is elongate, head sloping in profile, with short spines. Abundant in southern waters.

271. Honeycomb rockfish
        Sebastodes umbrosus
Also: Mottled rockfish, shaded rockfish.

Range: Southern California to Baja.
Size: Length to 16 inches.
Value: Rather rare.
Description: Color is dusky black back with hues of orange, shading to light on ventral surface; fins dusky orange, several blotches on back and sides. Body is stout, spinous dorsal low, eyes large, head and snout covered with short spines.

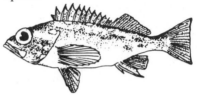

272. Flyfish
        Sebastodes rhodochloris
Also: Red rockfish, red flyfish, rainbow rockfish.
Range: West coast of Baja California.
Size: Length to 12 inches.
Value: Excellent food fish.
Description: Bright red color, with irregular green streaks on dorsal surface, turning to orange and bright yellow on sides, often mixed with light red. Green streaks radiating from eyes, several large spots on back, fins yellowish to greenish with red rays. Recognized mainly by color pattern and by elongated spines on anal fin. Jaws equal, sharp spines on head and snout, spinous dorsal low. Abundant over range.

273. Greenspotted rockfish
        Sebastodes chlorostictus
Also: Red rock cod, China cod, chucklehead, cernie, belina.
Range: Coastal areas from Oregon border to Cabo San Lucas.
Size: Length to 16 inches.
Value: Common bottom fish.
Description: Color is greenish on

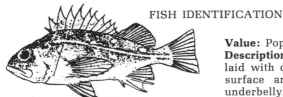

dorsal surface, lighter on ventral, several spots on back surrounded by rings of green, fins red with yellowish rays, base of dorsal fin green. Body is stout with rounded snout, large eyes, long spines on anal fin, high spines on dorsal fin, short spines on head and snout. Abundant over its range.

274. Pink rockfish
Sebastodes eos
Also: Rosy cod, rose rockfish.
Range: Southern California.
Size: Length to 24 inches.
Value: Popular sportfish.
Description: Color is pink to rose on back, head, and fins with brownish mottlings, several spots on back of lighter rose with brown rings. Body is elongated, caudal peduncle slender, spinous dorsal high, low spines on head, large eyes, knob on lower lip. Abundant in most coastal areas.

275. Rosy rockfish
Sebastodes rosaceus
Also: Corsair, due, rainbow rockfish.
Range: Baja to Gulf of Alaska.
Size: Length to 12 inches.

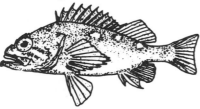

Value: Popular sportfish.
Description: Color is yellow overlaid with dark blood-red on dorsal surface and lateral line, whitish underbelly, whitish blotches ringed with purple, on upper sides, pink fins with black dots. Body is elongate, head slightly curved in upper profile, jaws about equal, small symphyseal knob, spinous dorsal high, spines on head and snout, three spines on anal fin, triangular-shaped pectoral fins. Similar in color to several other species of rockfish, but differs slightly in configuration. Abundant over range in moderately deep water to seventy fathoms and easily caught.

Family: Gasterosteidae
Common Name: Sticklebacks

These numerous small fishes include seven genera and twelve species in fresh and salt waters of North America, Europe, and Asia.

276. Threespine stickleback
Gasterosteus aculeatus
Also: Saltwater stickleback.

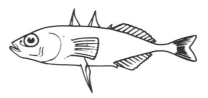

Range: Baja to Bering Sea.
Size: Length to 4 inches.
Value: Good for bait.
Description: Color is silvery green to intense blue-black in salt water, mottled brown in fresh or brackish; bright silvery when young. Body is elongate, moderately compressed, caudal peduncle slender, sometimes with lateral keels, head pointed, minute teeth. Dorsal fin

has two or three separated, serrated spines ahead of rayed portion, keel-like anal fin. Recognized by the large spines on the dorsal and pelvic fins, the slender caudal peduncle and the vertical bony plates on sides of body. Common along the coast of the eastern Pacific and in rivers and lakes, occurring in small schools in eelgrass and around pilings. Large numbers are also found far offshore. The spawning instincts of this species are well-known in fresh water, where a male builds a nest for one or more females to spawn in, and then guards the nest until the fry are able to forage for themselves. Sticklebacks feed on small crustaceans and aquatic insects, and, in turn, are eaten by other fishes and birds.

Family: Clinidae
Common Name: Kelpfishes

These are small tidepool fishes, usually very colorful, found in temperate and tropical tidal zones.

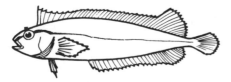

277. Striped kelpfish
Gibbonsia metzi
Also: Blenny, striped butterfish.
Range: Baja to Gulf of Alaska.
Size: Length to 5½ inches.
Value: Of interest mainly to those who like to explore tidal pools.

Description: Color is red or brown with stripes of lighter hues to darker shades. Recognized by size, color, the extremely elongated dorsal fin with elevated rayed portion, and by the elongated anal fin. One of the many kelpfish.

278. Kelpfish
Heterostochus rostratus
Also: Butterfish, kelp blenny.
Range: Baja to Gulf of Alaska.
Size: Length to 16 inches.
Value: An excellent food fish, with good flavor.
Description: Color varies from brown to black-brown, purple and green, with blotches. Pointed snout, protruding lower lip, extremely elongated dorsal and anal fins. Found around kelp and coral.

Family: Anarrhichadidae
Common Name: Wolffishes

Large fishes found in northern waters at moderate depths, which prey on a wide variety of invertebrates and fishes, grasping and grinding them in a vicious looking mouth.

279. Wolf-eel
Anarrhichthys ocellatus
Also: Wolf fish.
Range: Baja to Gulf of Alaska.
Size: Length to 8 feet.

Value: Nil.
Description: Color is gray, brown, or dark green, sometimes orange in young, with black round spots covering body and dorsal fin..Body is extremely elongate, compressed, head deep and compressed. The mouth is large, with thick lips, numerous strong conical canine teeth; dorsal and anal fin low and extremely elongated, with no pelvic fins. Frequently caught in traps and seines, and is voracious and predacious. Few are caught on sport tackle, however.

Family: Stichaeida
Common Name: Pricklebacks

280. Rock-eel
   Xiphister mucosus
Also: Blenny, slick eel, rock blenny.
Range: Southern California to Bering Sea.
Size: Length to 24 inches.
Value: Collectors only.
Description: Color is greenish-black with lighter bars. Body is elongate, slender, with extremely elongated dorsal and anal fins, snout blunt, no pelvic fin. Found in ledges and rocky areas and taken with regular sport gear or with "poke poles."

Family: Blennidae
Common Name: Blennies

281. Sarcastic
   Neoclinus blanchardi
Also: Fringehead, kelp fish.

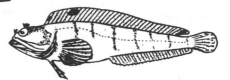

Range: Baja to northern California.
Size: Length to 10 inches.
Value: Nil.
Description: Color is red, brown, or green, or mottled with dark shades, with light bars on sides, often white spots, and reddish stripes. Body is elongate, with large mouth and extreme gape. Males have branched cirrus in front of eyes. Dorsal and anal fins are extremely elongated. Seldom taken by sports anglers.

Family: Ptilichthyidae
Common Name: Monkeyface eels

282. Monkeyface eel
   Cebidichthys ciolaceus
Also: Blenny, blenny eel.
Range: Southern California to Oregon.
Size: Length to 4 feet.
Value: Of interest to collectors only.
Description: Color is brown with dull green on dorsal surface, shading to lighter, with irregular spots, often ringed with orange, vertical fins tipped with red. Body is elongate, slender, eellike, snout blunt with fleshy appendages, dorsal and anal fins continuous. Usually found in tidal zones.

Family: Stichaeidae
Common Name: Pricklebacks

283. Giant wrymouth
Delolepis gigantea
Also: Wrymouth, congo eel.
Range: Northern California to Alaska.
Size: Length to 4 feet.
Value: Can be taken on sport gear and is considered a good food fish.
Description: Color is light to dark brown, yellowish sides with bluish tinge, dark stripes along dorsal fin. Body is elongate and slender, mouth large, head flattened, eyes small, dorsal and anal fins continuous and attached to caudal fin. Found in rocky areas, in moderate depths.

Family: Batrachoididae
Common Name: Toadfishes

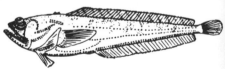

284. Slim midshipman
Porichthys myriaster
Also: Singing fish, toadfish, midshipman.
Range: Baja to northern California.
Size: Length to 16 inches.
Value: Considered edible but mainly taken for bait.
Description: Color is dark purple or bronze back, with lighter shading on sides, yellow, orange, or tan ventral surface, with dark blotches. Body is elongate, slender with continuous dorsal and anal fins; head broad, mouth large, lower jaw projecting, teeth large, eyes extended. Found in shallow, rocky areas.

285. Northern midshipman
Porichthys notatus
Also: Singing fish, bullhead, toadfish.
Range: Baja to Alaska.
Size: Length to 16 inches.
Value: Considered edible, taken on the usual bait and gear in deep water banks or in shallows during spawning.
Description: Color is blue to brown fading to lighter hues on sides with yellowish-bronze belly, white under eyes, with black crescent below. Body is elongate, slender, extended eyes staring upward, with rows of small lenslike buttons on head and body, teeth numerous and sharp in large mouth; caudal fin rounded, dorsal and anal fins continuous; no scales. The name midshipman apparently comes from the photophores, or buttons, similar to the old-time naval uniforms.

Common Name: Milkfishes

286. Awa   Chanos chanos
Also: Milkfish.
Range: Tropical waters of Pacific and Asia.
Size: Length to 5 feet, weight to 50 pounds.
Value: A great fighting fish, and a leaper. Considered an excellent food fish.
Description: Color is grayish-green on back, turning to silver on sides and white on belly. Mouths are

very tender. Bread is a popular
bait for them. They feed in schools
in bays and inlets, mostly on plant
life.

Common Name: Morays
287. (Moray) eel
            Uropterygius knighti
Also: Puhis.
Range: Tropical Pacific.

288. (Moray) eel
            Anarchias leucurus
Also: Moray.
Range: Tropical Pacific.

289. Puhi-oa   **Muraena pardalis**
Also: Puhi-kaulhila.   t
Range: Tropical Pacific and Japan.

290. (Moray) eel
      Enchelynassa canina canina
Also: Dog eel.
Range: Tropical Pacific.

291. (Moray) eel
            Gymnothorax eurostus
Also: Moray.
Range: Tropical Pacific.

292. Puhi-paka
      Gymnothorax flavimarginatus
Also: Moray eel.
Range: Tropical Pacific, Red Sea.

293. White eel
            Conger marginatus
Also: Puhi-uha.
Range: Tropical Pacific.

294. California tonguefish
            Symphurus atricauda
Also: Tonguefish.
Range: Sea of Cortez north to Ore-
gon border.

295. Humuhumu-nukunuku-a-pua'a
            Rhinecanthus rectangulus
Range: Tropical Pacific and Indian
Ocean, Hawaiian Islands.

296. Humuhumu- 'ele'ele
            Melichthys buniva
Range: Tropical Pacific, Hawaiian
Islands.

297. Humuhumu-hi'uKole
            Melichthys vidua
Range: Tropical Pacific, Hawaiian
Islands.

398. 'O'ili unwiwi
            Peruagor spilosoma
Range: Tropical Pacific, Hawaiian
Islands.

Family: Ammodytidae
Common Name: Sandlances

A school fish occurring in shallow water, often in surf, sometimes
partly buried in sand.

299. Pacific sandlance
            Ammodytes hexapterus
Also: Arctic sandlance, sandlance.
Range: Baja to Bering Sea.

Size: Length to 8 inches.

Value: It furnishes an important food to salmon, lingcod, halibut, and even seals. It is considered an excellent food fish for humans, having a delicate, delicious flavor.

Description: Color is pale green on back, silvery on ventral. Body is elongate, very slender, head pointed, lower jaw projecting, dorsal fin continuous, anal fin elongated, no pelvic fins. An abundant forage fish, occurring in large schools, sometimes buried in sandy beaches. It feeds on plankton, small crustaceans, barnacle larvae.

Family: Molidae

Common Name: Ocean sunfishes

A large, grotesque, pelagic fish that is found on the open seas, drifting with the current, although known to dive to great depths. They grow to a length of nine feet, weighing a ton or more.

300. Ocean sunfish   **Mola mola**

Also: Millstone fish, headfish.

Range: Temperate waters of North Pacific.

Size: Length to 9 feet.

Value: Occasionally taken on surface.

Description: Color is dark gray on back, gray-brown on sides, silvery reflections, light gray band at base of dorsal, anal, and caudal fins. Body is short, deep, ovate, greatly compressed. Head is deep, compressed, mouth small, teeth are beaklike, eyes small, no scales. Recognized easily by the body which appears to be all head, with a tall narrow dorsal fin on top and an equally long narrow anal fin directly under, no pelvic fins, small pectoral fin; caudal is broad and wavy in outline. Usually found in open tropical and temperate seas, but occasionally found near shores and around islands drifting with the current. It is a prolific fish, the female producing as many as 300 million eggs, which are set free in the ocean, the larva growing from a tenth of an inch to its enormous size as an adult. **Mola** means millstone, a descriptive name, but often called headfish.

Alphabetical Index
of Common Names

Key No.

Key No.

Key No.

Key No.

Key No.

Key No.

Additional Sources

Major Books In Print:

Pacific North! by Don Holm. (The Caxton Printers, Ltd.)
McClane's Standard Fishing Encyclopedia by A. J. McClane.
(Holt, Rinehart, Winston.)
How To Fish The Pacific Coast by Ray Cannon. (Sunset Books.)
The Sea of Cortez by Ray Cannon and *Sunset* Staff. (Lane.)
Northwest Passages by Bruce Calhoun. (Miller Freeman.)

Periodicals:

Saltwater Sportsman
Fishing World
Outdoor Life
Field & Stream
International Game Fisherman
Western Outdoors
Sea and Pacific Motor Boat
Sportfishing
Alaska (formerly *Alaska Sportsman*)
Walkabout (Melbourne, Australia)
International Fish & Game

Newspapers:

Vancouver *Sun* and *Province*
Seattle *Times*, Seattle *Post-Intelligencer*
Honolulu *Advertiser*
The Oregonian, Portland
San Francisco *Chronicle, Call-Bulletin, Examiner*
Los Angeles *Times*
San Diego *Union, Tribune*
Anchorage *News, Times*
Juneau *Empire*
New Zealand *Herald* (Aukland)

These are only a few of the daily papers that offer current fishing news. In addition, there are dozens of local weekly newspapers in coastal towns, many of which are devoted almost entirely to fishing, boating, and beachcombing news.

Special Publications:

Fishing & Hunting News, a weekly tabloid with Northwest and California editions, published in Seattle, Wash., is one of several papers entirely devoted to outdoor sports. In addition, annual "guides" to local fishing are published regularly in British Columbia, Washington, Oregon, California, Hawaii, New Zealand, and Australia.

Government Publications:

Coast Pilots, published by the Coast & Geodetic Survey, are available at nominal cost for the West Coast of the United States, including Alaska and the Hawaiian Islands. *Sailing Directions* for the open sea and all parts of the world outside U.S. territory, are published by the U.S. Navy Hydrographic Office, now called Oceanographic Office. *British Columbia Coast Pilots* are published by the Canadian Hydrographic Service.

Official Agencies:

Sport Fish Division, Alaska Department of Fish & Game,
    Juneau, Alaska
Government Tourist Bureau, P.O. Box 527, Rotorua, N.Z.
British Columbia Information Center, 652 Burrard St.,
    Vancouver, B.C., Canada
Oregon State Highway Department, Salem
Washington Game Department, Olympia
Washington Department of Fisheries, Olympia
California Department of Fish and Game, Sacramento
Hawaii Visitors Bureau, Honolulu
Australian Consulate-General, 1 Post St., San Francisco, Calif.

Airlines

Quantas
Western
Northwest Orient
Pacific Northern
Wein Consolidated Airlines
Alaska Airlines
Canadian Pacific
Air Canada
Air France
APSA Peruvian Airlines
Air West
United Airlines
Avianca Airlines
Braniff International
Aeronaves de Mexico
New Zealand Airlines

CREDITS

Wholehearted thanks and congratulations go to E. Bruce Dauner, of *The Oregonian*, who did many of the line drawings of fish species in the second half of the book.

Also, for the use of photographs, the author wishes to thank: Leonard Bacon (p. 36), U.S. Army Engineers (p. 43, p. 48), California Dept. of Fish & Game (p. 45), Washington State Dept. of Fisheries (p. 75), Braniff International (p. 86), Oregon State Highways (p. 97), Quantas (pp. 108, 109, 112).